P9-BJA-957

NORTH-WEST OF SIXTEEN

TO KNOW TO UNDERSTAND TO PARTICIPATE
THE CANADIAN HERITAGE IS YOUR HERITAGE

**ALBERTA HERITAGE
LEARNING RESOURCES
PROJECT**

A Project of Alberta Education
Funded
By
The Alberta Heritage Savings Trust Fund
and
Dedicated to the Students
of Alberta
by the
Government of Alberta
1979

We acknowledge the co-operation
of the publishers and authors in
including their works in the Alberta Heritage collection.

MEMBERS OF THE SELECTION COMMITTEE

William F. Lockhart/*Managing Editor, Alberta Education*
Leslie L. Aitken/*Alberta Education*
Louis Burke/*Lethbridge Separate School District*
Heather-Belle Dowling/*County of Strathcona Municipal Library*
Shirley I. Paustian/*Edmonton Public School District*
Hilda Ross/*Freelancer and Instructor of Creative Writing*
John N. White/*East Smoky School Division*

David Shaw & Associates Ltd./*Project Cover Design*

NORTH-WEST
OF
SIXTEEN

James G. MacGregor

Western Producer Prairie Books
Saskatoon, Saskatchewan

Complimentary Copy

Alberta Heritage fund

971.23

79-0075

May 1977

Copyright © 1977 by J. G. MacGregor
Western Producer Prairie Books
Saskatoon, Saskatchewan

All rights reserved. No part of this publication may be reproduced, stored
in a retrieval system, or transmitted, in any form or by any means,
electronic, mechanical, photocopying, recording or otherwise, without the
prior permission of the publisher.

First published by McClelland & Stewart Limited in 1958
Republished by M. G. Hurtig Ltd. in 1968
First softcover edition by Western Producer Prairie Books in 1977

Canadian Shared Cataloguing in Publication Data

MacGregor, James G., 1905-
North-west of 16

First published in 1958.
ISBN 0-919306-83-7 pa.

1. MacGregor, James G., 1905-
2. Frontier and pioneer life — Alberta.
I. Title.
FC3694.3.M23A3   971.23'3
F1076.M13

AUGUSTANA LIBRARY
UNIVERSITY OF ALBERTA

J im MacGregor was already a well-known author when *North-West of Sixteen* was first published in 1958. Starting out nine years earlier with *Blankets and Beads, A History of the Saskatchewan River*, he went on to produce *The Land of Twelve-Foot Davis* in 1952, and *Behold the Shining Mountains* in 1954. These were printed in Edmonton and had a brisk circulation in the northern Alberta area.

But *North-West of Sixteen* was different. Not only was it his first book produced by a national publisher, McClelland & Stewart of Toronto, but it was the story of Jim's own boyhood. Where his other books had been accurate and readable histories, this one was a literary triumph. It was warm and vibrant and carried with it a feeling of deep love for the 160 acres of bush, slough, and pasture that made up the north-west quarter of Section Sixteen, Township Fifty-Nine, Range One, west of the Fifth Meridian.

This homestead, where Jim's parents settled in 1906, was twelve miles from Westlock, Alberta, but as he says in his book, "One quarter was much like another. I have written about our quarter and our family because I know more about them than about the others." In telling about the MacGregor quarter, he paints a picture of homestead life with its chattering squirrels and scolding whiskey jacks. He tells of clearing the wilderness, building the log cabin and "proving up". He also tells of school life and of the sacrifices made by his parents to ensure that their children got a good education. Fittingly, his first book, *Blankets and Beads*, is dedicated to his pioneering father and to his mother "who, every morning, carried her five-year-old son over the floating corduroy of the quarter mile slough, so that he might not have to sit in school all day in wet clothes."

It is a warm story about the kind of pioneers who opened the West and, while it may be the tale of one family as seen through the eyes of a boy, it is really a much bigger story. In it are reflected the pleasures, hopes, terrors and sorrows of many nameless homesteaders, some who stayed and some who didn't.

Since the national acclaim accorded this book when it was first published, the author has gone on to write *Pack Saddles to Tete Jaune Cache* (1962), *Edmonton Trader* (1963), *Peter Fidler, Canada's Forgotten Surveyor* (1966), *Edmonton, a History* (1967), *Vilni Zemli, the Ukrainian Settlement of Alberta* (1969), *The Klondike Gold Rush Through Edmonton* (1970), *A History of Alberta* (1972), *Overland by the Yellowhead* (1974), *Paddle Wheels to Bucket-Wheels on the Athabasca* (1974), *Father Lacombe* (1975), and *The Battle River Valley* (1976). In addition, *North-West of Sixteen* was reprinted by M. G. Hurtig Ltd. of Edmonton in 1968. In recognition of his contribution to Canadian literature, Mr. MacGregor was awarded the Order of Canada, an honorary doctorate from the University of Alberta and several historical and literary awards. His books have established him solidly as one of Canada's leading historical authors, but not one of them has equalled *North-West of Sixteen* for literary style and warmth. For that reason, it is fitting that this book should be reprinted so that others may enjoy the author's finest work.

Hugh A. Dempsey

Calgary, Alberta

This is a story of pioneer days in Northern Alberta. Using some of the experiences of my father and mother and their neighbours, I have gone back over half a century to trace the development of a typical pioneer community through its first twenty years until railroads, gravelled highways, telephones, and radios entered what had once been a dense forest.

Once a year now I drive out to the old farm. As I look at the hillside with its wheat nodding in the wind, I am proud that my brother Bill and I cleared that hillside, foot by foot; it used to be covered with heavy green spruce timber, and many of the trees were as much as three feet in diameter. The road past the farm is now straight and graded. When Dad and I and Henry Paulson cleared the first straight road through here, it could be travelled only in winter when it was frozen; then, year by year, mud-hole by mud-hole, corduroy by corduroy, ditch by ditch and culvert by culvert, we built it up.

Our little community of Eastburg, nestled on the slope that rises from the valley of the Pembina River, was not very different from the other communities one used to pass on the highway between there and Edmonton. The twenty years from 1906 to 1926 saw it develop from minute clearings amongst the trees to two-hundred-acre fields adjoining each other and spreading out under the spring rains and the August sun. There is no Eastburg now. Several years ago the post office there gave up competing with a rural route coming out from Westlock and another from Picardville. But once Eastburg meant something, and its post office, which for years took up a corner of our house, came alive twice a week when Gerry Hoogers brought out the mail. Eastburg was my home for twenty years. Mother and Dad lived on the farm for many years after that, and shared in the life of the community which they and their neighbours had built.

I had a farmer come to see me recently on business, and I asked: "Where do you live—what quarter?" I was taken aback when he did not know the number of his own quarter-section. Thus far have we come! And for those of my readers to whom even the term itself may be strange, I am going to end my preface with an explanation, as brief as I can make it, of the system of survey that was so familiar to the settlers of my father's day.

For the prairie provinces of Manitoba, Saskatchewan, and Alberta, the process of subdividing the land into homesteads started at the Red River Settlement near Winnipeg. A short distance west of that town a line was surveyed from the United States border due north to Lake Winnipeg. This line was called the Principal, or First, Meridian. Nearly two hundred miles west of it another north-and-south line was surveyed and called the Second Meridian; and so on. When, in 1905, the provinces of Alberta and Saskatchewan were created, the boundary between the two was placed at the Fourth Meridian. The Fifth Meridian (longitude 114°) passed through Calgary and through a point about twenty miles west of Edmonton.

The land between the meridians was laid out in squares measuring six miles on each side. The extreme south-easterly square of land in Alberta, right in the corner where the Fourth Meridian intersected the U.S. border, was called Township 1, Range 1, West of the 4th Meridian. The square bordering it on the west was called Township 1, Range 2; and so on, with the numbers of the ranges increasing towards the west. The square immediately north of Township 1, Range 1 was called Township 2, Range 1; and so on, with the township numbers increasing towards the north until with Township 126 the north boundary of the province was reached.

Each of these large squares, known as townships, was then divided into thirty-six small squares, called sections. The numbering of the sections began likewise from the south-east corner but continued from west to east along the second tier, and so on alternately west and east until the north-east section in the township became number 36. Under the homestead regulations a settler could file on a quarter-section of 160 acres.

One quarter was much like another. I have written about our quarter and our family because I know more about them than about the others. But you could move half a mile west and call this family the ter Horsts, or a mile or so north and call it the Skaalens, or east to Finnegan's, or south to Napoleon Brault's. Only the details would vary. Or you could move six miles west to Manola instead of Eastburg, or east to Hazel Bluff, or north to Rossington, and you would get the same picture. But I knew Eastburg and the MacGregors, and that is how I came to centre this story around the black iron survey-stake marked:

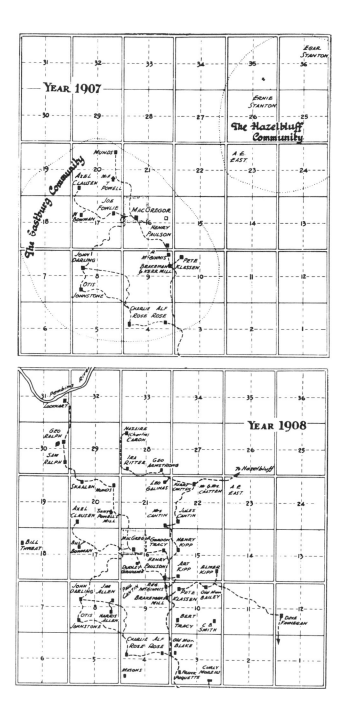

The MacGregors—Mother, Dad, and I—
arrived in Edmonton in October 1906. At that time the city,
huddled in a crescent close to the old fort, contained eleven thousand
souls. We came as immigrants, with eyes wide, doubtful and staring
at the strangeness, the newness and the rawness of this frontier civilization. Our problems were simple only by comparison with those
of the newly arrived Galicians, Germans, Scandinavians, Dutch, and
others, for although half the people around us spoke strange languages the other half, including the merchants and railwaymen and
immigration staffs, spoke English. It was however a strange English,
all mixed up with oaths and chewing tobacco, and full of terms
that were familiar on the frontier but new to my parents.

Our problems as newcomers—at least Dad's and Mother's
problems, since I was one year old at the time—were compli-
cated by a difference of outlook. This coming to Canada, this
idea of a quarter-section of free land, of 160 acres of waving wheat-
fields and peach trees (so the literature said), was all Dad's. I don't
think the riches appealed unduly, for Dad had an army pension of
thirty-five dollars a month; but the freedom and adventure did.
New lands, new people, new customs did not bother an old soldier
who had seen twenty-one years' service in the Scots Guards.
He had marched to the relief of Gordon at Khartoum; in the
famous British Square he had knelt on the sand to repel the attack
of the men he had always admired, the charging Fuzzy-wuzzy;
he had staggered along half dead with dysentery; he had slept
for three years under the open sky of the African veldt. This Canada,
to him, was just another new country.

But it had freedom, doubly precious after the disciplined life of soldiering, and now this freedom lay before him. He was like a boy out of school, a boy old enough to put his foot up on the brass rail of a bar. Dad, I think, was akin in spirit to some primitive ancestor who, after a wet night, came out of his rock shelter, stood on the hilltop, and stretched as he looked up at the rising sun and out at the leaves of spring, new washed by the night's rain, and then down the valley to the river shining far below. This was the freedom Dad wanted; freedom to stretch and, if necessary, to scratch; freedom to get away from the babble of the crowd; freedom to sit and do nothing if one wanted. These were Dad's riches.

So this country—rough perhaps, but free, beautiful and peaceful—was Dad's country from the start.

Eventually it became Mother's country too, but that is a long story. Certainly at first she hated it. Dad was a Scot, and though his many years in London had toned down a burr that was never very marked, nevertheless a discerning man could tell that he had been born in Scotland. Mother was English and her accent was noticeably so. To be English in the Canadian West in 1906 was a hurdle difficult to overcome. Everywhere she went there was something or someone to remind her that out here the English were not wanted. Many of the Help Wanted signs said: "No Englishman need apply." Down-East Canadians seldom missed a chance to comment on her English accent. Most of the Americans were bitter in their denunciation of it.

To Mother, who, I'm afraid, played a rôle of passive resistance, the trip from Scotland to Edmonton had been strange and hateful. The old *Carthagina* wallowed around in the seas, and Mother no sooner got over a bout of seasickness than I came down with croup or some other childish disease. Dad found more congenial company in the ship's bar.

Montreal and firm ground was a blessed relief, but it seemed that practically everybody there spoke French. Mother had never realized this. A strange language always has a menacing quality, to insular folk. So Mother was glad to get on the train, but even it, with its ringing bell, its frequently blowing whistle, and its long colonist cars, was disturbingly different from the cozy English trains. At every station the crowds appeared to be chewing something, which Mother later knew to be gum, and this was another strange custom. Evidently I was still sick, but a woman on the train and her two kindly daughters helped Mother by looking after me. Some train delay must have ensued, for we were six or seven days getting to Calgary. Both the loneliness of Nothern Ontario and the vastness of the prairies were appalling; the sight of the mountains as the train came into Calgary provided the only relief from the universal October drabness. Then came the trip to Edmonton, the trip that left the prairie behind as the train plunged ever deeper into the forest country. Finally there was the journey down the Strathcona Hill by stage.

Somehow or other we escaped the Immigration Hall, and Dad was quick in getting the tent pitched on Ross Flats amidst dozens of other tents. Even at this late season, when the main flood of immigrants had slackened off for another year, there were still many prospective settlers camped on the Flats. Doubtless Mother was thankful to be there at last, with the prospect of staying in one place for a little while; but all night long the light October rain drummed on the canvas, and the plaintive notes of the pipers at the far-off Clydeside pier rang in her head—"Will ye no come back again?" The glory of the pipers in the march-past, the bugle calls on the Horse Guards' parade, the lively activity of Wellington Barracks, the roar of the traffic in Piccadilly—she heard it all again, and she had exchanged it all for the roar of rain on a tent pitched in a sea of oozy mud. How she hated Canada!

Next morning the sun shone, but it was a bleak sun, cheerlessly revealing the bareness of the trees and the sogginess of the camp grounds. Still, the air was fresh, and Mother had a busy day before her, washing a week's accumulation of clothes and arranging the tent for a two weeks' stay.

Dad was awake early, after a sound sleep, and was eager to be about. This was The Day—The Beginning. Most of the other passengers on the *Carthagina*, and nearly all those on the train, had been coming out to homestead, and for weeks this had been the main topic of conversation. Until now, all had been anticipation, but today, here at Edmonton, was the beginning of the reality. So Dad hastened up McDougall Hill to the town to get an idea of the procedure and to talk to everyone he could. That was easy, because everyone else seemed to have the same idea, and all the talk was about land in three forms—city lots, farm land for sale, and distant entrancing valleys in which one could homestead.

Edmonton, whatever it may or may not lack, is a thrilling

place in boom times, and it has had more than its share of booms. These, like great waves, have often reared so high that they have curled over into wild speculation and come down with a thud. In spite of that, they have all had a solid basis in fact. In 1906, of course, the present riches were unsuspected. What they had then was land, no less than 50,000 sections of it. That meant 200,000 quarter-sections, all tributary to Edmonton. That in turn, once these quarter-sections were settled up, meant 200,000 families, and that meant a million people all trading in Edmonton. Oh no, not all of them had arrived yet, but they were coming daily. As well as these farmers there would be all the small towns that would arise in the farming communities; and they would all be tributary to Edmonton. Moreover, this 50,000 square miles of land was rich and productive. You had but to take a shovel and walk half a mile out of the city, or fifty miles, or a hundred miles, and thrust the shovel into the soil and it would reveal a foot or so of rich black mould. Land! Get down on your knees and feel it! Let it run through your fingers! This was riches; this was the land that would make Edmonton a great city.

The fact that not all of the land was equally good had failed to penetrate many heads. There was no scientific land appraisal; trial-and-error was the only method. A settler filed on the quarter, and two or three years' experience would show him whether it was good or not.

Why this sudden excitement, this decade of excitement over land? Had it not always been there? Yes, but now a wheat had been developed that would grow on this land, and the hungry of Europe had heard of it. Many from Europe came to grow it, and the rest stayed home as a market for it. The emaciated of Europe came out here by the thousands. The well-fed of Europe, who thirsted for land of their own and for freedom, came out by the hundreds.

And settlers came not only from Europe, but from Eastern Canada and the United States. In the spring of 1906, according to Charles Sutter, Dominion Immigration Agent at Edmonton, daily arrivals had averaged between three hundred and five hundred. The immigration building was crowded and the hotels were full. New immigration quarters were opened at the Exhibition Grounds, and a new immigration hall north of the C.N.R. tracks was finished that summer. The agent spoke of a contingent of United States settlers that had recently started from Chicago. In this contingent were nine train loads all bound for the prairies; and it was only one of hundreds.

Mr. Harrison of the Land Office had difficulty in keeping up with prospective settlers; some mornings a long line-up of them was waiting outside his office, which was then on what is now 100th Avenue, between 105th and 106th streets. Most individual settlers—that is, those who had not come out in colonies—naturally wanted to see their land before filing on it; so as soon as they arrived in Edmonton and had arranged for their families to be temporarily cared for at the immigration buildings or elsewhere, they would rush to hire a team and make straight for the Land Titles Office to get township plans and see what land was still available.

There were many officially registered guides to take these people out. Some were good, others merely mercenary. Many settlers were met at Edmonton by relatives or friends who had already taken land and were prepared to suggest good land adjoining their own, but the settler going out with a guide found that it was well to select four or five quarters, because by the time he got back to the Land Office someone else, who had visited the land two or three days ahead of him, might have filed on the quarter he wanted. Many came back with a list of quarters, only to find that all of them had been taken. Then, in desperation and at random, they selected vacant quarters in the same vicinity, sometimes with devastating results. From those who filed sight-unseen there often came woeful stories of filing on quaking marshes or stony hilltops where, as someone said, "There was very little land to the acre."

By 1906 most of the quarters within forty miles of Edmonton had been taken. All those along the Calgary and Edmonton Railroad, of course, had been filed on shortly after the railroad came through in 1891. Most of the area immediately adjacent to the Canadian Northern Railway from Lloydminster to Edmonton was also homesteaded. A few miles back from that, north or south, however, the land was open. One of the districts being discussed at the time Dad came on the scene was that along the Pembina River from Entwistle downstream. It was rumoured that a railroad was to go out to Whitecourt, and that made settlement in this area interesting. The district along the Paddle River and up Barrhead way also had its advocates, and others were loud in their praises of the soil around Athabasca Landing.

The attitude of those who were not going to farm was that

they had better get in on the ground floor of the booming city—get into business or contracting, or buy lots, or merely do the labour that had to be done. The big stores of the day were doing a roaring trade: the Hudson's Bay Company, McDougall and Secord, Larue and Picard, Blowey-Henry, Johnstone-Walker, Gariepy and Lessard, Revillon's. And so were many smaller stores, not the least of which was Henry Wilson's across from the market square. There were thirteen hotels, of which the Alberta, the Queen's and the Windsor stood out. There were eleven banks; and as for real-estate offices, they were beyond counting. Everyone was selling land in a new subdivision, or selling land in Vegreville, Vermilion, Mundare or Entwistle. If they weren't doing that, they were selling farm lands. They were even selling summer-resort lots at Whitesand Beach on White Whale Lake (Wabamun). Edmonton had come a long way from the days when the real glass in the windows of John Rowand's Big House was one of the wonders of the West. Even its successor, Hardisty's Big House, which stood where the Legislative Building is now, had fallen on evil days. It had become, of all things, the Club House of Edmonton's nine-hole golf course.

The selling of lots was a brisk business. Corner lots down in the business section on Jasper Avenue were selling at $20,000 to $35,000 each. Ordinary lots on Jasper and on First Street sold for $600 a frontage foot. This, of course, was down town. Out on the extreme end of Jasper Avenue, away out in the bush—at what is now 17th Street—the price was lower.

Edmonton's incorporation as a city was as recent as 1904, but it had acquired an electric light plant in 1891, and had owned a waterworks system since 1903, when about seven miles of water mains and five miles of sewers had been run. Five more miles of water mains were added in 1906, and the city council held lengthy discussions about paving streets with wood-block paving. A plan was afoot to build a high-level bridge, and a street railway was mooted. Other modern facilities were not lacking; on July 31, 1906, the penitentiary was opened (on what we know now as the Penn Site) and served its first meal to its first customer that day. There seemed no end to the progress that lay in store.

Motor cars had invaded the streets of Edmonton, and even whizzed along the roads leading to it. The first to come had been Joe Morris's, in 1903, but others had followed quickly. On March 24, 1906, the Edmonton *Bulletin* said: "Carriveau and Manuel, who are doing a large business with their benzine buggies, have ordered another carload of automobiles from Chicago—they are ordering Fords this time, all high-potential machines, capable of making great time on the good roads which converge on Edmonton."

Some weeks later on, an advertisement in the *Bulletin* listed twenty-seven second-hand cars which could be had by mail-order from Toronto, and stated: "A modern car is as easy to run as it is to drive a horse—and actually safer than most horses and actually less expensive to keep." Apparently all you had to do was fill in the coupon below, send a draft for your money, and in due time your benzine buggy would arrive.

Dad, in reading a current issue of the paper, was amused by a letter from an irate citizen complaining of the conduct of those in high places when in charge of an automobile. The writer had been out driving with his horse and buggy on the Cooking Lake Trail when he heard the chugging of a motor car behind him. He had looked back to ascertain from the driver on which side the car wanted to pass; at that moment the car had pulled out around him, nearly striking his back wheel, and then, as it slipped in front of him, some part of the roof of the car caught in the ring of the horse's bit, yanking the bit out of its mouth, breaking the bridle and causing the horse to gallop down the road out of control. "Something," said the letter, "should be done about this."

Well, it appeared that the recently elected members of Alberta's first legislature had already planned to do something, for Mr. J. R. Boyle, the Member for Sturgeon, had moved in the House on April 23, 1906, "an Act to Regulate the Speed and Operation of Motor Vehicles on Highways." This Act provided that the owner of a vehicle must "register with the Provincial Secretary and take out a permit. He is given a number and a licence and is requested at all times to carry the number exposed and to carry lights at night, bearing the number on the glass . . . twenty miles per hour in the country, except when passing from the rear vehicles drawn by horses, when it is required that the speed be cut down to ten miles an hour. When meeting a rig, the speed limit is five miles an hour." Yes, indeed, these benzine buggies would have to be cooled down a bit.

This, then, was the bustling city that Dad entered when he walked up McDougall Hill in October 1906. It did not take him long to get his bearings and to decide to leave Mother and me camped on the flats while he went out to the country north and west of Edmonton to select a homestead.

To Mother, the two weeks in the tent were a welcome relief. While Dad was away, Mother was able to rest and to get some of the travel weariness out of her bones. The camp on Ross Flats grew smaller as families moved out to their homesteads. All sorts of people, mostly women and children waiting for the return of their menfolk, surrounded her: Germans, Norwegians, and Americans; people from "back east"; English, Irish, Scots, Galicians. All the women were uneasy, yet they were all friendly because they shared the experience of awaiting the unknown, some with hopefulness and others with grim determination; and these feelings were mingled with loyalty to their venturesome husbands, who were trying to better their own and their children's chances, even though there might, as in Mother's case, be some resentment at the uprooting of their lives. The Canadian and American women were the most confident. At most they were only two generations removed from the frontier and the majority had already moved ahead of civilization once or twice in their lives, just as their mothers before them had done.

Up McDougall Hill there was a world even stranger than that of the camp, and Mother, taking me with her, went for walks along the streets of the city. She saw buildings going up everywhere, a few with steel framework covered with brick, and dozens of wooden ones with false fronts. The sound of hammer and saw and the redolence of newly sawn spruce lumber filled the air. Mother had never smelled that before, but she enjoyed its clean wholesome pungency.

The men she saw on the streets were dressed in a great variety of clothes, with overalls predominating but with buckskin jackets and hobnail boots very much in evidence. Here and there a mounted policeman in his service uniform and stetson hat stood out smartly. But the crowds were composed mainly of women. A few were nicely dressed women whose husbands were already established in the town, but most of them were newcomers wearing plain, serviceable clothes. The scene was enlivened by the bright plaid scarves and blouses of the squaws and half-breed women, some with papooses on their backs and most with one or more black-haired, button-eyed cherubs in tow. The Galician women wore their invariable shawls, white, yellow, or a subdued red.

The streets were a babble of languages. These varied all the way from the soft accents of Negroes, coming in to take up land, to the sing-song of Chinese immigrants and the gutteral accents of Indians. Broad Scots brogues competed with the idiom of Yorkshire and Lancashire, and Cockney voices challenged the dialects of the western, central, and southern United States.

Hither and yon along the muddy streets, teams drew huge loads of lumber that had been cut at Walters' Mill, and Fraser's, and other mills all over the country to the east, north, and west of Edmonton. Mother was no judge of horses, but she noticed these fine teams, and noticed too the fast-stepping ponies that pulled the light carriages—the buggies, as she heard them called. She saw also some ill-matched teams driven by settlers who, it was only too obvious, were trying it for the first time. Indians rode by on their ponies, or belaboured their despondent, half-starved horses. Ox-teams plodded along, slobbering and slow, pulling not by means of a yoke but in ordinary harness. On the less muddy days an occasional car chugged past, a forlorn pioneer like Mother herself.

About a week went by, and then, one evening, Dad came back to announce that after travelling north and west for three days into the valley of the Pembina he had selected a homestead. Tomorrow he would go to the Land Titles Office and file on it. He and his new-found friend, Tom Pirie, had taken adjoining quarters, and had arranged for teams to travel together to take both their families out. That night the MacGregors visited the Piries, who were also camped on the Flats, although Mother had not yet met them.

The next few days were busy ones for Dad and Mother; he filed on the land and then bought supplies, while she packed again. On the morning of October 18, all was ready, and we set out on the last leg of our journey.

"What will our new address be?" asked Mother. "I'll write home to Dolly and tell her, and she can let the others know."

"There's no post office," stated Dad, who hadn't thought of it before. "Just tell them Edmonton, I suppose."

"But we shall be sixty miles away from Edmonton, you said. Your next pension cheque will be due in January. There's one due now, if only we knew where it was. How will you get them? How shall we get our letters and the newspapers?"

"We'll get them in the spring," said Dad.

2

"This," said the teamster, "must be about the centre of your homestead."

"Well, here we are, Mother," said Dad, with a brave display of optimism. "Here is the farm."

"Good Heavens!" was all Mother said.

If I had any comments, no one thought them worth remembering.

There were, however, two other reactions. The first came from the edge of the stand of magnificent spruce which had effectively blocked the team's further progress into the forest. "This grove," a squirrel shouted, "is my domain. Go away!" And he continued to scold and chatter. The second was from a whisky-jack, who appeared the minute the unloading started. He extended the wing of welcome and chirped confidently as he flitted from branch to branch. "This," he prattled, "looks like a good place to spend the winter."

And that is how, at four o'clock on the afternoon of October 21, 1906, we entered upon the North-West Quarter of Section 16, Township 59, Range 1, West of the 5th, to possess it. It took but a few minutes for the teamster to unload and to help Dad set up the tent. It took him longer perhaps to turn the team and wagon around amidst the trees and fallen logs. In the space of a quarter of an hour we had arrived, unloaded, and set up housekeeping. The teamster, waving good-bye, followed his previous wheel-marks in the moss and disappeared along the way we had come. For a few minutes more we could hear the rattling of the receding wheels as they rolled over logs, and the whack of whiffle-trees as they smacked against stumps. Then all was silent, all but the October breeze soughing in the trees.

"Here we are," said Dad. "Farmers."

"Here we are," replied Mother, "cast adrift."

She gazed along the way the teamster had gone, and listened in vain. Then she sat down on a log and cried. The tears were a mingling of fear of this dreadful forest, bitterness at leaving the comforts of civilization, and anger at Dad that he could have brought us to this pass. For, she reasoned, we had been very comfortable and secure in the Old Country. Now we were neither.

Dad, contrite as any man in the presence of tears, built a little fire and in silence set about preparing supper. If this adventure miscarried he knew that he alone was to blame; the idea of coming to Canada was his idea and his alone. But even if his thoughts were grave, even if he felt on his shoulders this heavy responsibility, the burden of melancholy was not added to the load of his cares.

As soon as supper was eaten, Dad cut spruce branches and fashioned them into a comfortable mattress. Then, by the time he had lit a fire in the small cook-stove and had disposed everything for the night, it was dark. Before long the full moon, riding along the treetops, cast the shadows of bare branches on the roof of the tent—clutching, menacing shadows that moved as the giant trees swayed in the breeze. Within, all was dark and silent; dark, except for the bright glow from the damper-hole of the stove; silent, except for the quiet breathing of a year-old baby. Dad settled himself near the door, with Mother next to the wall, and me in the middle. Between the MacGregors and the unknown forest stretched the canvas of a tent ten feet square, erected just three hours before. The night of October 21, 1906, had fallen on the homestead—the first night since time began that man had laid claim to it and had said, "This is my land."

The comfort of the bed after the fatigue of the day, the warmth and aroma of the boughs, the smell of the fresh-cut spruce mingled with the hint of smoke from the little stove—Dad relished it all. What if he was forty-one? Maybe the venture was foolhardy; time alone would prove or disprove that. What did the Bible say of the man who vacillated?—"No man, having put his hand to the plough, and looking back, is fit for the kingdom of God."

In the flickering glow of the heater, as Dad puffed at his pipe, he thought of the immensity of this land. We have not covered many miles today, he mused. By the map, in a straight line, we are only forty-six miles from Edmonton, the last outpost of civilization. By the trail, Edmonton is four days away. To the north lies the forest. A straight line from Edmonton to the tent could be extended a further four hundred miles before it passed out of Alberta, and hundreds of miles beyond that before it passed from the last stunted trees to the barren lands. Along all that line to the north, not one settler would be found. We are on the frontier—nay, beyond it!

Mother's thoughts were vastly different. We were in the middle of this hateful, alien bush. So was Edmonton, for that matter. So was all this malign country from Montreal west. Tomorrow she would make Dad pack up and go back to civilization. But, she remembered, he could scarcely do that, having neither team nor wagon. All right, then, he could walk back somewhere and get a team, and take us away.

Mother lay staring glumly at the shadows that leered at her from the roof of the tent. A few short weeks ago she had left London and now that rasping, coughing squawk she had just heard was an owl—so Dad said—an owl in the Canadian bush. As she tossed and turned on this much overrated bed of spruce boughs, Mother thought she would never again get the ache out of her back. For four days she had sat in that wagon, lurching in the mud-holes, swaying over the corduroyed sloughs, jolting over logs which the teamster did not want to chop out of the trail, rocking as first a front wheel passed up and over a tree root and then bumped down, and then a back wheel repeated the motion. The ship had been miserable, the train from Montreal wearying, but this wagon trip had been four days of torture.

The teams had arrived at the Flats first thing in the morning. One of them went for the Piries while the other came for us. Huge horses drew a lumber wagon with a green box; there were canvases to cover everything, and two spring seats perched high in the air. Soon all was piled in our wagon: Dad's salmon rod on the floor, his fishing creel somewhere in the load, and, lashed on top, his Sunbeam bicycle, brought all the way from London. Dad and the driver sat up in front while Mother, holding me, clung desperately to the second seat.

"We're off, Mother," said Dad. The teamster drove around by Pirie's tent and waited until their load was in place, and then we were really off. The rains of the previous three or four days had left mud puddles in the road, and in the early morning each had a thin skin of ice over it. The weather was slightly colder; the warm sunny days of a week ago had gone.

Around by old Fort Edmonton the procession went, past the Catholic hospital and other buildings, across Jasper Avenue about 16th Street, and finally its wheels were set on the St. Albert Trail. That this was the old Fort Assiniboine Trail, which everyone knew as the Klondike Trail or the Dawson Trail, Mother didn't know and probably didn't care. As far as St. Albert it was a good graded road, with culverts over the little streams, and it wound past a dozen snug-looking farms. They had that restful appearance common to farms in the bush when the fall work is over and they are settling down for the winter. The fields were not large, but scattered over them two by two were stacks of grain, waiting for the threshing-machine. Other fields had piles of fresh white straw. All had remnants of what appeared to have been lush gardens, and all had pigs and some cattle. "See, Mother," said Dad, "that's what our place will be like next year."

In the morning sunlight they looked rather attractive, and Mother was optimistic, especially since Dad had told her that they would reach St. Albert for lunch. This town, he said, was older than Edmonton in point of settlement and was the seat of the Roman Catholic bishop. As we followed the trail down to the little town, Mother had another disappointment. So this was St. Albert! *This* was the seat of the Bishop! She had conjured up a vision of something rather different. However, it was a busy stopping-place, alive with settlers coming or going. Some, like ourselves, were in charge of a teamster, others were driving their own ox-teams, and still others, the fortunate ones, were driving their own horses. But ox-teams predominated.

After lunch the trip was a repetition of that of the morning, except that the farms were better and all of them looked cosy with their neatly stacked woodpiles. The road was not so good, but it was straight for as much as two miles at a time, possibly the first straight road of that length Mother had ever seen. At dusk we reached Riviere Qui Barre with its two hotels and a few other buildings.

Lying in the tent among the trees, Mother remembered how gratefully we had all gone to bed in the hotel there; and now she wondered what had possessed Dad to pick this particular spot for the homestead. It was obvious that he could have chosen one closer to Edmonton. Some of the land on the way had looked good and had been covered with only light brush. How were we ever to get the great trees off this? To "clear" it appeared to be the expression. Except for the Piries, who were in like straits, we were miles from any neighbours. What had possessed him? He was "bugs," that was it—just "plain bugs." A good expression, she thought; an American one, which she had heard in the camp, and the teamster too had used it. Then in a flash she was transported back into that bed at Riviere Qui Barre, for she had just now realized the full import of the word. She remembered again how tired we had all been; we had fallen asleep almost instantly. But Mother had awakened in short order. Something in the bed had bitten her. . . .

It had been a long trip, from Riviere Qui Barre to the homestead. We gradually left the good farms behind, and the road no longer ran straight north or straight west. Fences had disappeared, and the trail wound this way and that, going, she was sure, two miles around to make one mile of progress. Like an English road, she thought—in respect to its crookedness only. It was still muddy after the recent rains, and the further north we went, the more closely the forest hemmed it in. Only occasionally was there a little space cleared and fenced with picturesque rails. Nothing else was picturesque. The trees, although there were millions of them, bore little resemblance to the dignified oaks and elms of the English countryside. There were poplars with their tall white trunks, bare of branches except for the topmost ten feet. There were spruces, equally straight but with branches all the way down to the ground, shutting out the sunlight. Here and there, of course, there were little meadowlike openings in the forest, but the meadows shaded almost imperceptibly into slough and muskeg, and in those stretches there were mud-holes along the trail.

The second night after leaving Edmonton we reached Johnny Williams's place at Independence. It was a recognized stopping-place with a large log house and some log buildings. A small saw-mill showed at the edge of the clearing amidst great piles of spruce logs and huge mounds of white sawdust. Independence, even at that time, had a post office, which, if we had realized it, was the nearest one to the homestead. It took Mother some time to find out that usually a post office in Northern Alberta was kept by some homesteader, so that the places marked on the map were not necessarily villages or hamlets at all. In fact, north of St. Albert there were no villages.

On the third day the road became worse, and our progress slower. We wound through the great belt of timber in the area that is now known as Picardville. There appeared to be no sign of civilization in this area but Sanderson's mill and the ubiquitous cutlines. After leaving the thickest of the forest the teams passed a formidable slough, and finally ascended a hill. There beside the trail in a sheltered spot where there was plenty of dry wood, we camped. The night was fine, so the tent was not erected. Lying there watching the brilliant stars above and the bright moon gradually passing through some light clouds, it took Mother a long time to go to sleep, but she was cheered by the promise that tomorrow we would reach the homestead.

The next day we did reach it. The trail continued west down the hill for some distance, crossing more muskegs, but by this time it was scarcely recognizable as a trail. Finally it turned north for some hours, working its way along the cutline. Late in the afternoon we passed a neat little log shack with a sod roof, but the owner was not at home; Dad found out afterwards that it was Paulson's shack. At that point Pirie's teamster turned off in the direction of the hilltop, where the land appeared to be a little more open. Our teamster followed another cutline west for about half a mile, and then, abandoning this, plunged north into the bush. On this last stretch there was not even a pretext of a trail, and he skirted around trees, trying to pick the more open places. At four o'clock he stopped.

"And here we are," sighed Mother, thinking back over it all, while beside her Dad snored away without a care in the world.

We slept late next morning, and were awakened by the sun streaming through the door of the tent. Mother was woefully stiff, but in spite of that it struck her as being a good morning, even if it was a little cold around the edges—the sort of morning which in the past she would have called wintry. She walked around the tent to see where we were—to see some of our 160 acres of free land. When Dad remarked that we were lucky, because the survey map showed that our quarter contained 161 acres, Mother laughingly prophesied that he would curse that additional acre before he got it cleared. The forest looked so formidable that, try as she would, she could not visualize it ever being transformed into waving fields of grain.

The tent was at the south edge of a grove of stately spruce trees. To Mother it was only bush: to Dad it was a sacred fane. While breakfast was cooking he walked into it, gazing at each huge trunk in turn, down this long aisle and down that one, and then upward. As Dad looked up, it was thirty feet before a branch marred the symmetry of the great rugged columns. It was seventy-five feet to where the branches arched out and interlaced to form the living tracery of the cathedral roof, that roof through which no sky appeared.

Then the solemnity was shattered by the chattering of a squirrel, loud and clear, warning all denizens of the grove that an intruder had come among them. From somewhere, as Dad turned to retreat, a bush partridge clucked nervously, and then its steps became audible on the thick carpet of leaves. "Pat, pat, pat," sounded the steps, and drew Dad's attention to the bird strutting away, its out-ruffed throat and wide-spread tail jerking in time with each step.

"Well, what did you see?" asked Mother. He tried to tell her of the squirrel, the partridge, the yielding moss, the soaring columns, but what you feel often differs vastly from what you can express. "Fine lumber," he said. "Spruce trees so thick"—he held out his arms to show her—"thirty feet up and not a branch or knot on them. Worth thousands. We'll be rich, Mother."

After breakfast he left Mother to unpack her treasures while he went out to get his bearings, as he said—to establish in his mind the boundaries of his estate. Taking an axe, he followed the wagon tracks about half a mile back to the east-and-west cutline which we had left on the previous day. The cutline, when he reached it, stood out clearly, a gash in the forest three feet wide, with all trees cut to fall right and left of the line. Slashed through but a year ago, it was easy to see but hard to follow as it ran westward across ridges and creeks, sloughs and meadows. He had to detour around the sloughs because many of them were full of water. Around their banks and on little islands were muskrat houses.

Finally he came to an intersecting cutline running north and south. At the intersection were four pits about two feet square and eighteen inches deep, and full of water. In the centre was a mound of clay which one year's growth of grass had not covered. Out of the mound stuck an iron stake, proclaiming to all the world that it marked the north-east corner of VIII.LIX.I. It was therefore the south-west corner of Section 16, and Dad knew that, half a mile north of it, he would find the south-west corner of his own quarter-section.

North from the survey mound the new cutline crossed two sloughs in quick succession, then rose to higher ground and denser forest. Then another slough barred Dad's way; he detoured, and came back to the line at the top of a long slope. Looking down it he saw yet another and bigger slough in the path of the line. There was no lack of water, that was certain! Beyond, the land took another drop to a low-level area, and beyond that again, nearly a mile away, it fell rapidly to a still larger flat. Then, several miles further on, it rose again and gradually merged into the horizon fifteen miles away. Flowing in the bottom of the valley, Dad knew, would be the Pembina River, and somewhere away over the horizon lay the mighty Athabasca. But what a queer way to have to look at the country, through this narrow slit of the cutline! It was like looking through the sights of a rifle.

He made his way down the hill where the cutline passed through a magnificent stand of spruce trees. He recalled what he had read of the surveyors' description: "The surface is rolling, nearly hilly towards the south part, with no prairie or very little spots of it. It is covered with a new growth of small poplar and willows easily cleared. On Sections 26–17–16–9 and 10 there is heavy bush. . . . There is a large island of heavy spruce on Sections 9–10–16 and 17. We saw there five spruce measuring as much as thirty inches in diameter and sound. . . . The sections or quarters containing these spruce might be turned into a timber reserve for the use of settlers."

In a short distance he came to his objective: four pits, a mound, and, this time, a wooden stake marked merely "$\frac{1}{4}$." This was it, then; sixty-six feet east of this stake was the corner of his quarter. He carefully stepped off this distance, which was the "road allowance," and came to another great spruce at the exact corner of his land. He blazed the tree and stood there a moment, lost in thought.

He owned this land, this 161 acres. Half a mile east from this tree it stretched, and half a mile north. It was all his to do with as he willed—or as he was able. He was the first man in all time who had set foot here with the intention of tilling this soil. For thousands of years to come, men would live here, but to him was given the privilege of being the first. Strangely enough he thought of William the Conqueror who, when he landed at Hastings, had knelt down and seized the land. Legal documents still referred to that. Did they not say that a man was "seized of" a piece of land? Should not he, too, kneel down and with his hands seize this rich soil?

From the big spruce tree he walked east along the south boundary of his land, keeping as straight a line as he could and blazing the trees as he picked his way along. After advancing a quarter of a mile, he crossed the wheel-marks in the moss, and there, not a hundred yards away, was the tent. The teamster had said that this spot would be about the centre of his land. Actually he had brought us to the very edge of the quarter.

While Dad had been locating his estate, tramping over it and gloating over it, Mother had been looking to hers. She had been unpacking and she had no cause for gloating. Some of the trunks had been stored in such a position in the ship that they had filled with sea water. Many of her clothes, pictures and souvenirs, and her two clocks, had been ruined. When she opened the last trunk she found that what the sea water had spared, the four days' jolting in the wagon had stricken. Most of her china, her ordinary cups and saucers, her Dresden and Doulton ware, and many other treasures lay in little fragments at the bottom of the trunk. Possibly a dozen pieces of china remained. When Dad arrived from his surveying, Mother was throwing away the broken bits behind the tent—her first sacrifice, the first of her offerings to this new homestead. If today you start from the barn and walk south 150 yards and a little east, you will find mixed with the soil of the field many blue, red, and creamy fragments of china.

Each time she carried a load of broken pieces out of the tent she walked by the tree against which leaned the bicycle and the salmon rod, and on which hung the fishing creel. These things had been spared by the trip; it was her china and her clocks that had been destroyed.

Dad looked in on the process of unpacking, but as wisdom dictated a hasty retreat he went for another reconnaissance. This trip took him along the edge of the meadow, past the thick spruces, and on to the bank of a little creek. It was dry, except for ice-covered pools. Following the stream a short distance he entered another grove, through which the creek in its rapid descent had cut a miniature gorge. The banks of the creek were thick with chokecherry bushes, still heavy with their ripened, wrinkled fruit. This little gorge, then, would be where the creek flowed off the bench to a lower level. This bench with its brook would make an ideal building-site. Moreover, it nurtured some splendid poplar and balm trees which could be cut and rolled into position for the house. The higher knoll a hundred feet to the south, where birch trees eighteen inches in diameter grew, was to be reserved for the permanent home which would be built a few years hence.

Two hundred yards to the north-west was another grove of tremendous spruce trees. As Dad walked into it he came to six trees of immense size, one of which stood out as a giant. The surveyors had mentioned five spruce trees measuring thirty inches in diameter. Well, they had missed this grove. Many of the trees here were more than three feet thick and the huge one easily spanned four feet. Dad returned to the building site and cleared out a place in which to pitch the tent, and another on which he proposed to build the log house. On his way back to Mother he slashed out a path.

After lunch Dad took down the tent and he and Mother carried it to its new location and set it up again. Then they returned for our other possessions. I was quite a problem. If one of them carried me, very little else could be carried, so they solved the difficulty by shutting the tent door and leaving me in it while they made their short trips back and forth.

To the whisky-jacks fluttering along ahead or behind, they must have made quite a spectacle as they carried the stove, trunks and other goods along the newly made path. The squirrels, too, took a critical interest in the proceedings. Each time Dad and Mother arrived at the site with a new load, the squirrels burst out afresh. " Here they come," they shouted, and chattered away until the bearers departed. Then they appeared to be notifying the squirrels at the other end to look out. These squirrels would be silent for a while and then they too started scolding, as much as to say to the others, "You're right, they're back here again."

The job was finished before dusk, although Dad had taken time also to mark out the boundaries of the cellar and dig away some of the surface layer, thus revealing an intricate mass of roots which required much chopping and digging to remove. On the last trip of all he slung his creel over his shoulder and, carrying the salmon rod in one hand, guided the bicycle over the logs with the other.

After supper (dinner we called it, though, until I went to school) Dad took Mother and me down to the new grove to see the giant spruce. As we returned to the tent the sky in the west flamed out into the radiance of an autumn sunset. The calm strength of the rugged trees silhouetted against the magnificence of an Alberta sunset impressed even Mother. "It will be a fine day tomorrow," said Dad—an observation which he was to repeat nearly every evening for over forty years.

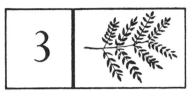

3

The building of the house went slowly, although Mother and Dad worked hard, and even jubilantly. In spite of Mother's resistance to the whole idea up to this point, it was, nevertheless, an accomplished fact now; so, like another man, she worked beside Dad. She was twenty-seven then, and strong. Three things, however, conspired to delay them: they had no team, they were inexperienced, and they placed too much reliance on the immigration literature.

The lack of a team, though a severe handicap, was partially offset by the proximity of building-logs. Fine straight poplars and balms a foot in diameter grew all around the spot selected for the house. In fact, two of them were chopped off it before Dad commenced digging the cellar.

Willingness is a poor substitute for experience. Dad and Mother finally built a house, but two French-Canadian axe-men would have erected it in a twentieth of the time. Moreover, had they realized, on October 23, how little time they had, they would have built a small shack of light poles, one that could have been thrown up in three or four days. For they would have known that winter was almost upon them, and they would have known what sort of winter Alberta might produce. So much for experience.

The rest of the blame lies with the immigration literature. Dad knew that Alberta winters sometimes reached sixty below. He knew that occasionally missionaries, trappers, and traders had frozen to death in blizzards. But these things, he thought, occurred in January and February, while this was only October. All the literature and advertising had spoken of the salubrity of Alberta's autumns. It admitted the possibility of a little snow perhaps, even in October, but very rarely; and then extolled the glories of Indian summer. This, according to the advertising, was a magic season, warm and free from snow and lasting till the new year. Having experienced nearly fifty Alberta winters, I find it hard to believe that Dad could have been so optimistic.

Now, if you are going to build an orthodox house—a home, even though it be of logs—you must have a basement. So Dad laid out his house on the ground, twenty feet by thirty feet, and commenced to dig the basement. Fortunately he started at one end, lengthening the excavation as he went. By nightfall on the first day he had done little but remove one stump and raise a fine crop of blisters. The night fell early, and without any glorious sunset. The sky was low and grey. A brisk breeze stirred the brittle leaves on the forest floor, and whirred those left on the willows. High overhead it roared through the tops of the spruces, which bent and creaked but shielded the tent below from all but the momentary gusts that slipped through their guard.

The canvas of the tent, bellying in and out, strained at the guy ropes. Before morning its struggles had ceased and it hung drab and grey, soothed by the patter of rain. For four days the rain, cold and dismal, poured on leaf and log, and dripped from branch and bough. On the fifth morning Dad awoke to silence. "Good," he thought. "It has stopped raining." He opened the flap of the tent on his first sight of the snow-covered forest. This, then, accounted for the silence—snow, still falling ever so quietly.

Oh, well, a little snow in October maybe, the literature had said, and then Indian summer till Christmas. In the meantime, one could work in the snow, so he returned to his digging. In a day or so more he had a hole nearly ten feet square and five or six feet deep.

As he was felling a tree an old man with a long white beard appeared at his elbow.

"I didn't know I had neighbours so close," he said. "I was following a deer and heard you chopping. I'm over on the north-west of Eight. We came out in July. My name's Darling."

Then he advised Dad to forget about his big house, stop digging that cellar, and put up a small shack.

When Dad suggested that Indian summer was coming, he wagged his white beard. "I was born in Canada," he said. "You can't rely on the weather. This could be winter. To be safe, you'd

better assume that it is. Listen," he said, pointing skyward. "See
them. Hear them. That's the wild geese going south, hundreds,
thousands of them going south for the winter. They know. They
are fleeing from winter and it will follow them closely."

With that, and a further shake of his head, he stepped back into
the bush and was gone.

Dad's experience had taught him that if he was doing something, the first five people who happened along would give advice
and each would advocate a different policy. He that putteth his
hand to the plough—should go right on ploughing. Dad returned
to his digging.

The rest of the afternoon the sky was alive with geese. They
flew over in wide spreading V's, sometimes fifty or seventy-
five in a V, one formation following close behind another. Sometimes five or six of these flocks could be seen at once. When they
flew thus in orderly formation their cackling sounded as if they
discussed quietly the things they saw below, and their discourse
started at the head of the line and rippled back along the wings
of the V. Sometimes their regular formation broke and they flew
over in wild disorder, swinging in great circles around the sky,
milling around, up and down and in and out, as they sought to
regain their discipline. Out of these flocks came discordant crying,
querulous, searching, and plaintive. It was long after dusk before
quietness again reigned in the heavens.

The next morning dawned to the cry of more geese, and all
that day they flew over, seeming to be more disordered than on
the previous day. Maybe, thought Dad, they do know something,
the geese and the grey-beard, both natives of this country. Maybe
he had better abandon the basement and start building the house.

So for the next few days he felled big trees parallel to the proposed walls of the house, cut them into logs, trimmed them with
a broadaxe and mortised their ends. Then he and Mother rolled
them into place. By the night of November 14 they had three logs
up all around the house.

That night, in howling fury, winter struck. For eight days we
were cooped up in the tent. The temperature dropped below
zero. Some snow sifted into the tent, but on the whole we were
comfortable enough, although somewhat confined. But the storm
treated the house and the cellar harshly. First the cellar and then
the space inside the logs was drifted full of snow. The old man
and the geese had been right.

During the storm the forest was a strangely desolate place. The squirrels, normally so inquisitive, had disappeared. Nothing moved in the forest but the whirling wind and the sifting snow. Even the red rose-hips, contrasting with the whiteness of the snow, seemed to shiver. We belong to the summer, they seemed to say. The bicycle and the salmon rod were covered with snow, and the creel, crammed with snow, swung forlornly from a branch. Everything was stilled but the howling wind and the creaking trees. Even the whisky-jacks had left us to our fate.

On November 23 the storm subsided. The weather warmed up and the sun came out. The squirrels, too, came out of their nests, and the whisky-jacks returned to see what we had to offer. The obvious thing to do now was to dig the snow out of the cellar, move the tent over it, and live in the cellar for the balance of the winter. Once the tent was moved, Dad could go on building the house round it. He flattened the faces of small poles for the floor of the cellar, and in due time we moved into our second home on the farm. About this time we had a visit from Tom Pirie, who told us that he had built a small shack and was relatively comfortable.

Thinking you might accuse me of exaggerating what kind of winter the MacGregors fought, I have looked up the official weather reports. If you are an old-timer, I don't need to tell you about the winter of 1906–7. Even at that, though, you might like to see the figures to refresh your memory.

"October 1906: Weather warmer than usual to the 17th, sometimes reaching 70°, balance of month cooler, rainfall heavier than usual. Rains from the 3rd to the 5th, on the 11th and 15th, from 24th to 28th, with considerable fall of snow on 28th. Trees were bared early in the month.

"November 1906: Weather fair to the 14th, with occasional snow. Severe storms and heavy snow and much colder from the 15th to the 23rd, dropping below zero on the 16th. Mild from 23rd to 29th, getting much colder on the 30th.

"December 1906: Exceedingly cold. Snow fell 4th to 10th, 13th and 14th, and 28th to 31st. More snow than average.

"January 1907: Exceedingly cold weather in January. Coldest January on record, 18·6° below normal for January. Average temperature January 12·3° below. Snowfall at Edmonton less than usual."

February relented somewhat, but still it kept its hand in. "First six days exceedingly cold," say the Alberta figures compiled at Ottawa, "next two weeks unseasonably mild, balance of month moderately cold. Snowfall for the month light."

On the whole, February was not bad, and the settlers that had endured thus far had hopes of living through till spring.

March took any fancy notions out of their heads, and plunged them right back into winter:

"March 1907: Temperature slightly below normal. Snow-fall greater than usual."

April and May followed suit. Homesteaders less than a year out from England recalled with dismay what the old-timers had said about Alberta's winters—ten months winter and two months poor sleighing. They had thought the old-timers were joking. Now they weren't certain. "Can't always tell when these Canadians are spoofing and when they are not."

Here is the report:

"April 1907: The outstanding feature of the weather of April was the unusual cold experienced in Alberta. Temperatures below zero recorded as late as the 28th, precipitation light.

"May 1907: The month of May was very cold in nearly all portions of Canada . . . vegetation was very backward and did not make much progress till nearly the end of the month. Temperatures 10° to 15° lower than normal."

Then June came, and the reports say: "Weather returned to normal." One of the months of poor sleighing, no doubt.

These, then, are the statistics for the winter of 1906-7—our first winter on the homestead, the winter we spent in a tent. But of course I don't remember it. Those who do will recall its severity not in such figures but in terms of the ice around the well and in the water trough—in terms of pulling up bucket after bucket of water with mitts so iced they slip on the rope, which, like an icy stick, is stiff and crackling.

When the bucket is so coated with ice that it holds only a cupful of water, and the rope is so stiff and slippery you can't get a grip on it; when the bucket breaks off the rope and you have to fish in the well for it, while the old red cow stands there soaking up the water and never gets enough, and the howling wind freezes your cheeks and nose—that's how you measure a cold winter.

When, one by one, the ears and tails of the cattle fall off from the frost, and those that live till spring are a sorry sight; when the hay and then the straw gives out and you buy straw at fabulous prices and haul it for miles; when the snow is so deep that hay racks upset two or three times on the way home and when you get there you find two more cattle dead—that's how you measure a cold winter.

When each morning towards spring two of you go out to the cattle, and five or six of them are down and can't rise; while one of you lifts on the head and the other tugs at the tail and one by one you get them back on their feet; when the one you have just raised staggers a few steps and falls down while you are lifting the next one—that's how you measure a cold winter.

When you have done all this and have prayed for green grass, and then it comes a month late; when the tailless, earless relics that have come through the winter gorge themselves on what grass there is, and you find them next morning bloated and dying— that's how you measure a cold winter.

But the MacGregors didn't have any cattle that winter of 1906–7. We wouldn't even have had a well at which to water them. If we had had cattle, we would have taken the biggest cow into the tent to keep us warm. Our livestock consisted of two whisky-jacks and several squirrels. When the weather became severely cold, the whisky-jacks disappeared, but when it moderated they returned to be fed. I think that it was only our help that got them through the winter. The squirrels, so voluble in the early fall, gradually fell silent and curled up in their nests fifty feet high in the spruces. They were no company to us at all. I fear that some of them froze in their nests that winter of 1906–7. Those that escaped, however, appeared in the spring just as chipper and saucy as ever.

So in the winter of 1906–7 we had no cares over our livestock. We had just ourselves to look after. Except for the fact that some mornings our hair froze to the wall of the tent where our breath had condensed, we suffered little. One or two nights of that and Mother made us all flannel night-caps.

Dad oftened bemoaned the fact that he was a slow sleeper. Many a night, he said, it took him twelve hours to sleep as much as an ordinary person did in eight hours. Mother complained that he was not only a slow sleeper but a sound and even sonorous one. She soon tired of trying to arouse him to replenish the fire when it died down in the early mornings. It was easier to do it herself. One morning about daybreak after filling up the heater and jumping back into bed she was asleep again almost before she realized she had been awake. Her sleep did not last long. In a few moments she woke up choking. Something had blocked up the stovepipe and the fire was filling the tent with thick smoke.

"Wake up, Dad," she shouted, at the same time beating a tattoo on his ribs. No answer.

"Wake up," she cried, using unkind names. "Something's gone wrong. The baby will choke."

By this time Dad was aroused, injured in spirit but not yet perceiving the reason for all the fuss.

"We'll all die of suffocation!" shouted Mother.

"Well," retorted Dad, "it's a quick, easy death."

Mother was flabbergasted. So was Dad, for the next thing he knew, he found himself and his flapping nightshirt out in the snow in bare feet, closely pursued by Mother with a stick of firewood. The pipe was soon righted, but Mother and Dad each felt aggrieved until breakfast had cheered them up and they could laugh at the excitement.

About this time Mary-Ann was added to our household. I have often wished that we had kept Mary-Ann. Unfortunately I don't remember her. By December that year I was eighteen months old, and for Christmas Dad carved me a doll out of a spruce log. Mother dressed it and Dad painted it. Mary-Ann was its name. I played with Mary-Ann all that winter. For the first two or three days, they tell me, she was treated like a doll. After that I found Dad's hammer and some shingle nails. Mary-Ann stood by me well, in spite of being pounded so full of nails that there was no space for more. We were inseparable companions.

Much of Dad's entertainment that winter was provided by Mother's efforts at making bread. You see, until Mother left Edmonton for the homestead she had never been more than a block or so away from a baker's. Dad had taken out what he thought was a plentiful supply of "Strong Bakers" flour, and during the first week on the homestead Mother and Dad discussed the fine art of making bread. He knew nearly as little about it as she did, but somewhere back in his childhood he had picked up the idea that yeast was a factor in making bread and that it was followed by a process called kneading. In any event, Mother set to work to bake, but they tell me that the loaf, when finished, was difficult to digest and hard to recognize as bread. Her next few attempts were dismal failures. Dad laughed and Mother nearly wept, and each time they had to throw it out, and then for a few days they reverted to biscuits and pancakes. Then Mother would try again.

Anyone who has broken up land in the forested portion of Alberta knows that every now and then you turn up a lump of grey material which is similar in appearance to a half-dried and decayed deer's paunch. Some people think that is what it is. Every so often someone ploughs up a piece of this stuff, which is actually a fungus growth like that on rotting birch trees, and takes it into his house, confident that he has found a piece of Indian pemmican that has been preserved all through the years. Anyway, you know the stuff I mean. Mother's bread was said to have resembled that. In after years her early attempts at making bread formed a favourite joke of Dad's. He would come home in the evening from breaking, carrying a piece of this stuff which the plough had turned over, and say: "Mother, I've just dug up that old loaf of yours again!"

But what I started to say was that one night there was a feeling of great expectancy in the tent. The previous night Mother had put on a cake of yeast and in the morning had mixed up the flour and the yeast and some salt, and was now being studiously careful to keep the batch warm. Towards ten o'clock that night the bread gave indications of rising, so Mother kneaded it and wrapped another sweater around the mixing-pan and stoked up the fire. It could get pretty cold in the tent. This bread showed signs of success, and it must not be allowed to get a chill, so she stayed up, hovering over it like a hen over her chicks, while Dad and I slept. She arranged with Dad that at midnight she would wake him up so that he could cherish the bread while she slept. At midnight she stoked up the fire, kneaded the bread, and decided that in about two hours it would be ready for baking, so she called Dad to do his stint of nursing along the promising dough, and then she crawled into bed. Dad got up, rubbed his eyes, pulled on his pants and, still only half awake, staggered over in the general direction of the bread pan. Mother turned her face to the wall and was beginning to stretch out and relax when Dad tripped over something in the crowded tent. He fell against the bread, and the pan ended up face downwards in the dust of the cellar floor. Another attempt at bread-making had literally bit the dust.

But even if they lacked bread, the MacGregors ate well. They had porridge and beans, biscuits and scones, and rabbits and rabbits. They had stewed rabbits and steamed rabbits, fried rabbits and fricasseed rabbits, boiled rabbits and baked rabbits, day in and day out. Once in a while Dad killed a deer, and occasionally a partridge added variety to the menu. On the whole we all ate very well, but, as the winter wore on, our stock of flour diminished alarmingly. Mother's attempts at bread-making had caused terrific inroads, and it finally appeared that something would have to be done about our food supply. Our cash, however, was exhausted. Dad could have borrowed enough from our scattered neighbours to get us by but that would have been only a temporary expedient. Call it stubbornness, pride, or independence, or what you will, Dad and Mother thought it necessary for Dad to walk to Edmonton, get a job, and then send a team out for Mother and me. They discussed this for two or three days, although there was no alternative. On a night near the middle of January the decision was made.

The next day was mild; but the sun, surrounded by a wide ring, peered bleakly through low clouds. All day Dad sawed and split wood. By evening the space between the front of the tent and the half-raised walls of the house-to-be was filled with wood, split and neatly piled. A narrow passageway led from the tent door. Snow had begun to fall, and as dusk closed in a white mantle, light as feathers, softened the harsher outlines of the woodpile.

In the morning it was still snowing and the piles of wood were two soft ridges, while the passageway was a shadier hollow in the snow. At daybreak, after a good breakfast and a hasty farewell, Dad started for Edmonton. As he slipped through between the two big spruce trees, twenty-five yards away at the edge of the clearing, he turned, waved, and disappeared. Mother stood looking at the huge tracks he had made in the fluffy snow and listening until she could no longer hear the sound of his progress through the underbrush. Then she turned and ducked through the door of the tent. For a while she sat down on the edge of the bed, watching me as I lay fast asleep. She busied herself doing the small jobs of housekeeping around the tent in a valiant effort not to feel the intensity of her loneliness and helplessness. But increasingly as the day wore on it was borne in on her, and by dusk it loomed over her.

A score of times that day she stepped out of the tent to look along Dad's tracks in the snow—the last link with security and the life she had known. The snowfall was fast blotting out even these. That night it erased them.

The following morning the sun shone on a scene of sparkling whiteness and beauty. Around the clearing on four sides rose the gigantic spruce trees, poplars, and balms, their branches heavy with snow not yet whisked off by any breeze. No track or depression marred the fresh whiteness. Even the untidiness of the branches and tops of the trees that had been cut to make building-logs was now enfolded and hidden. The scene was radiantly beautiful, but to the young woman from London it was filled with menace.

It would have been different if she had been brought up in the Canadian forest, or even with a knowledge of it, or of this pioneer life. Except for three years in a small town in the north of Scotland, where I was born, she had spent all her life in London. Today, here she was in this clearing, alone with her baby and a whisky-jack and surrounded by the intense cold whiteness of this faceless snow. Four days away by team lay Edmonton. Somewhere between, she knew, Dad was walking to that frontier town—that town which in October had disappointed her so, but which now would have seemed like Mecca. Ten days hence, or possibly two weeks, a teamster would come for her—maybe.

Half a mile to the east—"That way," Dad had said, pointing past the leaning poplar—was Piries' place. We had all gone there on Christmas Day. But there was no path. Dad knew the way; he could find his way anywhere in this enveloping forest. For her, the snow was too deep; there were patches of windfall; and besides, she knew she would get lost. Wolves, coyotes, lynx, and for all she knew, bears, would bar the way. These animals, unknown to her but cunning and fearsome and magnified into hideous monsters, were by their very unknownness enough to keep her from venturing.

In any other direction there would be the same terrors, and greater distances. No one lived to the north. Old man Darling lived two miles south-west, and the Dodsons lived five miles south-east. Henry Paulson's place was only a mile away, but he was away for the winter. Dad had said that he had met a man named Clausen who lived somewhere off to the west.

Mother's Church of England upbringing stood her in good stead. Each night, at least, she prayed long and fervently, if somewhat incoherently. Then she stoked up the heater and made sure that the guns were just where she could put her hands on them. The heater worried her; a fire too large was dangerous, but one too small might go out. Her stock of matches was low, and the tales she had read about numbed hands trying to start a fire. . . .

There was nothing to do; no work to occupy her time. Cooking for me, caring for me, talking to me, stoking the stove, took such little parts of each day. Stoking became more frequent as the bitter cold descended on the bush; but that lasted only five or six days. It was probably a good job that the thermometer had been broken. Later she learned that it had been sixty below at Edmonton; but what you don't know doesn't hurt you.

During the days of intense cold, even the whisky-jack failed to appear. The coyotes' barking and wailing had stopped also. The forest was unutterably still. Mother slept in her clothes, and made another night-cap for me. So the first week went by, marked off every morning on the calendar. Dad would be working in Edmonton now, and perhaps the promised team had already started out for her. She tried to picture them as they would appear at the edge of the clearing after the tinkle of the heel chains had apprised her of their coming. It was incredibly lonesome.

In a few days the weather warmed a little, the wind began to breathe through the trees, and the animals stirred again. The rabbits came out from the shelter of brush piles and hopped across the clearing. One morning Mother saw huge tracks circling the tent and stopping at the door—tracks of the tremendous feet of some fearsome animal. Not till she described them to Dad, weeks later, did she know that the tiny rabbits made them.

Once as she went out for firewood a rabbit shot across the clearing with a coyote hard on its heels. Neither noticed her, but she dropped the wood and dived back into the tent. In a minute came the agonizing scream of the stricken rabbit. Count yourself lucky if you have never heard the anguish and fear in that scream, and its ending in a final sobbing moan. Coyotes still catch rabbits in the fence rows, and, if you are standing with a group of friends in a modern farmyard, that scream stops all conversation and makes the hair on the back of your head tingle. It nearly prostrated Mother. Many times in the next three weeks it was to be repeated.

And at intervals all day long the coyotes yapped and howled. Just before dusk they would start again, and keep it up for as long as thirty minutes in blood-curdling unison. Their wail, rising and falling, and coming from all directions at once, seemed to form a ring closing in on the little clearing. A ring of awful portent. These were, Mother knew, coyotes and maybe timber wolves. Dad had said that they would not come near the sight or smell of fire—but was he sure?

Then for more than a day—she had not noticed it before—

from somewhere back of the tent rose an awful moan, then silence for five or ten minutes, then the groan again. It was something like the short wail of a ship's siren but not so deep or vibrant. All night it went on, and well into the next day, this moan, the silence, and the moan again. Mother did not notice that it lasted only as long as the wind was moderate. Not till the next winter did she hear it again, and then Dad told her that it was a branch of one tree rubbing on that of another.

According to the calendar, two weeks had gone by, and there was still no word. There was plenty of firewood and food, but fear was taking its toll. Mother began to dwell on the possibility of accident to Dad. She prayed much and slept little. Again she surveyed Dad's treasured guns. His loaded army pistol was there, and the ·303 Lee Enfield which the Sergeants' Mess had presented to him when he left the Scots Guards, and beside it three boxes of shells. There too was the fancy Alex Martin double-barrelled shotgun—for grouse-shooting on Scottish moors. Dad had carried the ·22 rifle with him, but had laid these out and had tried to explain to Mother how to use them in case of emergency. Never had she fired a shot and, God help her, she hoped she never would. But loneliness and fear were making her desperate.

One night after the ominous silence which always followed the howling of the coyotes, the canvas of the tent shook and bellied in deeply, while a heavy animal clawed its way to the top.[1] Beside the roof-jack it lay all night, and there, showing in the light of the lamp, was the bulge it made in the roof of the tent. Occasionally it stirred, and its claws scratched the canvas each time. Mother did not sleep that night but held me close and hardly took her eyes off this new terror. At daybreak, with much scratching and flapping of the canvas, this thing jumped off into the snow and was gone. Mother went out to look at the tracks in the soft snow, although she knew that she could not identify them anyway.

Mother said she cried most of that day.

The thing returned again at dusk, climbed up to the roof-jack and remained there until daylight. Mother resolved that if it came once more she would shoot it.

It came, and climbed to the pipe, and stayed there. For hours

[1] All my life I have wondered about this incident. I find myself almost unable to believe that a wildcat or lynx would venture to do this. Maybe it was a weasel or a squirrel, but Mother always maintained it was a large animal. The story of her testing in the tent for three weeks was harrowing enough. It needs no fabrication such as this might appear, to embellish it.

she did not dare to move, but sometime before dawn she picked up the loaded ·303, pointed it at the dent in the canvas, shut her eyes, and yanked the trigger. For days after, her shoulder was black and blue from the recoil. The noise in the small tent was deafening. When the smoke cleared, the animal was gone. Mother had been knocked across the bed; her shoulder, neck, and jaw were numbed, and she bled from a scratch on her face. Many months later when Dad examined the tent there was a hole through the canvas two or three feet from where the animal had lain.

This was the last straw. Half hysterical, Mother soothed me and talked to me for an hour or so, breaking into crying spells, she said. I'm glad I don't remember. But that was the last night on the homestead that winter. Dad had then been gone twenty days.

It took an hour next morning to feed me and get her own breakfast. Then Mother bundled me up in coats, sweaters, and a blanket, dressed herself warmly, for it was twenty below, and started out for Piries'. Past the leaning poplar she went, over fallen logs and around trees. Here and there, early in the winter in blithesome mood, Dad had blazed a tree. For some distance she was able to follow these signs, but after going around a deadfall she was unable to find any more of them. She knew, however, that the Piries lived in the general direction of the low sun ahead. She struggled on, often falling in the deep drifts, tripping over a branch or straddling a reclining log, and now and then dropping me in the snow. She was lost, except for the sun; and judging by the time she took to travel that half mile, she must have wandered far from the direct way. Finally she came on tracks in the snow and followed these into the little clearing surrounding the Piries' log shack.

In a burst of sobbing and tears she kicked on the door. Kindly Mrs. Pirie opened it. They had not known that Dad had left. The comfort and the company in their little shack, aided by a drop of whisky, which normally Mother would never touch, and a hot meal, brought new life to her. It was arranged that Pirie would go for Axel Clausen and get him to bring his team over and take Mother to Edmonton. He came the next day and we returned to the tent long enough to pack a few belongings. Amongst the things she did not take were Dad's guns, and these were a source of worry to Dad until the spring.

Three days later we were in Edmonton hunting for Dad. At that time of year he had found it hard to get a job, but after a few days had obtained one at the city warehouse. Some days later he had sent a teamster out for Mother, but this man had got mixed in his directions and several days elapsed before he called at Piries' place and then found that we had gone.

So ended our first winter on the homestead.

As you drive by the old quarter now, you can see our farm buildings, there, well back from the road. To the left of the big house stood the old log shack, which once had the tent over its cellar. See the alfalfa field beyond, and then the line fence further up the hill, and the field of barley beyond it? Piries' shack stood well into that field. The day Mother stumbled along, dropping me in the deadfalls, that distance took two hours to cover. Do you wonder that I can still see the forest growing there where the barley beards dip to the breeze?

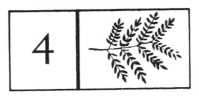

4

Bunty came into our lives in the spring of 1907. Bunty was a cow, a nondescript brown cow, with one horn awry and one blind teat. She gave milk. It is true that it was in limited quantities and for short periods only, each year, but it was undeniably milk. She was a docile, friendly beast, although on occasion she made it plain that she had a mind of her own and that, contrary to any notions we might have, we in reality were the servants of Bunty.

For a while Mother and Bunty were dubious of each other. Dad, however, rejoicing in his new-found rôle of farmer, milked Bunty in the beginning. Indeed he milked her for nearly a week. Somehow from then on that task fell to Mother, and a lasting affection grew up between these two. At times, of course, a coolness developed. Sometimes we would see Bunty flying out of the barn door while Mother, with uplifted stool and the milk running off her skirt, leapt after her in resolute pursuit. Then we would know that the flies had bothered Bunty, and that her flailing tail had slashed Mother across the face three or four times before it was tied down to Bunty's leg. Bunty's next move had obviously been to kick and upset the bucket of milk all over Mother's lap.

Poor old Bunty—the first cow in the township. I don't remember how she ended up. I suspect that we sold her when beef prices were high during the first war. I suppose, however, that her great-great-grandchildren must be around somewhere at the moment, unless of course her line was cut off by the hard winter of 1919.

In February 1907, when Mother reached Edmonton and found Dad, his plan was to return to the farm as soon as spring came.

That was supposed to happen early in April, so when April arrived we were ready to start. Dad's pension cheques for the previous three-quarters of a year had caught up with us, and this money, added to what he had earned during the winter, was available for the purchase of farm equipment.

Our trek back to the farm was very much the same as the first trip out, and the same as that of hundreds of others who were on their way to their homesteads. The main difference, as far as we were concerned, was that this time Dad drove his own team. Unlike most of the settlers who set out behind a slobbering snail-like ox-team, we had horses.

Dad's money had stretched over a multitude of purchases. We owned a second-hand wagon, but we could not afford the luxury of a spring seat. We also had a breaking plough, a few bundles of shingles, some nails, and enough teeth to make a set of harrows. We had some additional household utensils, some garden tools, and a further supply of flour and other food. Horses were in great demand and Dad had paid an exorbitant price for our team which, while they were good travellers, were very light for farm work. As well as the horses and Bunty, our livestock included ten hens and a rooster.

So, with all our farm piled on or about the wagon, except for the actual land and except for Bunty, who was tied behind, we took our place in the line of homesteaders striking out west along Jasper Avenue and swinging north about 16th Street to follow the old St. Albert Trail. Dad, the optimist, proud as Punch, enjoyed himself as he drove along. Mother, the pessimist, very dubious about Dad's prowess as a charioteer, hung on for dear life. Bunty, the sceptic, with many a shake of her head, protested in vain against this journey and sought incessantly to break the rope that was dragging her out to the frontier.

As we left St. Albert along the old Fort Assiniboine Trail, the ground was still snow-covered. The further north we went into the woods, the less the winter's snow had melted. During the afternoon of the fourth day we re-entered our little clearing. Although this was about the middle of April and Mother had abandoned the place at the end of January, there was little apparent difference. The snow was still there, although now it was old and packed down; the trees were still totally bare of foliage; and in the centre of the clearing the tent still stood.

Dad had worried about the guns Mother had left in the abandoned tent, and felt certain that he would never see them again. The first thing he did was to run into the tent to see if they were still there. They were. Nothing had been damaged, except that squirrels and other animals had gnawed their way into some of the food containers and had scattered much of their contents around.

The one thing to which all these months Dad had scarcely given a passing thought was the thing that had suffered most in its contact with the forest. This was the bicycle. Curious rodents, most likely squirrels, but possibly a porcupine disgruntled because he had come out of hibernation before the land had come out of the grip of winter, had gnawed away the leather seat of the bicycle. That the animals had seen fit to molest the bicycle, the most useless of all our possessions, struck Mother as amusing.

A fire was soon lit in the stove, and before long we were snug and comfortable again. Bunty and the horses, however, had a very slim two or three weeks. Dad had brought along some hay and some oats, but according to the calendar it was springtime and the animals should have been able to forage for themselves.

Dad and Mother set to work cutting logs for the house, but this time they had the assistance of the horses to move them the few feet from where they had grown to where the house was being erected. The walls of the house went up with reasonable speed. When, towards the end of April, the first real thaw came, the cellar began to fill with water, so the tent and its contents had to be moved to a drier location.

Spring hardly managed to arrive, even in May. As the weather report said, "vegetation was very backward and did not make much progress until nearly the end of the month." A spring like that dampens the optimism of newcomers. The literature had spoken of spring coming in March. It was very disappointing and discouraging. With the approach of June, pussywillows were in evidence and the buds on the poplars were swelling; nevertheless, snow remained in the shadier parts of the forest, and most of the forest was shady.

Then spring came. It came suddenly in the night. The evening before, the sun had set in a clear, cold sky, and ice formed on all the puddles of water. The starved creek slunk along, half-choked in the brittle remnants of the snowdrifts.

During the night a wind rose. Dad woke to hear it slapping the canvas of the tent and straining at the guy ropes. As he lay listening, the honking of geese filled the air. When he jumped up and peered out, it was daylight, but the sun was still only a promise in the eastern sky. The breeze brushing past the tent door felt soft and warm. The sky above the clearing was filled with clamouring geese flying north in great flocks. No sooner had one flock on his left disappeared over the treetops than another swept straight over the clearing. And then this was followed by another on his right. He shouted to Mother and me to come out, and see, and hear. For a long time the three of us stood in our night clothes watching in awe these great mysterious birds hurrying north on their annual pilgrimage.

"Spring is here," said Dad. "Let's get some breakfast."

Soon the sun rose and flooded the clearing. It rose over a land basking in the warmth of a spring day. Twenty-five yards away the creek, rippling and jubilant now, swept away the snowdrifts and capsized the snow bridges. The buds on the topmost twigs of the great balm trees responded first, for the rays of the rising sun caressed them first, and they swelled and opened and flooded the clearing with their fragrance. The crows were the first of our birds to respond. Yesterday, with crabbed croaking and drooping wings, they had hovered low over the snow, dejected and desultory. This morning, with cheerful cawing, they sat high in the trees, soaking up the grateful sunshine. "We've made it," they said. "Spring is here and we've lived through these last dreadful weeks to see it."

The fragrance of the bursting buds settled lower in the trees and reached the nostrils of the red squirrels. This was the signal for which they had waited all winter. It was the signal that set them into frantic activity. In groups and in pairs they celebrated. Out along this branch they raced, across to that limb they leaped, up this trunk they scampered, and then scrambled down to the forest floor. Up and down they raced, across the mossy dell and through the hollow log. Then they darted back up the tree, only to swoop from branch to branch and start all over once more. If, for a moment, they came to rest, it was to cheer and chatter. "It's spring," they said, "spring and green things, spring and toadstools."

Embarrassed for weeks now since their white coats had turned brown and made them conspicuous against the lingering snow, the rabbits rejoiced in silence. What they lacked in vocal prowess they made up in mad capers on the mossy floor. For spring is an enchanted time for a cotton-tail ever ready for amorous adventure. The brook the rabbits had leaped so easily the day before brought them up short now. It ran bank full, sweeping away the snow as it gurgled and purred on its way to the Pembina River. And every hundred yards, tinkling and chuckling, some little rill drained off the springtime flood from thawing meadow or pond newly freed from its icy cage.

New life had returned to each pond. At its edge waded snipe, dipping and bobbing. Along its fallen logs raced Sora rails, while overhead woodcock whirred by, and a pair of mallards splashed in for a landing or swam about seeking in every cove for a nesting place. In the centre of the pond, on willows where green buds pushed wintry pussywillows aside, sat red-winged blackbirds, singing and exultant. "Spring is here—there will be no end of worms and bugs and butterflies."

From far back in the misty green recesses of the forest came the boom, boom, boom of the bush partridge, thumping away. Over all the forest, with its new life, came all the sounds of spring's awakening. The forest, once so silent and foreboding, enveloped even Mother in its new aura of expectancy.

The MacGregors, too, had lived through the long frigid months. Winter's weary burden had dropped from their shoulders, and this forest adorning itself with the sights and sounds, and above all, with the smells of spring, held out a tantalizing new hope.

Perhaps all this did not happen in one day, but so it seemed. Yesterday had been winter. Today was spring.

Each day some new marvel unfolded as spring, so long overdue, hastened into summer. The grass at the warm edges of the ponds grew an inch a day. The trees sprang into leaf and their branches bowed with their load of feathery catkins, red or silvery. As the water receded in the ponds, the dark green lily-like leaves of the buttercups [1] pushed up through the shallow water, followed in a day or so by their gladsome yellow flowers. Yellow, a favourite colour of our forests, is the symbol of brightness and hope and cheer. These yellow buttercups, the first flowers of the year, brought a new lilt to Mother's voice and a new lightness to her step.

But if spring raised the MacGregors' spirits, it also raised up their most troublesome enemy. Each warm day brought from the grassy bottoms of the sloughs millions of mosquitoes. Each sultry night brought from the surrounding bushes myriads of them to attack the occupants of the tent. The mosquitoes were another

[1] Marsh marigold (Caltha palustris).

new thing in this new land to which we had not yet built up an immunity. Arms, faces, ears, eyes, and ankles swelled from bites as profuse as the spots of a bad case of measles. We had no protection from them and no escape.

The work of building the house had to go on in spite of the mosquitoes. There was no time to waste slapping at insects or gaping at the marvels of spring. The first three logs in each wall, of course, had been in position since the previous November when winter had struck. Now, with a team to haul the logs and to pull them up into place, Dad and Mother made rapid progress with their building. Soon even Mother's critical eye could discern the rude semblance of a dwelling. Building a medium-sized house with lumber is relatively easy, though it would be a tedious labour for one man working alone. Building a small log shack is also fairly easy. But our farm home was to be more commodious than a shack, so that big logs nearly a foot through and about thirty feet long went into its walls. Dad proposed to get enough lumber for sheeting the roof, but, cheap as lumber was in those days, he could not afford to buy two-by-six planks for the rafters. When the walls and the central log partition had reached the required height, he cut logs for the gable ends and laid these one on top of another until on each of the end walls, and on the central partition, he had three logs in place. Then on each side he ran a log stringer the long way of the house, resting it on these gable-end logs and the central partition in such a way that its finished surface would be in the plane of the roof when the time came to lay that. Above this first set of stringers he raised three more logs on the gable ends and the partition, and then placed another pair of stringers higher up in the plane of the roof. After that, a few more short gable logs carried the ends of the house high enough to support the ridge pole. The word "pole" is not a happy one in this connection. As I remember this so-called ridge pole, it was a good big log. Dad believed in strength in his structures and ruggedness in his roof tree.

We did get lumber for the roof. The homestead regulations made it possible for a settler to get a permit to cut ten thousand feet of lumber on his own place or on Crown lands for his own use. It was possible to go to a sawmill and turn this permit over to the mill owner; many settlers who made their buildings of logs needed very little lumber and sold these permits to various sawmill operators, and this gave the sawmill owner the right to cut timber off Crown lands. Dad decided to save his timber and arranged to pay for fifteen hundred feet of lumber for the floor and the roof. This lumber, which today would cost about a hundred dollars, cost about ten dollars in those days. To pay for it, Mother did the washing for several of the men who worked at the mill, and by some financial juggling the laundry was offset against the cost of the lumber.

The sheeting and shingling of the roof was soon done. A rough board floor completed the house for the time being. The central partition, which was made of logs, divided the house into two large rooms. Some time later, before winter set in, Dad acquired some more boards and made a ceiling, thus converting the house into one with two rooms downstairs and two upstairs, and at the same time making it much less draughty.

Mother, of course, had helped Dad to erect the logs; in fact she had worked at every stage in the construction. From a small peat-bog down in the bush, Dad brought up loads of moss with which to chink the cracks. These were then plastered with mud both inside and out. The finished house was warm and comfortable, and, if it lacked aesthetic values, it nevertheless stood staunchly between the MacGregors and the lashing rain or the driving blizzard. Even though it was large, sturdy and durable, it was not neatly done, and the cracks between the logs needed careful chinking. The spaces along the eaves, though stuffed with moss and packed in some mysterious manner with tar-paper, admitted enough air so that we were never in danger of suffocating.

The tar-paper in the eaves was a problem. When winter gales blew, it refused to suffer in silence, but instead sent forth lamentation. It vibrated and vocalized with a loud wail that was continuous and eerie. If anyone in the house were ill or sleepless, its constant moan would nearly drive him mad. It nearly drove Dad mad too, because he could never locate and correct the source of this noise. Even though the tar-paper's lament was explained to me, I never got used to the moan. Many a night when I woke up and heard it wailing away in the darkness I knew for certain that the Banshee had come.

In those early days I think we had much more rain than we have now. All the settlers spoke of a "rainy season" in June. Dad had to get the roof on the house before this rainy season came. At the same time there were dozens of other necessary tasks to complete. A garden had to be cleared, ploughed, and planted. So did a small bit of land for oats for the horses. The magnitude of the task of clearing up 160 acres of free land began to have meaning for Dad after he and the horses had worked several days to clear and break up a selected patch. Dad was a bit of a mathematician, so one evening after this first effort at farming had been completed, he measured the patch and computed its area. The result of this calculation was unbelievable; but after he had checked and re-checked he was forced to give in. Whereupon he threw the paper in the fire without telling Mother how much land all that effort had brought under cultivation. Truly the mountain had laboured and brought forth a mouse. The cultivated land on the MacGregor farm had reached a total of one-sixth of an acre.

Little as it was, this scratch in the forest was a beginning—an accomplishment. Dad planted and tended it, hovered over it and and enjoyed it to the full. The years proved that he was not to be a very successful farmer. He was inclined at times to mix medi-tation with his mowing, cogitation with his clearing and philosophy with his ploughing. What was the good of clearing out a clump of trees and dragging them over and building them into a huge pile, if you couldn't sit and watch them burn and see the roaring flames and rising sparks, and savour the fragrance of burning birch and sniff the aroma of smouldering willow ?

So many pleasures were inherent in life on a bush homestead. For forty years two of these never lost their fascination for Dad. He revelled in the smell and the sight of blazing brush-piles, and he relished equally the trickle of running water. In the earlier days at least there was a surfeit of moisture on our quarter. So Dad often enjoyed himself draining this little pool into that and diverting this little rill into that one, until by degrees he had streams of water running all over the place towards the central creek, which in turn drained to the Pembina River three miles away.

The patch of grain and garden led inevitably to the need for a fence, because Bunty expressed a gustatory interest in this cleared spot with its growing things, while the horses found it an ideal place in which to roll. Here was a new-found pleasure, a new art, building a rail fence which was the forerunner of untold rods of rail fences on our quarter. This first fence was built of spruce posts and spruce rails all cut within a stone's throw of the house. There was no muskeg on our homestead and, therefore, no tamarack.

If the garden needed a fence to keep the horses out of it, they and Bunty needed a place of their own, or rather, would need one when winter came. This need led to the erection of our second structure, a rude barn made of logs and slabs.

There were so many novelties and needs on this 160 acres of free land. As spring changed into summer the ponds dried up and a scum of green algae covered them. So, some twenty-five feet away from the house and higher up the hill, Dad dug a well four feet square and twenty feet deep. Its water was clear, cold, and palatable, and there was a definite satisfaction in hauling it up with a rope and bucket. Hitherto, Bunty and the horses had been content to drink of nature's bounty at any creek or slough, but now they too fell under this new influence of civilization which was entering the forest. They, too, had to drink at this new fountain. Since you can't have a gentle old cow like Bunty or even affectionate horses drinking out of the only bucket on the homestead, it became necessary to devise a watering trough. This, like many of its successors, was made by hollowing out a large balm log with an adze.

By the time all these tasks had been accomplished the summer was wearing away. This was in spite of the many hours of daylight that each summer day provided. The length of the days in Northern Alberta was something of which Dad boasted all his life. He could never resist calling attention to them. But Mother could not see any special virtue in long summer days or late summer evenings. A few extra hours of daylight, pleasant though they might be, could not be of much help in the long battle which she foresaw with the bush. All the hours of daylight from here to eternity, she thought, would be few enough to make much of an impression on the work that loomed ahead in clearing up the homestead. Moreover, long hours of daylight combined with multitudes of mosquitoes made it nearly impossible to get young Jimmy asleep each evening.

Mother was always a hard worker. If, as seemed likely, this mad mood of Dad's persisted—this mad desire to become a farmer at the age of forty-two—she would co-operate. In spite of pointed references to the folly of the whole undertaking, Mother was beginning to enter into the spirit of the thing. In fact, as the farmstead began to show signs of occupancy, she rather enjoyed the feeling of accomplishment, although she would never admit it. She worked side by side with Dad at everything he did, and worked more consistently than he.

One evening, while Dad quietly perused the *Glasgow Herald*

in the fading sunlight, Mother and I were busy weeding the garden. In reality, she weeded while I waddled around getting in her way and pulling up many of the plants which she was trying to assist. Mother, down on her knees, kept working along row after row, while I followed behind. At the beginning of each new row Mother would say, "We'll quit, Sonny, when this row is finished," but somehow or other when that happened she would always start on another. At the end of one of these rows she stood up to take the kinks out of her back. When she did so, all the sounds of summer in the forest became audible to her. Wrens were singing to and fro, while flickers talked back and forth, and wood-peckers shouted to each other. The whole forest was a medley of music. Gradually, however, her mind focused on a sound rising above all these others. Away off in the forest a strong, not unmusical, burred voice was singing—

"Too-re-loo-re-loo-re-lay
    On the Braes o' Killicrankie."

For a moment Mother listened before the full significance of it struck her. This was not someone on the trail, because the trail did not go that way. This song was coming from the dense bush off to the west. It must be a new neighbour, and a Scotsman at that.

"Dad," she yelled, dropping the hoe and running towards the shack. "Dad, there's someone down in the bush and he's Scots, and he's singing 'Killicrankie.' "

"Go on, woman, you're daft," said Dad, but he came to the door and both of them listened to the voice rising and falling.

Up to this time our nearest neighbours (starting at the south and running in a circle clockwise) were a Swedish bachelor, an old Canadian couple—regular Down-Easters—a Danish bachelor, a stolid German family, and, further off to the south-east, a French-Canadian family. The Piries, the Scots family with whom we had trekked to the homestead, had abandoned their land and returned to Edmonton. And here from out of the wilderness came this voice with the tang of the heather. The voice came no nearer, but continued to sing with a hearty goodwill.

"Dad, it's new neighbours!" said Mother. "I'll put on the kettle and you go and get them. Bring him up here, and bring his wife along. Poor soul," she added. On the chance of seeing a rabbit or partridge en route, Dad took his ·22 rifle and disappeared into the bush. He made his way through the trees for about half a mile before he found the voice. Stepping lightly on the moss, he came quietly upon the singer and, at the first pause, spoke up. "You're far from home, Jock."

The singer nearly jumped out of his skin. He whirled around. "Man," he said, "where did you come from?"

This was the beginning of a friendship of many years, that ended when Joe Fowlie was killed in 1916 at the Battle of St. Eloi.

"Come up to the house. The wife's put the kettle on."

"Bide a wee till I get this pitch off my hands," said Joe, as Dad followed him into the small tent. In the corner amongst a miscellany of clothes and tools Joe unearthed a stone crock of Hudson's Bay Whisky. During the next ten minutes it came out that, while Dad had served in the Scots Guards in Egypt and Africa, Joe had served with the Black Watch in India and Africa. After that he had been to the Klondike, and then he decided to take up a homestead in Alberta.

Soon, toting the jug of whisky, they arrived at our log shack. Mother was so glad to see someone that she sobbed while she poured the tea. It was daybreak before Joe was permitted to leave for his tent, and from that evening the homestead never returned to its former isolation.

By degrees, fall came on. As the leaves turned yellow, the edges of the meadows abounded in wild currants, black and red. Further back among the trees, raspberries ripened in wild profusion. Chokecherries reddened, then turned to black glistening clusters. Saskatoons hung heavy on bowed branches. These fruits, said Dad, were inexhaustible; there was no limit, save our inclination, to the amount we might pick. Mother, however, while agreeing that these were new and interesting fruits, was apt to compare them with the plums, apples, and cherries that surrounded our house in Dornoch, Scotland. She also pointed out that these Alberta fruits arose from the beneficence of nature, and that little claim could be laid to them as the first-fruits of our farm.

"Here we are," she used to say, "stuck out here, four days' travel by that awful wagon from even a town like Edmonton. Goodness knows it's a terrible place, and it's hundreds of miles from any proper city, and thousands of miles from London. And we came here because you wanted to be a farmer. Well, we've been here nearly a year now and where are your crops? Never mind the peach plantations, never mind the apple orchards, but where are these 'grain fields of golden opportunity' they yarned about?"

Dad would evade these remarks with a grin, and remind Mother of all the radishes we had picked from our garden. But Mother, deadly accurate as always in such matters, would point out that we had had radishes only three times before the worms got at the rest of them. And the lettuce that had promised so well had been found by the rabbits. "Radishes, lettuce, cabbage—we could get them at home from the greengrocer's for a penny an armful."

"Next year, Mother," Dad would say. "Next year we'll grow wheat. Tomorrow, though, I'll have to start putting up some hay—enough to feed Bunty through the winter and to keep the horses in good shape."

Mother challenged that idea too. Bunty was not pulling her weight. It was true that she was gentle, friendly, and companionable. She also expressed an interest in all we did, particularly in the garden, as well as devising ways to get over, through, or under the rail fence so as to demonstrate her appreciation of the vegetables. But her milk, if good, was not copious, and now she was beginning to dry up, just at the time when milk would be most beneficial, especially since our family was to be augmented about December.

"Hay for Bunty!" Mother snorted. "A barn for Bunty! And what do we get from her?—Limpid looks. And those horses, we really work for them. What do they do for us? They wander around the yard. They hover over the trough waiting for us to draw water for them instead of going down to the slough to get their own. Yet when you try to catch one of them to ride down to the river to go fishing, where are they?—Out of sight all day hiding in the bush. And now we must put up hay for them. Why, they haven't worked a week all summer!"

Chappie and Charlie did indeed live the life of Riley. They were our first horses and were little more than ponies. Compared to the draught horses we owned later on, or judged by the standards established in the 'twenties in Alberta, they really were scarcely worth their keep. Viewed in relation to their times, however, they were a team well worth having.

When in the spring of 1907 they picked their way in the footsteps of the horses which the fall before had broken trail taking us to the homestead, they were the second team to take up residence in the whole of Township 59-1-5. Axel Clausen over on 20 had the other team. What other settlers there were either had no motive power but their legs or else had oxen. To own any team was noteworthy. To own a team with the speed of Chappie and Charlie set their owner above everyone else for miles around.

Chappie and Charlie were neither draught horses nor drivers, but they were soon to show that they had stamina and speed. Through the mud-holes of the summer trails, pulling the rough old lumber-wagon, not even they could make good time, but when the steel-shod runners of the sleighs slipped along the snow-packed winter trail on the way to Johnstone's for Christmas or to Rose's for New Year's, Chappie and Charlie showed their mettle. When on an errand of mercy they sped tirelessly through the night pulling the light "jumper" Dad had made, they proved their pluck. The time an old man was found in his shack all but dead with a ruptured appendix, Chappie and Charlie's famous run to Edmonton in less than twenty-four hours was talked of for years. The time when a man came galloping up from the sawmill to get Dad to do what he could for the Swede who had run foul of the saw and was said to be nearly cut in two; the time when we did not see Dad for five days while he took the man to Edmonton over the old Riviere Qui Barre trail and saved his life—at these times they earned the respect of all men isolated in the bush on Township 59. The time they made the flying trip to Morinville for groceries when we started the store is still not forgotten—but that is a tale for later on.

At times like those, in emergencies, Chappie and Charlie entered into the spirit of things; but farm work—drudgery—they viewed dispassionately. Chappie wasn't so bad. He was an energetic little fellow who leaned forward into his collar and pulled. Charlie was the sly one, who ever so gradually eased back his end of the evener until it rested against something, thus leaving the willing Chappie to pull the whole load. Charlie had to be watched all the time to be sure that he did his share of the work. As Dad said, they were willing workers. Chappie was willing to work, while Charlie was willing to let him.

Maybe modern psychologists are right when they say that horses are not very intelligent. It is one thing, however, to test a horse under laboratory conditions, and a far different thing to live with one for many years and to have his horse-sense get you out of difficulties, his loyalty carry you through when the going is tough, and his affection greet you each morning as you enter the barn. It's still another matter, of course, to cope with his ability to hide silently in the trees when he knows you are in a hurry to find him and make a start on the spring seeding.

Charlie, even if foxy, was the steadier of the two. It was Chappie who started the numerous run-aways we had with the hay rack, when it went lurching and banging against the trees as the horses galloped in mad circles. Charlie only aided and abetted. But it was sly old Charlie who could be depended on to "snake" logs out of the bush. You know, when logs are needed for something you select whatever trees are suitable, and cut and trim them. When enough are cut, you skid them in one by one to a central pile, where later they are loaded and carted away. In doing this, two men work together, one out where the logs lie, the other at the pile. As the go-between you need a steady horse. He is led out to the nearest log, hitched to it and given a slap on the rump, the implication being "Get to blazes out of here and take that log to the pile." So back and forth Charlie went, dragging logs out and wandering back along the path alone; if a log got hung up on a stump or a root, he would change his angle of pull and try to work it free, and generally did so. He was a handy horse in the bush. But when noontime neared or when Charlie thought he had done enough, instead of returning along the path for another log he would wander up a path from which the logs had already been taken out, and then stop at the end of it as if he were completely confused.

I mentioned Axel Clausen as also having a team of horses. Axel was possibly twenty years of age. I am not certain whether he came straight from Denmark or had spent a few years in some other part of Canada or the United States. He was of short stature, but nimble physically and mentally. Like most Danes, he had a better than average education and was adaptable and friendly. As the years went by he took his place in the community.

I saw Axel some time ago. He is over seventy now, but the years have been kind to him. His eyes glowed with the ardour of youth as he told me that he was expecting to start in two or three weeks on an extended visit to Denmark, which he had not seen for at least fifty years.

By the fall of 1907 we had several neighbours. The first of the township plans used in the endpaper design of the book shows the trails running from one homestead to another. This group of settlers, with A. E. East over on 23, was the nucleus of what later became the Eastburg Community. All of these settlers except Mr. East had entered the area along the trail from Riviere Qui Barre. He must have come in from the north-east, as by that time there was a trail from Edmonton to George MacLachlan's and Jack Edgson's place near what is now Clyde. The trail was continued west nearly fifteen miles along the top boundary of Township 59. There were other settlers in the north-east of Township 59, Range

I, particularly Egar and Ernie Stanton; these people were the nucleus of the Hazel Bluff Community. Between the MacGregors' shack and East's place stretched majestic spruce forest which at first prevented all intercourse. Within two or three years, however, when other settlers came in and began to grope their way towards their quarters and to cut paths from one homestead to another, a trail was opened through to the north-east.

Joe Fowlie threw up his quarter after a while, and in the following year he filed on the North-West of 34 in Township 58. But, while it lasted, his presence on the next quarter west was a blessing for Dad, and the footpath between the two clearings became well worn. To Mother, also, his companionship was a godsend. He was always welcome, and many a happy evening was spent talking of the army and the Old Country. Usually Dad would get out his violin and play while Mother and Joe sang. The two months that Joe stayed on the North-East of 17 were the happiest months Mother had spent since leaving Scotland.

By this time, of course, we had moved into the house and were protected from the elements. The evolution of our thinking about the house is interesting. At first it was "The House," meaning the castle. Then, in conformity with local usage, it became the shack. "Shack" has become a term of disparagement, and we often refer to shack-towns in this manner. To the homesteader the word "shack" meant his log home in the bush, no matter how elegant it might be. In our case it was but a few years before we began to refer to it as the log shack, and finally, before we converted it to a garage and machine-shop, it had fallen to the status of the old shack. To a two-year-old boy a newly built log shack is a fascinating place. First of all it smells of clean, new wood—the tart odour of green poplar, the sour smell of fresh-cut balm and the incense of spruce sap. Then, for many feet around the walls, in a pile two feet deep, lie the chips and bits of bark. Eventually Mother gathered all these for kindling, but while they lasted, I revelled in them. The joys of homesteaders' children are many, though simple.

I don't remember it, but at this time I was at the pull-toy stage. I went everywhere dragging behind me a fascinating collection of tin cans, bits of roots, washers and buttons, and a host of other miscellaneous items, all tied together with string. This came to be called my Jingling Johnny. When I did not bring some new thing to Dad to be fastened to it, he found some other oddity to increase its length and its clatter. Everywhere I went, Jingling Johnny went too.

Our "boughten" furniture was as scarce as Jingling Johnny was long. It consisted of a proper bed with a spring and mattress, and a stove. Possibly in that category we should also include the framed pictures which helped to cover up the walls. We had many of them, but they were all of Dad in uniform or of various groups of soldiers or military formations. The rest of our furniture consisted of boxes. Fortunately this was in the days before card-board containers, so we never lacked for boxes.

Dad made all the rest of the furniture. The immediate neces-sities were knocked together quickly and then for many years during winter days and evenings he enjoyed himself making furni-ture. First of all, of course, in addition to a cot for me, we needed a table and stools or benches. These were soon made. Within seven years we built a new frame house and filled it with furniture, but, until about 1920, the only "boughten" furniture even in the new house was more beds, a bigger kitchen range, some air-tight heaters, one rocking-chair, and an overstuffed chair. The rest was home-made, and well made too, out of the birch trees which in those homestead days grew to such a tremendous size outside our windows.

I shall never forget those great white birches that grew on the knoll south of the old shack and on the site of the new house which was built in 1913. Many of them were eighteen inches in diameter at the butt and all were over twelve inches. They formed a majestic group. Like all Western birch that lives to grow up to a large size, they were not straight and slender as were the spruce and poplars, but leaned this way and that and spread grace-fully against the sky. Even at that, we were able to cut logs from them ten feet long and ten inches in diameter at the top. Dad cut out what little underbrush there was around these trees and fashioned a rude bench under them. There in utter contentment he smoked many an evening pipe. In 1908, when Tinny Powell started his mill on Mrs. Mund's place, Dad felled these old trees and had them sawn into lumber. This was carefully stored against the time when the new house should be built. There were a few other groves of large birch trees on the quarter and these too were converted into lumber as soon as possible, for there was always the chance that a forest fire would destroy them. There were also a few nice birches over on 17, and I fear that after Joe Fowlie abandoned that quarter, Dad hastened in with his little axe and cut them too. All of this birch made superb furniture. Many of the boards had a bird's-eye-maple effect and these were husbanded for panels in sideboards and china cabinets. A most attractive floor for Mother's bedroom in the new house was fashioned from the birch later on, and the rest of it supplied us with wagon reaches, double-trees, eveners, and baseball bats for many a year.

Great spruce trees, as I have said, grew all around the little clearing, but on the north-west side they were particularly grand. In height and girth one of these stood out from all the others. When this one was cut for lumber, it was sawn off about five feet above the ground, and for years afterwards the stump was one of my favourite haunts. I remember Dad and the neighbours discussing the first log cut from this tree, because it was of record size and had cut into more than five hundred board feet of lumber although it was only ten feet long. Even so, this tree may not have been the largest one on the place; when the north-east corner of our quarter was logged off, many butt logs had to be left simply because they were too big for the mill to handle.

Something about this huge spruce appealed to Dad from the first, and he chopped out a path winding down to it from the shack. Often in the evenings when the day's work was done, he and I used to repair to the foot of this steadfast giant. The yielding green moss, the yellow toadstools, the bright red pigeon-berries, and the piles of spruce cones shelled out by the squirrels, all were enchanting. Through the surrounding forest everything else might be scorched and dry, but this shadowy grove was always cool, fragrant, and inviting.

When the forest floor began to dry up and twigs and grass crackled underfoot, Dad was reminded that we needed a fire-break. It was a wise precaution to surround a farmyard with a strip of ploughed ground as wide as circumstances would permit. So Dad set to work widening our clearing on all four sides until a narrow strip of ploughed ground surrounded the yard and at last we were safe. It was a good job that at that time we had no conception of the might of a forest fire. Later experience was to prove that this fire-break was of psychological value only.

I have already dwelt on the building of the house and mentioned the throwing together of the slab barn and the lining up of the rail fence. Early in 1907 Dad had erected another structure, which lasted until it was thought to be out of keeping with the grandeur of the new frame house. This edifice was what Mother, carrying over into Alberta her English pattern of thought, called the Water Closet, or, when she wished to be particularly refined, the W.C. As the years went by this came to be referred to as the Little House, and finally in complete surrender to Canadian ways, the Toilet. The other term used by many of our neighbours, "privy," never gained acceptance on the North-West of 16, although on occasions of extreme levity Mother fell in line and called it the "biffy."

Dad did not lavish on this first structure the affection that subsequent W.C.'s brought out. Using slabs, he built a primitive single-holer facing south into the sun and away from the cold winds. Not having any metal hinges, he dispensed with a door, and the W.C. smiled blandly on wild honeysuckle and hazel bushes, and harboured an egg-shaped hornet's nest in the peak of the roof. When, however, winter breezes wafted snowdrifts onto the seat, a door was hurriedly added.

Do not think that the whole of that first summer was given over to toil. Mother and Dad both worked very hard, but Dad varied this labour by exploring into every nook and cranny of our quarter. He extended these trips to take in the surrounding quarters, and soon knew all about them: where the raspberries were heaviest; where the smell of mint rose on the air as you brushed against branches heavy with wild black currants; where good-quality building logs, not too big but uniform, might be cut; where the thick stands of young, slender spruce fit for fence rails were; where lay all the hay meadows and the sloughs that harboured ducks, as well as the coverts haunted by deer.

The Pembina River was only three miles away, and Dad loved to fish. The sluggish Pembina, grey with mud in spring and tea-brown from muskeg run-off most of the summer, was a far cry from the rippling, stony salmon streams of Scotland. The stupid jackfish was far removed in spirit and flavour from the silvery salmon of Sutherlandshire. Nevertheless, these jackfish were accommodating, and a couple of hours' fishing would often catch more than we could eat. Some of these fish were big ones which, according to our spring scales, weighed twenty-two pounds. More and more, Alberta was proving itself to be all that Dad had expected of it. And during the long days of summer he enjoyed it to the full from the peep of the morning's earliest bird to the final sleepy croak of the evening's last frog.

Any trail to a settler's shack had to keep on the high ground as much as possible, and in order to do so and at the same time avoid going through the heaviest timber, it had to wind hither and yon until you were never certain that it was always trending in one direction. Dad worked over the trail by which he had reached the farm until, as far back as Paulson's and the mill, it had been widened and improved. He hewed a path down to Joe Fowlie's shack. Keeping in mind the need for putting up hay, he cut a trail from the yard to the nearest meadow. From here the track was extended a few hundred yards to the next one. Soon a network of trails ran from meadow to meadow.

When haying time came, Dad was ready for it. In the cool of a fall morning, armed with scythe, whetstone, and a five-pound lard pail of drinking water, he strode off down the trail past the giant spruce, until he came to the first meadow. The little meadows in the bush all follow the same pattern, whether they are as small as a tennis court or as large as a landing field. Around them on the higher ground grow spruce and poplar, but as you get down to the damper ground these give way to a ring of balm trees, huge and individual, twisted, broken, and gnarled with the buffeting and sorrows of centuries. Still lower down, the alders grow in clumps of eight or ten trunks, up to five inches in diameter, which all rise from one central root—a delightful tree with smooth, speckled bark and regular glossy green leaves. The alders share the fringe of the meadow with giant willows which revel in moisture, so that they extend into the meadow even further than the alders. Then the meadow grasses and the wild mint take over. Here and there the white blossoms of the water hemlock shoot up above the grass, and down below, hiding the racetracks of mice and moles, grows the big-leaved Arrow-leaf Sweet Coltsfoot (*Petasites sagittata*).

I think all our little hay meadows were the work of beavers. These animals were extinct in our area, but their handiwork remained. Even now, forty years after these meadows have been broken up and cropped, if you look carefully you can see where their dam was and you can make out most of their canals. The beavers builded better than they knew. When we first mowed these meadows, the beavers' engineering works stood out plainly. At the lower end, fifty feet or five hundred feet long, depending on the size of the meadow, stood the bulwark of the deserted beaver dam now covered thickly with willow and alder. Intersecting the meadow were canals generally full of water and bordered by a thick growth of rank horsetail and hemlock. The series of canals was carried well beyond the meadow up into the growth of balm and poplar. On these slopes the furry engineers had cut their food supply of juicy poplar and succulent balm, and along these canals they had floated their logs into the pond.

In later years, after the forest was swept away, these beaver meadows could be seen at their best when the slanting rays of the setting sun brought out in the high relief of shadows the ridges and depressions of old dams and canals. If you want to see a fine example not yet erased by civilization, drive out nine miles west of Westlock along the highway to what we used to call Agnew's Corner. There the highway turns north to go down to Rossington and the bridge over the Pembina. As you swing around the long curve, slow down, for just where the highway straightens out again you will see a long beaver-dam winding through the trees on the east side of the road.

But let's get back to Dad, his scythe, his whetstone, and his lard pail. As he descended the trail the meadow spread out before him. Setting his pail in the shade of a big tree where he was certain to be able to find it again, he stood surveying the meadow over which the morning sun cast long, cool shadows. The smell of mint filled the air. Here and there a late fireweed was still in full bloom, but most of them had gone to seed, and the fluffy white of fireweed cotton had replaced the reddish purple flowers. The hay before him grew waist high. Off to the right a bench of slough hay— dark green and coarse, and the edges of its leaves as sharp as knives— stretched across what was undoubtedly a wetter region of the meadow. In bays, mostly on the west side and shaded from the afternoon sun, grew Red Top, the glory of the wild hay meadows. In places it was six feet high with its tassels waving and rustling in the breeze.

Dad whetted his scythe and began what he hoped was the rhythmical swing of the practised mower. Somehow the rhythm was faulty but the exercise was rapturous. The sharp blade sang as it swished through the grass. Soon a respectable swath rewarded his efforts. He paused to whet his scythe again, to wipe his forehead, and to slip into the shade for a drink.

Sitting on a log in the shade he savoured the meadow afresh. The scent of new-mown hay and of bruised wild mint filled the air. Butterflies flitted here and there. A flicker cheered from a nearby tree, then relapsed into silence. The silence and the solitude brought a sense of infinite well-being and peace. Dad thought of the burning sands of the Soudan and the charging Fuzzy-wuzzies, of the barren parade-ground at Wellington Barracks, of the crowded streets and the slums of London. All these he had escaped, and here before him lay this hay in his own meadow. The silent, companionable forest. was his home and estate; his children and their children forever would enjoy it.

But contemplating a hay meadow did not cut hay. So Dad resumed the task and kept at it till well towards noon. After lunch he returned, but the spell had gone from the meadow. The heat of the afternoon lay heavy upon it. Sweat ran down his face, blisters broke on his hands. His nostrils, filled with the fluff of fireweed, itched intolerably. His muscles ached, and each swing of the scythe aroused another swarm of mosquitoes to add to the myriads that buzzed and bit unceasingly. Oh well, he'd cut one more swath and quit.

That swath was Dad's undoing. While cutting around the branches of a fallen tree, the scythe sliced neatly through a hornet's nest about five inches in diameter. All hell broke loose. He flung the scythe fifteen feet into the grass, leapt wildly, tripped over the concealed branches of the tree, and fell face down in the beaver ditch. He got up and ran, with arms flailing futilely at the pursuing hornets. At the edge of the meadow near the water bucket he outstripped them, and then stopped to pack wet clay on a dozen stings. Only then did he realize that in tripping he had skinned one shin from knee to ankle. "Charging Fuzzy-wuzzies, bah," he muttered, and limped home, forgetting the pail.

But, in spite of mosquitoes, hidden branches, and hornets, this meadow and one or two others, were cut. The smell of hay curing in the golden sunshine made up for a few bruises and stings. With a fork and a home-made wooden rake, Dad gathered the swaths into cocks and soon the day came when he brought the hay home. For this he used the wagon box. Our hay rack was still in the future.

Chappie and Charlie were hitched up. Mother and Dad and I climbed into the wagon. Bunty, attracted by the excitement, followed along behind. The wagon lurched and rocked over the tree roots and bumped against the trunks beside the trail, but no one, least of all Mother, complained. The box was soon filled with hay and the three of us returned to the yard to stack it. Bunty, to show her oneness with us in this great enterprise, capered and danced, tossing her crumpled horn. All six of us, Mother and Dad, Chappie and Charlie, Bunty and I, were one happy and united family.

With our harvest of hay safely stored, Dad had time for further pleasures. New neighbours, the Otis Johnstones, had moved in on the South-West of 8. Dad and Otis liked each other immediately. Both were men more imbued with the freedom and loveliness of this land than with any thought of taming it. Soon a trail was blazed down through the meadows on the South-East of 17 and out past Old Man Darling's place to Johnstone's. At times Otis worked on his end of it while Dad cleared away at our part. Sometimes they worked together.

Otis was from Eureka, California, while Sofie, his wife, still retained the accent she had brought with her from Germany via New York and California to Alberta. Lloyd, their older child, was about five, and Pearl possibly three. A strong friendship grew up between Sofie and Mother. For a time these two were each other's sole feminine companions, and every few weeks they visited back and forth.

One by one, as fall came on, the bachelors left for Edmonton and some outside employment. Homestead regulations demanded that for three years all settlers should live on their quarters for at least six months in each year. They also had to bring fifteen acres under cultivation and to erect some sort of abode. (Carrying out these obligations and getting title to the land was termed "proving up.") So as to provide a grubstake for use on their homesteads during the summer when they could clear and break land, the bachelors went out to work each winter. Some, like Pete Klasson and Alf Rose, worked in the mines at Cardiff. Others, like Henry Paulson and Charlie Rose, went to work on the sewer ditches of the booming city of Edmonton. Still others, like Axel Clausen, took work in lumber mills, while a few helped to build the Grand Trunk Railway which was then pushing its way towards the coast. The fact that mines and sawmills worked only during the winter months made this form of employment ideal for homesteaders.

In that same fall of 1907, Tinny Powell began setting up his mill on the South-East of 20—about a mile away by the trail. As I have said, it occurred to Dad that he had better begin to convert some of his forest to lumber before a fire carried it away; so he and Otis

Johnstone cut many of the best spruce trees on the west side and in the north-west corner of our place. In return, Dad helped Otis build his barn and supplied him with lumber. Bill Bowman, a bachelor, who had just built a shack on the North-West of 17, also helped cut the age-old trees. This business of lumbering went on nearly all the winter.

As Mother had foreseen, the problem of getting mail was a difficult one. Any mail we might expect came, of course, from Great Britain—letters from Dad's two sisters in Glasgow and from Mother's sisters in London. As well as this, we had a subscription to the Glasgow *Herald*; and, most important of all, every three months Dad's army pension cheque was due. In those days mail took a month or more to travel from England to Edmonton. Then it lay there sometimes for months more, until a homesteader emerged from the bush to get it, or a neighbour, returning from town, brought it.

Eventually a store and post office was opened at Sunniebend, which, if one could have travelled in a straight line, would have been about ten miles to the north-east, but was many more miles by the trail. In fact, at first there was no trail. The splendid forest to the north and east of us cut off all communication in that direction, despite the fact that this bush was intersected by cutlines. During the fall of 1907 or the following winter, A. E. East started his mill over on Section 23. A year or so later, Egar Stanton started his store on the North-East of 36, in the extreme corner of the township, and Hazel Bluff post office was established at the same location. (I'm a little vague about these dates, but any error cannot be greater than a year.)

Once East's mill was operating, a trail was cut through to it from the north-east. To get to Letts' store at Sunniebend then it was necessary for Dad to follow cutlines until he came on to the logging trails leading to East's mill. Beyond that, definite trails led north-east to the post offices of Edgson and Clyde, as well as straight north to Sunniebend. In the winter of 1906–7, before we had Chappie and Charlie, Dad had once walked over to Letts' store. A year later, having Chappie to ride, he found this trip much easier to make, so we began to get our mail there.

As the fall of 1907 came on, everything was secure around our farm. Our food supply seemed adequate and there was enough fodder for the horses and Bunty. Dad viewed the approaching winter with equanimity. Not so Mother, who still dreaded the loneliness and the callousness of the forest. She was heavy with child. Moreover, she was still having trouble baking palatable bread. With great care she set the yeast and mixed the dough. In the sweat of her brow she kneaded it and fought with it and finally put it in the oven. From that point on it was out of her hands and beyond her control and prediction. Once in a rare while, when the allotted time had elapsed, she opened the oven door on bread as light as a feather, brown-crusted and smelling as only good newly-baked bread can. I don't know how many kinds of mediocre and even terrible bread there can be, but in those early days Mother's oven produced them all. And she could never tell until she opened the oven door what surprise she was going to get this time.

If the bread was uncertain, rabbit stews were not. Here, although I have mentioned them already, I should like to pay tribute to what we called rabbits; I think they are properly called hares. In any event, they were the little snowshoe bunnies and not the big jacks common to the prairies. In those days there were none of the latter in our area, although I believe they are to be found there at present. Rabbits kept us alive in the winter of 1906-7 and again the following winter. These meek creatures may be a nuisance in some ways, but in the years in which they are plentiful they support all the other fur-bearing creatures. When the rabbits are at the top of their cycle, weasels, lynxes, coyotes, and wolves are plentiful. Fortunately they were near the top of the cycle when we and all the other settlers first homesteaded in the Westlock country. Many an Alberta farmer and business man is alive today because of rabbits.

Early in November, when Otis Johnstone started building his barn, Dad spent many days helping him, and in spite of Mother's rather nervous state Dad decided to save travelling-time by sleeping at Johnstone's every other night. The new baby was not expected for two or three weeks. By that time Otis and Dad hoped to have the barn finished.

One morning when Otis and Dad went out to work, six inches of snow had fallen and the temperature was dropping rapidly. The pair worked hurriedly all day and Dad decided that he had better not stay for supper that night. Instead, he saddled Chappie and turned his head for home. Chappie, his curiosity aroused by the new appearance of the forest under its snow blanket, picked his way along the path more carefully than usual, so that it was long after dark when he cantered up the little rise into the yard. Dad looked expectantly for the lighted lamp in the window, but this night the window was dark. Suspecting what was wrong, he jumped off Chappie, leaving him to fend for himself, and rushed into the shack. Not only was it dark, but the fire had gone out. A tired voice from the bed explained it all. Mother, alone except for her two-year-old son, had been long in travail. Even with her directions I had not been able to keep the fire going. Hunger and and fear beset me. The baby, a girl, had just been born but was already dead.

Next morning Dad carried out the little body and buried it. If Mother ever knew the location of its grave, she never told us. That burial on some hillside of the farm, attended by Dad alone, was the first in the community.

As I drive by a prosperous farm I often wonder how many are buried on it. Nearly every quarter-section contains some pioneer's grave. On four contiguous quarters are buried the Byvanks' year-old boy, the two Dunkelaar children, my baby sister, and Mr. Mund, father of a hungry brood. Within a mile of these is the grave of Mrs. Hewer, mother of four or five young children. These graves are not marked. People buy and sell these quarters now and never realize the graves are there. Not that it matters to anyone. Yet with nearly every quarter-section go not only the labour and the courage, the clearing and the cultivation, but also the long-forgotten dead of the pioneer men and women who, step by step, cut the trails into the forest—who, far from the help of doctor or preacher, carried out their own dead for burial.

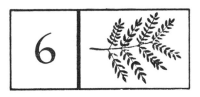

Much was accomplished, that winter of 1907–8, including the cutting of a great deal of timber, which was sawn into planks and rough boards and in due time formed great piles of lumber off to the east of the house. The smell of newly-sawn spruce is still one of my delights, and probably this stems from the days when I played over or fell off those lumber piles.

The little pioneer sawmills, nibbling away at the edge of the great forest, were fascinating to a small boy. They were run by an antiquated steam boiler that was always on the verge of blowing up, yet never did. When enough of the bush was cleared away so that we could look down from our hill towards the green forests adjoining the river, we could see the great columns of steam that rose every winter from the boilers of three or four sawmills. I believe it is technically possible for a steam boiler to operate without a whistle, but it seems to be humanly impossible. At starting or quitting time the whistles blew, and at various times in between, depending on the whim of the engineer. Starting-time I believe was eight in the morning, and you could set your watch by the eight o'clock whistle—so long as you remained loyal to one mill. For eight o'clock arrived at Powell's mill five minutes sooner than it did at Renton's, and twenty minutes later than it did at Sanderson's.

One of the transcendent moments in a boy's life was to climb astride the huge logs on the sleigh and, hanging on to Dad for dear life, to ride with him down to the mill. The sleighs slipped along the trail making little bumping noises while the heel chains jingled. After swinging around the hundreds of bends in the trail, the near approach to the mill was heralded by the piercing shriek of the saw as it ran through a log. Then, all of a sudden, the trail issued from the bush into the sawmill clearing.

What a sight! Was there ever such a busy place? There were so many things to see. Most important, of course, was the huge steam-engine in a slab shed, with its towering column of steam rising far into the heavens, and with its crackling fire that belched out when the door was opened to throw in more blocks of wood. There stood the engineer with his gauntlets—great god that he was—who pushed levers and with a touch of his hand on the cord could blow the whistle. And all the while the boiler grunted and gurgled, governor balls spun around, and the huge flywheel swirled the slapping belt that raced endlessly back and forth.

At the other end of the belt was the saw, a fearsome thing to be watched from a safe distance. Always as it spun it sang a quiet, swishing song, exulting while it waited. Under the watchful eye of the sawyer—the other god of the clearing—men bustled around it. From a huge pile of logs men with peaveys and canthooks rolled one on to the carriage. The sawyer, serious of mien, clamped it here, stood back and sized it up, then clamped it there. Then he pulled one of the many levers that sent the great log slowly towards its doom. The carriage inched along and the slavering saw spun and sang to itself. A great scream rent the air as the saw bit into the log. Was it a shout of victory from the saw, or a shriek of anguish from the log? And always the log was pushed into it until it seemed that the mad saw was wheeling itself into the log. Then the cut was finished, the slab fell to the platform, the carriage was reversed and back came the wounded log, while the snarling saw remained in its place singing away and waiting gloatingly until once more its victim was pushed on to it.

A stream of sawdust flew into the pit below. The dust built into mounds while a man and a wheelbarrow fought to carry it away fast enough and to dump it at the end of the huge, white, aromatic pile. Meanwhile the pile of glistening lumber grew, board by board, as more logs were rolled on to the sacrificial carriage. Why, a boy sitting on a log, well back out of harm's way, could watch forever.

By and by the busy cook would beckon. He always had cake and canned fruit. Steam rose from his bubbling potato-pot and from his boiling cabbage caldron. As he pulled them out of the oven to baste, the roasting meats gurgled and sputtered. Soon the table was set: piles of potatoes, heaps of cabbage, great bowls of turnips. And there were cakes and pies and biscuits. To a boy, maybe fresh from some weeks of scanty diet at home, the cook-house was an even greater miracle than the steaming engine and the screaming saw.

All too soon the mysterious calculations that were the basis of exchange of logs for lumber were over, the logs unloaded on to one of the many skidways, and the sleigh bunks piled high with sticky white lumber. Too soon it was time to go home. All too short was the visit to the mill, even though the memory of it lingers over nearly half a century.

Don't tell me that you, a grown-up, have seen these trifling mills in the back woods and that their very smallness bores you, or that the engineer is not the most wonderful man in the world, and that his engine is not the biggest. Don't tell me that the sawyer is just a man like other men and maybe lousy to boot. Just permit me to see this mill again with the eyes of childhood. I can still take you to where the great piles of sawdust stood shining. It was right here between us and the creek. Here was where the steam-engine stood. Over there was the saw, and back here the sawdust pile. Well, maybe it was a little bit further along, maybe around the next bend of the creek. It is hard to tell now, standing in this clover field. Fires have long since burnt up the slab pile and most of the sawdust. The rest just rotted away and was ploughed up. No, I can't find any trace of it, but a chemist could tell you that this soil was once sawdust from great spruces that bowed before the storms of Columbus's time.

But Tinny Powell's mill must have been here, because here's where old man Mund's grave was. Well, it was about here some-where. They buried him here after the great fire of 1908 had burned up lumber and mill alike. For years the useless, rusted steam-engine stood here—until during the First War they hauled it away for scrap. The fence around the grave was renewed two or three times, but the Munds are all gone now—have been for years.

There used to be so many mills. There was the one over on McGinnis's place, and one hard by on Pete Klasson's place, and this mill of Tinny Powell's, and Renton's mill further down there, and East's mill, and the one over on Section 24, and half a dozen more in the township.

Christmas of 1907 was celebrated in the log shack and made

merrier by a visit from Axel Clausen. On Christmas morning when we huddled around the tin heater to get dressed, standing by it was the most wondrous rocking-horse. Dad had carved it out of a log. With its leather ears, its red buttons for eyes and its flaring red nostrils, it fairly pranced about the room. Its mane was black like Chappie's and its tail long like Charlie's. I've always suspected that Chappie and Charlie begrudged this sacrifice to a boy's Christmas. But it was a wondrous horse, with a little leather saddle and a real bridle.

Except for my pleasure over the rocking-horse, I don't think it was much of a Christmas for Dad and Mother. But for me—well, Christmas was what it always has been to children, no matter what worries their parents faced.

As well as getting out lumber during that mild winter, Dad divided his time between chopping down the bigger trees on a piece of land across the creek, east of the house, and cutting logs for a barn he intended to build when spring came. This was the log barn that is still in use on the farm. It is about thirty-five feet by thirty feet, if I remember correctly, and Dad selected huge logs for it. Even after being hewn down with a broadaxe to a rectangular cross-section, many of them are twenty inches thick at the butt end. The roof of the barn and the hay loft are of lumber cut on the quarter.

Dad had a peculiar pride. While he had helped many of the neighbours put up their log buildings, and while they would have helped him gladly, he felt that we should do all these things for ourselves, so, instead of asking for help, he and Mother built the barn. If you have never built a large log building with green spruce logs thirty-five feet long and nearly two feet thick, you will have little conception of the labour involved. When, however, there are only two people to try to roll one of these logs into place, and they finally succeed in getting it there, they have really accomplished something, particularly if this is about the sixth or seventh log from the ground. To do it you cut about four lighter logs, lay them with one end on the topmost log of the building, and use them for skids. Upon these, with canthooks, you try to roll the building-log, turning it up half a turn and blocking it so that it will not roll back while you take a fresh bite with your canthook and roll it again. It's hard and irritating work. At the least indiscretion on the part of anyone, the log slips, rolls back to the ground and goes rollicking half way across the yard. This is annoying, and also dangerous, as a rolling log of this mass can crush anybody in its path. If it slips and gets away from you once, well that's all in a day's work. When, however, it does so half a dozen times, tempers flare. At the very least there is a tendency for each of the perspiring labourers to accuse the other of incompetence.

In spite of these difficulties, Mother and Dad put up one or two logs every day. That was all that they would want to see of the barn or of each other for one day. The fact that Mother was pregnant again did not make the work any easier for her. By spring, however, the log walls of the barn provided an eastern boundary for our farmyard.

That spring, they tried out a scheme of Dad's for cutting trees out by the roots while Chappie and Charlie pulled at the trunk. The idea was that Dad would fasten the rope well up the tree and then, while he chopped at the roots, Mother would drive the horses. Theoretically, this was a fine arrangement, but Chappie and Charlie were apprehensive of the tree behind them. Mother was downright afraid of it and, moreover, she was afraid of the horses. Though productive of sweat, tears and profanity, this attempt failed.

In really difficult, dangerous, and painful situations, Mother could be as bold as a lion. Nevertheless, the strangest things frightened her. A hen partridge, for instance, had but to look sideways at her and then advance one step, and Mother's resolution vanished. Any height scared her, or any vehicle going fast, or a falling tree.

After the method of pulling the trees over with the horses failed, a variation of the same method was tried. This time Mother was to supply the motive power. The rope had been left attached to the tree, and while Dad did some further chopping at the roots, Mother piled up other brush or was an interested applauder of his efforts. When Dad thought that the roots had been cut enough, that a good smart pull on the rope would drag the tree down, Mother went out to the end of the rope and started pulling. Pulling as hard as she could, however, she could not stir the tree, so Dad started chopping and digging again. While this was strenuous work, Mother was really in no danger even though she was afraid that the tree would fall on her. After a certain amount of tugging on her part and of chopping on Dad's, a root of the tree would snap with a loud crack and the tree might lean two or three degrees towards Mother. When this happened it generally required another half hour's chopping and pulling before it could be made to lean over any more. When it did finally fall, it would drop so slowly that one need only step sideways a few feet to avoid it. But Mother's nerves were as taut as the rope. When the first root snapped she would drop the rope and run like mad, three or four times the length of the tree, and would then look back fearfully—"In case," as Dad used to say, "the tree were chasing her."

There are two versions of the story. According to Dad's, the rope was so long that had the tree fallen flat on the ground its uppermost branches could not have fallen on Mother. According to Mother's, the rope was little longer than a halter shank. In any case, at this particular tree, the one that put an end to this method of clearing, Mother went to the extreme end of the rope and tugged. Nothing happened. Dad chopped and dug a little more.

"Try it again," he said. Mother, looking back fearfully at the great branches swaying against the sky, heaved on the rope. "Crack," went a root, and the tree leaned over ever so little. Dad swung his axe at the root and then found that he couldn't remove it, for Mother had dropped the rope so that the tree swung back and pinched the axe. When he looked up Mother was streaking across the clearing, leaping over logs and flying madly. That "crack" had been too much for her. Dad stood marvelling at Mother's fleetness of foot until, a hundred yards away, she slackened her pace and looked around. Exasperated almost beyond words, he shouted, "Run, you beggar, run," and Mother swept on like a fleeing stag until the full import of the sarcasm penetrated. Then she turned around, and marched up to Dad and his tree and his rope. In no uncertain terms she expressed her opinion of him, of his forbears, of his 160 acres of free land, of Alberta, and of Canada, returning frequently to dwell on the demerits of this particular quarter. And that was the end of Mother's attempts to do Chappie and Charlie out of a job. She marched back to the house, leaving Dad to extract his axe by himself.

Dad continued to work away with a will, feeling that it might be just as well to get quite a patch of land cleared before he ventured back to the house for supper. Finally, however, Mother came out to say that supper was ready, and there in the clearing they stood and laughed. In later years, of all their early experiences in the bush, this was the story that Dad and Mother liked best to tell.

Somehow or other, Bunty had conceived. Isolated in the bush

as we were, not even loyal old Bunty could have accomplished this by herself. I suspect that Mother had a hand in it. I suspect she insisted that, if we were to keep a cow, the cow (without mentioning any names) should pay her passage. So I suppose that one day the previous fall Dad and Bunty must have taken a long trip, because there were no bulls within many miles of us.

In any event, one morning in 1908 when the balm of spring spiced the air and the song of a thrush at sunrise awakened Dad, he looked out to see our Bunty nudging her calf from its birthplace in a thick clump of alders, home towards the barn. Here was something indeed. More first-fruits of the farm! And such a delightful little calf. I forget what we called him, but, being a most important member of our family, he had a name. Yet from the start he was doomed. While we enjoyed the company of this calf, he, being a male, was destined to a life-expectancy of about three years before he was converted from steer to stew.

From somewhere, early that spring, two black pigs arrived to swell the family circle. They, too, were welcome additions and were also given names. Unfortunately, of these names I can remember only "Belinda." She outlived the other pig and year by year presented us with offspring, until with the passage of time she became disillusioned and then disgruntled, and was finally consigned to the pork barrel.

Dad soon abandoned his method of pulling the trees over, in favour of chopping them off three or four feet above the ground. After the trees and the lesser brush on any patch of clearing had been cut down and piled, the piles were burned some day when the wind was just right and the forest not too dry. The clearing then became a barren spot, blackened where the fires had been and studded as thick with stumps as seats in a circus tent. These stumps had to be grubbed around later and pulled out with horses, and this was back-breaking work. Some people, when they cleared land, cut off the willows and poplar saplings flush with the ground, leaving the breaking-plough to deal with these small roots. On the North-West of 16, however, each willow and sapling was cut out by the roots. This method, if much more laborious, was nevertheless more thorough.

As the years went by and the forest fires killed the timber, clearing became easier. Even then, although the trees were killed and most of them fell over or were burnt off, their roots were left in the ground. Now poplar and balm roots soon rot. Eight or ten years will take all the resistance out of them. But spruce and tamarack, being resinous, seem to lie preserved in the ground forever. Before the ground can be ploughed they must be grubbed out by hand or dynamited or shattered by the tremendous power of a tractor.

No matter how carefully you dig or grub or pull out a stump, nearly all of the lateral roots remain in the ground. Only the central core is completely taken out. Those that are left must be torn out by the breaking-plough. Two horses cannot cope with work of this description. Four horses do a fair job, but even then there are many times when the plough smacks solidly into one of these roots and will not budge. Then you either have to leave the root and plough around it, or else you have to chop it out.

When summer came and the land dried up, Dad tried his hand at breaking the patch of about three acres which had been cleared. One morning he hitched Chappie and Charlie to the plough. Well, you might as well have hitched up two grasshoppers. Chappie and Charlie had neither the strength to do the breaking nor the inclination to tackle it. They were stymied when the coulter hit the first root as thick as your wrist. It brought them up short after the first five feet of furrow. Then Chappie lunged ahead, pulling Charlie back on his haunches. This hurt Charlie's pride and he bore onward, yanking a surprised Chappie back into a sitting position. Dad got this seesaw stopped, made the horses back up, worked the plough loose, and set to with the axe to chop out the root. This was the first root of somewhere between one and one and a half million roots on this one-quarter section. At the end of half an hour he had chopped it out, and he drove on. For about fifteen feet Chappie and Charlie turned a creditable furrow. Then the point of the ploughshare grated over a rock. It is a painful and a disconcerting feeling to hit a rock with a plough. Generally the horses are striding along at a good gait. Everything is going well. Suddenly the handles of the plough twist you nearly double and almost put your back out of joint, while with a resounding smack they hit your hip bone. If they don't do that, they fly straight up and you land over on a stump while the reins saw away at your raw neck and nearly pull your head off.

Dad got the plough back in the furrow and carried on. Fortunately there were few rocks, but the multitude of roots made breaking a slow process. The opening furrow of a piece of breaking is always the most difficult. By the time Dad had gone the length of the field, throwing a furrow one way, and then returned, casting the other furrow against it, he and Chappie and Charlie felt that they had done enough. Dad unhitched the sweating horses and drove them towards the barn for lunch. He paused once to look back. A whole morning's work was represented by these wavering scratches in the soil. "So this," he thought, "is farming."

In the course of a few days he broke a narrow strip of land. All he had to do now was to disk it, harrow it, and generally to reduce it to a fairly level patch of up-turned soil. Before that condition was reached, great piles of roots had to be picked and lesser piles of stones had to be gathered.

It soon became obvious that with Chappie and Charlie he was not going to get enough land broken to keep them supplied with oats. So he hired Bill Thweat, who came with three of his oxen. Bill's team grunted and puffed, slobbered and switched their tails, but by the end of day they had something to show for their labour. Before very long they had our three acres broken and lying over smoothly in a manner that gave rise to the hope that, after all, this field could be cultivated, and that with luck it might produce some of Canada's golden wheat.

Bill Thweat, a bachelor from Kentucky, was quiet, soft-spoken and friendly, clean in his person, and industrious. For the rest of his life he batched over on 18. No man that I ever heard had a hard word to say of him. Bill was a good hunter, and many a deer and moose fell to his rifle. By hunting he fed himself, in the early years. By trapping he paid for his machinery, and eventually became prosperous in a quiet sort of way. Once he entertained thoughts of marriage, but that is another story.

Bill was just one of our new neighbours. By the middle of 1908 we had three times as many as we had had a year earlier. These 1908 arrivals are included in the second township plan appearing in the endpaper design; they were among those whom we came to regard as the old-timers of the community. In succeeding years more people came in, until every quarter was taken up, but we always looked upon them as late-comers.

With so many settlers in the community, a post office became a necessity. Early in 1908, A. E. East applied for one and became the postmaster of the new post office of Eastburg.

Things were really beginning to look up. This was the year that Henry Paulson quit going away to Edmonton to work each winter.

From the spring of 1908 he lived continuously on his quarter. One or two of the other bachelors did the same, but most of them still had to work in the mines or mills or on railway construction during the winter in order to support themselves.

Henry Paulson was a young Swede, one inch over six feet. But there was nothing spindly about Henry. He was built like a bridge pier and was one of the strongest men I have ever known. Tall, powerful, with some of the stolidness of a bridge pier too, slow and deliberate of speech, with a long, unhurried stride, his bearing was apt to conceal his immense strength. One was also apt to under-estimate the tremendous amount of work he could do in a day. Everyone marvelled at the distance his apparently leisurely stride could carry his long legs in twenty-four hours.

At the beginning of the century Henry had sailed from Stockholm to New York, and then he had gone on to work in the mines in Pennsylvania. Those were tough times in the mines, and tough men laboured and fought there. Tough foremen had no mercy on weaklings. Henry, a most conscientious and law-abiding man, had teamed up with a wiry little Finn. A battle broke out at the mines between the Scandinavians and some of the other nation-alities. What happened Henry never told me, but in the dark of the night Henry and the Finn had to slip away for Canada. For a year or so they worked together on railroad construction and then, when they separated, Henry decided to take up a homestead.

By this time Henry had teamed up with Pete Klasson, another Swede, and they filed on adjacent quarters. Henry was the serious, thoughtful type. Pete, a short, slightly built, vivacious man, had those opposite characteristics needed for a life-long friendship between the two. Henry was a successful farmer. Pete had little interest in farming and sold his quarter to his friend as soon as he had proved up. Henry, from his great height, looked down on little Pete, enjoyed his follies and always affected to laugh at him. Henry became rich. Pete remained a poor labourer, but the glow of their friendship never diminished.

Henry and Pete, Axel Clausen and Ira Ritter, Paul Cantin and Charlie Caron were the avid poker-players of the community. All were bachelors, and during the winter they gathered at one or other of their shacks at dusk on Saturdays and played poker all night and all the next day. By the light of the coal-oil lamp they played, sustained by raw whisky. None of them could pull himself away from the game until Henry, the master-mind of them all, spread his great hands across the table and ordered all to desist.

Week after week, and year after year, the poker-players met, until their sacred circle was broken when Axel got married. That shook them, but they rallied and carried on. I believe that in such emergencies their circle included Harry Chatten, or Bert or Gordon Tracy, but these men were never part of the inner circle. The poker-players suffered another telling blow when Ira Ritter went to jail, but that, too, is another story. They played for pretty small stakes, especially in the earlier years. It was Henry Paulson with his slow smile and inscrutable face who was the most consistent winner. As the years went by it was also Henry who accumulated enough money to play the grain markets and had brains enough to win far more than he ever lost. Before his death he became one of the richest men north of Edmonton.

But besides his gambling instinct, Henry had other qualities that made for success. He had been well educated in Sweden, and excelled in mathematics. As the years slipped by and I started to study mathematics at the University, I began to appreciate how much Henry knew. He applied his mathematics to the stock and grain markets and followed their operation by drawing charts and graphs. In the early twenties Henry installed one of the first telephones in the community and, shortly after, bought the first radio. These were used almost solely to follow the market.

If Henry made a little money by poker and much by playing the markets, he acquired his early backlog of it by clearing up his quarter long before anyone else had half as much cleared. He was by many years the first man in Eastburg to thresh a thousand bushels of wheat in one year. A thousand bushels! Imagine that! Oh, I know that out on the prairies at the same time some farmers were threshing tens of thousands of bushels, but Henry's wheat came off the land he had won from the forest. Every foot of it he had cleared with his axe and grub-hoe. When the summer sun rose, it found Henry swinging his axe. When it set, it forced him to carry his axe home to be sharpened by lantern light, so as to be ready first thing in the morning. So, in a few years, Henry was rich. By the time the First War came, the forest on his quarter had disappeared. With 160 acres cleared and cultivated, he was ready for the high wartime grain prices. Even before this he had bought Pete Klasson's place and was rapidly clearing it up.

If anyone envies Henry his money, let him work for it as Henry did. For he was always a worker. In those early years when so many men flocked into the West, it was hard to get work in Edmonton. So many clamoured for one job. Each fall it was Henry's custom to leave the homestead and to go to Edmonton in search for work. Water and sewer systems were being installed in Edmonton, and hundreds of miles of ditches had to be dug by hand—a godsend to homesteaders needing work for the winter.

Henry told me how he got his first job in the city. Bright and early on the first morning of his arrival in Edmonton, he walked out along one of the ditches. All the way along, men were working steadily. For every man that worked, at least two others stood around hoping against hope that they, too, could get a job. But Henry did more than hope. Walking slowly along the ditch, he came to two men who were not working as hard as they should have been. Hunting up the foreman, Henry pointed to the two men. "Give me an extra dollar a day," he said, "and I'll do more work than both of them put together." The foreman, sizing Henry up correctly, took him at his word; and, as Henry said years later, "I never let him down, and he fulfilled his promise." How an employer would rejoice today if he could get men like Henry!

In the spring, when it came time to return to the homestead, Henry would quit his job in the ditches and walk the sixty miles back to Eastburg. Not many years ago the old man told me of one such trip in the spring of 1907. At six o'clock on a Saturday night when he had quit work and got paid off, he went over to the boarding-house, had his supper, and settled his account. Then he went to a store and bought a few odds and ends to complete his supplies, including, of course, a crock of whisky. Making these up into a pack, he set out for the homestead.

Some time after midnight he reached McNamara's Hotel at Riviere Qui Barre. Here he had a couple of drinks, a light meal, and plenty of coffee, and then set off again. All through the night Henry walked with that extra long, deceptively slow stride of his, knowing that if he stopped again that night he would be done for. Striding along until well after noon, he reached his shack. "Then," he said, "I flopped into my bunk for twenty-four hours. I was home. I could rest as long as I liked."

Henry, of course, was not the only homesteader who walked back and forth to the homestead. Nearly all of them did it. I think, though, that this was Henry's last long walk, because the next spring when he returned to the homestead it was to stay.

During the summer of 1908, Dad extended his haying operations to two or three more meadows. Now, you can't haul very much hay very far in a wagon box, so a hay rack was indicated. Dad believed whole-heartedly that, if a thing was worth doing, it was worth doing well. The hay rack was accordingly done well. Starting with two-by-eight sills and reinforced with two-by-fours and good heavy green boards all held together with many pounds of nails, it was, when completed, a noble structure. It was a heavy, unwieldy thing, and all the abuse and storms and run-aways of years, while they fractured and scarred it, never detracted from its weight. Many years later it was replaced by one considerably larger and lighter. Up to this point Dad had not given any particular thought to the fact that some day it would have to be hoisted on to the running gear of the wagon, a place now occupied by the wagon box. When the evil day came at last, the combined efforts of Mother and Dad could not set the rack on the wheels. The problem was solved only when Dad erected a tripod and managed to do the job with a block and tackle.

Chappie and Charlie came around to admire the rack as it sat on the ground. They even approved it when in all its virgin beauty it sat astride the wheels and glowed in the evening sun. Next morning, however, when it was time to propel it down to the meadow, they had a change of heart. When they started out, they found themselves pursued by a rattling monster. They headed for the tall timber with the wagon wheels bumping and rattling, and the rack creaking and swaying after them. It cracked into a tree, recoiled, and crashed into another. It bounced off this, only to run foul of a slight sapling, which bent before the sudden onslaught. But even a sapling will endure only so much. At first it bent, then, as one side of the rack slid up on it, it stopped bending. Then it fought back by springing up. All this takes a long time to tell, but only a twinkling to happen. In a few seconds the springing sapling had up-ended the rack and upset Dad. Both landed in the bush, while the wheels and Chappie and Charlie bolted down the trail.

Fortunately Dad was more chagrined than hurt. Salvaging the rack, however, and re-installing it on the wagon, kept him busy the rest of the day. In time the horses got used to it, and the hay was brought home and neatly stacked by the slab barn.

Good weather smiled on the haying, and continued afterwards, so Dad took further advantage of it to drive to Edmonton for supplies. As he followed the trail south he compared the fine fall weather with the rain of two years before. This, after all, was sunny Alberta—far different from the damp climate of England, he reflected, as the warm wind blowing from the south rustled the dry leaves. Two years earlier, this first fifteen miles of the trail had passed the homes of very few settlers. Now, nearly every mile there was a small clearing with a shack on it. Huge brush piles here and there made obvious the desire of the homesteaders to sweep this forest away. So, observing these signs of progress, he wound slowly along on his three days' trip towards Edmonton.

For the first two days after Dad's departure Mother and I led a leisurely existence, gathering eggs, feeding Belinda, and milking Bunty. For Mother the place had lost much of its dread. The sun setting through the trees cast a warm, mellow comfort over the clearing. The farm, thought Mother, was not such a bad place after all.

Next morning, while the sky appeared bright enough, the sun was only a luminous orange patch in the east and it cast only vague shadows. It was obscured by a smoky haze which thickened as the day progressed. By early afternoon, waves of acrid smoke billowed over the clearing. The air was filled with particles of white ash which, not many miles to the south and not many minutes before, had been dried leaves, twigs, and spruce needles. Far to the south a fire had broken out, and the fresh, warm wind was sweeping it our way. Mother began to worry. Apprehensively she wandered around the yard looking at the heavy grey column of smoke to the south, and then busied herself with some fancied job in the kitchen. Bunty, shut in the barn, was worried too. Soon she was sending out a persistent series of mournful bellowings.

It was at this point that my memory of events began. It may be that Mother's dread and Bunty's mournful misgivings communicated themselves to me. At any rate, I remember much about that fire. I can still see the slab shed just a few yards away, but blue and dim in the smoke. I can still hear Bunty bellowing, and remember Mother taking me up to chase her out of the barn.

Taking me by the hand, Mother went over to give Bunty her liberty. If we were all to fall victims to the fire, at least the three of us would be on an equal footing, and Bunty would be given a chance to fall back upon her animal instinct. As we returned through the thick blue smoke, we coughed and our eyes ran.

Mother went into the shack and got two or three blankets, and with these she climbed down the well. It was only about fifteen feet down to the water and there was a good broad ladder down one wall. Telling me to stand on the ground close to the well and not on any account to move away, she climbed down and soaked the blankets. When she brought them up again she left them lying on top of the well casing, where they could be reached from below. These were for the direst emergency, if the flames swept over us.

The air in the well was a little less smoky. Mother hung on to the ladder with one hand while she steadied me with the other. Occasionally a doomed rabbit raced past. For a long while, in spite of the menacing roar of the approaching fire, nothing could be seen but grey and black smoke belching by. Directly south, the roaring increased to the volume of a tornado, and only then, through the billows of smoke, could we see the angry, licking flames shooting high over the trees at the edge of the clearing. We were in the midst of an inferno.

Something—it may have been Dad's pitiful little fire-break— something split the fire. The hand of God can use such fragile instruments. One arm of the fire swung west, missing the house, and was then mysteriously deflected further west so as to miss the grove of trees which contained Dad's favourite giant of the forest. The other arm missed the barn, but it jumped the narrow strip of breaking east of it, caught on the brush north of that and then, well clear of the yard, swung back towards the west to link up with the first arm. The fire had completely encircled our clearing, to reunite and sweep on for miles until stopped by the Pembina River.

How long we remained in the well—whether it was minutes or hours—I do not remember. I do remember the beauty of the forest fire that night. All around the yard, even at its very edge, the great, swaying, friendly trees had been reduced to burning trunks and stumps. Little flames flickered up and down the cracks in these blackened trunks. Here and there, where for some reason the flames had burned more deeply, a ring of fire encircled a trunk. Another such ring might be seen five or ten feet above the first. The background was the jet black of a smoky night. And receding into the night as far as we could see were the fluttering lights of these burning trunks. The wind had dropped to a breeze, but the breeze fanned them gently so that they rose and fell, chasing up and down the cracks and playing tag with each other in a flickering symphony of blue and red flames.

Every few minutes one of these rings of fire would burn through the trunk and the top would fall. When it hit the ground, it threw up a cloud of sparks which flared up and then died out as they passed down the breeze. I remember all of this only as a spectacle. Its disastrous possibilities were beyond my comprehension or my care.

As soon as Henry Paulson could travel over the scorched track of the fire, he came running to see how we had fared. His visit was a wonderful solace to Mother. Many years later he told me of his own experience in this fire. From his shack the view was unobstructed down into the valley and to the top of the ridge a mile and a half away. Henry, too, had noticed the smoke in the morning, and he had been able to see the core of the fire as a column of black smoke rising above the ridge, and then crossing it. He knew that his well-built log shack, which was plastered with mud and had a sod-covered roof, would be hard to ignite. So, when the smoke got thick, he shut the door and lay down on the dirt floor. After the fire had passed and it was possible to breathe outside in the open air, Henry saw that his clearing too was surrounded with burning stumps. Some of them were so close to a pile of lumber that he was afraid the sparks might set it afire, so he decided to chop down the most dangerous stumps. He was hampered because his axe had already been dulled by some clearing he had done. There was no time to sharpen it, but right then Henry made a vow. It is characteristic of the man that, ever after, he kept the axe sharpened. As I remember Henry over the years, his tools were always in good shape. It was characteristic of him, too, that he soon set to work to chop out the logs that had fallen across the trail north to our place and south for a mile or so.

Bunty came through our fire unscathed, but of her actions during it I haven't any idea. Henry Paulson, however, told me how a stray dog, which had adopted him a few weeks before the fire, met the crisis. Two or three hundred yards south of Henry's shack, down on Reg McGinnis's place, there was one of the many flowing springs that used to be so common in that country. When things around Henry's place began to look ominous, the dog deserted him. He found afterwards that it had taken sanctuary at the spring, and had come through safely.

Three or four days later, when Dad returned from Edmonton,

he struck the beginning of the fire nearly forty miles from home. As he followed in its wake mile after mile and it did not show any signs of dying out, he began to worry. Urging Chappie and Charlie to their utmost, he passed farm after farm that was burnt out. No one that he saw, of course, had any idea how much further north the fire had gone, or any news of the damage it had done after passing his own place. Dad was nearly mad with apprehension. It was long after dark when he came galloping into the clearing and saw the reassuring yellow light of the coal-oil lamp shining out across the yard.

Bill was born on December 14, 1908. Otherwise it was a typical December day. Except for Bill's arrival, it was a nice day. The previous night many inches of snow had fallen. Long icicles hung from the eaves and were visible from holes scraped through the frost on the kitchen and bedroom windows. Snow covered the woodpile. Some of it had drifted through the slabs of which the porch was made, and on the shelf that held some tools and other farm gear it lay an inch or so deep. The glare of the sun on the snow was hard on the eyes, so that even in the shade of the porch it was difficult to follow the flickering movements of Dad's pet weasel. Even by watching the jet-black tip of his tail, it was hard to see where he went as he whisked up and down and along the shelf.

It was, then, a wintry day, like many others. I was three and a half years old, happy and quite content with the world as it was—the world that consisted of Mother and Dad and me and the weasel. (The weasel didn't count for much, it is true; he was only a minor member of the family and was not permitted indoors.) But on this day I was banished to the kitchen, while Mother lay in the bed in the other room and Dad was kept busy getting breakfast and lunch. I remember the loneliness of the afternoon as it gradually merged into dusk—that, and a sense of unease. Dad had gone somewhere. Little attention had been paid to me, and moreover, I was hungry.

Just before it got completely dark the tinkle of heel chains announced Dad's return, and the next moment Mrs. Mund entered. She spent a minute or so with Mother and then came to the kitchen.

In no time she had the stove burning well, a lamp lit, the kettle boiling, and supper under way. Then, after stabling the horses, Dad came in. Dad, the lighted lamp, Mrs. Mund's solicitude and the smell of supper cooking, satisfied my world. From there on, the rest of the evening fades out of my memory, but presumably I was soon put to bed, to forget the cares of the day and sleep until morning.

I do not remember the next day at all. I am alleged to have taken one look at Bill and to have requested that he be thrown out. But Bill had come to stay. According to the spring scales in the kitchen, he weighed fourteen pounds. These, of course, were the same scales that had been used to weigh the twenty-two-pound jack-fish which Dad caught down in the Pembina River. Mrs. Mund appeared dubious. She shook her head and declared, "Anyway, he's a fine, big baby."

Perhaps it's a good job that I looked at Bill and passed judgment on him, instead of the shoe being on the other foot, for, on that far-off day in Dornoch, Scotland, when I was ushered into the world, I had weighed three and a half pounds by the doctor's scales. No one believed that I could live—and I should not have been the first that Mother had lost—but they fed me hopefully with an eye-dropper and carried me carefully from place to place on a cushion. Old Andrew Carnegie, who happened to be home from America and was in the kirk at the christening, did not seem optimistic, as with delicate finger he pulled back my bonnet and looked at me. He must have winced a bit, not because of parting with the shilling he gave me, but from shock. But the old man quickly recovered his composure and, looking at Mother, said, "A fine braw laddie." Then with another doubtful peek at me he added, "A braw homely laddie." Whenever Mother told that story, she always hastened to add, "Now, 'homely' in the north of Scotland does not mean what it does here in Canada. Mr. Carnegie meant a fine lad that would be an acquisition in any home." In my darker moments I am not so sure.

All this excitement on the North-West of 16 carried us through Christmas 1908. During the winter the logs for the henhouse were cut from a group of fire-killed spruce on the west side of the quarter. The henhouse was quite large, and by far the neatest log building on the place. Dad was learning some of the skills of an axe-man.

When spring came, the desolation of the fire of the previous fall stood out in all its nakedness. Here and there some islands of green timber remained, but on most of the quarter one could walk for hundreds of yards and see nothing but blackened stumps and the charred trunks of trees. All living things were gone. The springy moss was replaced by scorched soil and ashes. No roses sprang into bloom. No ferns thrust up their hopeful heads. No hazelnuts swayed in the breeze. No honeysuckle twined over logs or scented the air. Where, before, the undergrowth had been alive with rabbits hopping about their business, now no flashes of movement caught the eye. Overhead, where graceful boughs had arched across the sky, nothing but charred spikes and blackened stumps stabbed into the blue emptiness. No chipmunks trilled in the bracken. No wrens warbled in the thickets. No robins rejoiced in the treetops. The forest was gone. Over hundreds of acres its skeletons stood silently. Dad's beloved forest was gone. Nothing of beauty now remained. These hideous stumps—the sooner they fell or were cut down, the better for all. No need now to hesitate about destroying this beauty and peace by clearing and breaking the land. The quicker the refuse was cleared off the land the better. So, whether he liked it or not, Dad was forced to become a more active farmer.

All the long spring, no green thing had the courage to take root in the black desolation. Yet, as summer passed, nature began to clothe hillside and creek bank with a carpet of green fireweed. Week by week it flourished and grew taller. Then, so suddenly that it seemed to happen overnight, the old aisles of the forest bloomed. For acres and acres, over hill and hollow, over bank and brae, stretched a purple carpet of fireweed. The forest was not to be denied its beauty. From the moment the fireweed bloomed, nature took heart again and new life quickened the quarter-section. In a few years the uncultivated land was once more covered with growing trees. Compared to the original forest, however, they were mere twigs.

The years 1909 and 1910 brought in enough new settlers to take up most of the available quarters in the township. Most of them were Dutch and came in a group from Enschede, near the German border. There were several families of them and all were more or less related. I want to list these Dutch people, for they were practically the last arrivals who completed our original Eastburg community. All but one of them were married. I've forgotten the names of some who left the community after the first few

years. I've not forgotten a thing about the fine people who settled
and who helped weave the fabric of Eastburg. Here they are,
together with their quarter-sections:

S.E.   7   Pete Hoogers
S.W.   9   Hulshofs
S.E.   9   Gerry Hoogers
S.W. 17   John ter Horst
N.E. 17   Old Man ter Horst
S.E. 19   George Wagelaar
N.E. 19   Ed Nyland
S.W. 21   George Donkelaar
N.E. 21   Barney Byvank

So you see what sort of community we had. There were these
Dutch people living next door to Norwegians from Minnesota or
Norway. There were Swedes playing poker with French-Canadians.
Here and there was a German cutting a trail through the bush
to the shack of his neighbour, a Down-Easter. There were two
kinds of Down-Easters, those from the Maritimes and those from
Ontario; each was as much superior to the other as the way they
did things down east was superior to the way people did things
out here. Then, of course, we had some Scots, one or two New
York Irish, and many English.

A whole book could be written about these English. There
were Cockneys and Yorkshiremen and Lancashire lassies. They
were of all kinds and all classes. Some were well educated, learned,
and refined. Some were not, but all of them could read and write.
Half of them soon left for greener pastures. Those who stayed,
whether clever or plodding, refined or rowdy, courteous or
churlish, blended, in time, with the rest of the community and
reaped from their land what they had sown.

All of these British, I have said, could read and write. This was
in marked contrast to most of the Americans who chose our
corner of Alberta. Of these, also, we had all sorts—Pennsylvania
Dutch, Hoosiers, New York Irish, and many others. Most of the
Americans settled in the adjoining community of Manola, and
most of these were pioneers still on the move—Californians moving
on, or early Oregon families still seeking that lush valley over the
next blue ridge. Many came from the ranching states. One had
even ridden with Buffalo Bill. The majority of them came of good,
sound stock, these American pioneers who would face up to anything or tackle any situation. They had two characteristics in

common; all of them rode horses, and all of them hated the English. In their provincialism they were quick to disdain those who knew less about the frontier than they did.

So, all these people made our Eastburg what it was. Each of them, Dane or Dutchman, Swede or Scot, Yankee or Yorkshireman, did his share. Eventually the sons of one race married the daughters of another. A bright moon after a dance, a horse and buggy, a boy and girl, and who cares who won at Bunker Hill, or who oppressed whom, or who spilled the Boston beans? So, Old Man ter Horst's boy married Gertie Skaalen; Pa Mason's Lancashire lass married Frank Paquette, and Daarchie Byvank's boy married the Stanton girl.

As the horse and buggy made way for the tin-lizzy, romance reached further afield and brought in new blood from the surrounding communities; German girls from Dusseldorf, full-breasted, flaxen-haired, and smouldering; French girls from Racine, trim-ankled, black-eyed, and impulsive; Italian girls from Naples, slim-waisted, sunburned, and impetuous. In this present generation, what races are mixed in the high-school children? Who can tell, except by guess, at what lies behind their names?—Lars, Tony, Duncan, Inga, Benicia, and Jean.

In those early days, for that matter, who could tell what history lay behind his neighbour? No one probed too deeply. What culture revealed the beauty of the world to the new family behind the big hill? It reminds me of a story they used to tell about "Old Jimmy" Adam, the talented draughting instructor in my day at the University of Alberta.

Jimmy, fresh from Scotland, arrived in Edmonton shortly before the new university opened. Times were hard, positions were scarce, but Jimmy was game. For months he of the many degrees, the skilful hand, and the trained eye, drove a cab, urging his horse over the rutted streets of Edmonton. One day at one of the downtown hotels he picked up a fare and took him over to the temporary premises of the new university to interview the president, Dr. Tory. On the way over, his passenger confided that he hoped to obtain the position of instructor in Mathematics and Descriptive Geometry.

While the interview took place, Jimmy waited; but not for long, because his passenger soon descended the steps, his face long showing that he had failed to get the job. "Haud the horses a wee, while I go in and get it," said Jimmy. And get it he did—and what's more, held it for twenty-five years. You could never tell, about the early pioneers in Western Canada.

Bunty crossed us up again in the spring of 1909, by bringing us another bundle from heaven that again turned out to be a steer. But probably that was just as well, because Mother was busy enough without the prospect of another cow to milk. What with milking Bunty, doing the housework, and tending the garden, which year after year Dad planted with such a flourish and then promptly forgot, Mother had her hands full. By this time also the Eastburg post office had been moved to our place; once a week the mail-carrier came, and this meant that many people, whom we would not see otherwise, visited us to get their mail. Its volume was very small, except twice a year when Eaton's new catalogue came out, and at Christmas, when parcels began arriving from the T. Eaton Company in Winnipeg.

A country postmistress receives many of the neighbours' confidences. For instance, there was the time that Bill Thweat sent the postal note to Eaton's for a blue serge suit. Shyly but proudly he explained to Mother that he and the vivacious girl in Egar Stanton's Hazel Bluff store were to be married. Mother, although surprised at the news and a bit dubious, expressed her genuine pleasure both for Bill's sake and because this fine girl would be our neighbour. The new suit, said Bill, was for the wedding. Bill Thweat, I think I have said, was one of our finest neighbours, although he may have lacked something in glamour and sartorial perfection.

Some ten days later, at the time the mail-carrier was due to arrive, Bill appeared again. As the mail sack was dumped out there were half a dozen letters and a bulky package for Bill. After a cup of tea, the mail-carrier went his way, and Bill opened the parcel to peek at his new suit. It was of very passable quality; Mother admired it, and Bill was elated.

We never saw Bill in his new suit. On Sundays for a few weeks he put it on to go courting, but, of course, he was too busy to come around by our place. It was not long, however, before some of the neighbours whispered that Bill's wooing had hit a snag. Gradually it dawned on everyone that it had gone awry, but Bill never explained nor complained. He visited us more frequently after this episode, but never in his blue serge suit. For nearly forty years it lay in the bottom of his trunk, carefully folded in tissue-paper. It was in 1948, I think, that his nearest neighbours, Ray and Jay Holmes, confirmed bachelors like himself, unpacked it so that for his last trip to the Manola cemetery Bill might be decked as a bridegroom.

While Mother added to her other cares those of postmistress, Dad busied himself with the worries of the Local Improvement District. Hitherto we had paid no taxes, but, if the Government asked no help from us, we received none from it. Our trails we had made ourselves. Much to the delight of all the boys in the area, we had no schools. We seemed to require no other services from the Province.

It was true that the Federal Government granted us a post office, which, even at the pittance Mother was paid, fell far short of meeting its trifling expenses. In one other way the Federal Government bestowed a boon on us. Every few weeks we would see, coming down the trail past the barn, a smartly dressed military figure with Stetson hat, polished shoes and well-groomed horse. A Mountie, of course—a member of the Royal North West Mounted Police, one of the constables who as often as possible patrolled the back-woods trails. No one was more welcome. For these men came not to ferret out niggling crime, but to watch and safeguard the inexperienced homesteaders. Their main purpose was to see that no one was ill and uncared-for; to keep an eye on the occasional pioneer whose loneliness was unsettling his mind; to make sure that in the back reaches of the forest no one disappeared without a proper explanation. There was no real crime in the Eastburg community. Stealing was almost unknown. Occasionally, however, an unstable father would just pack up and leave his wife and family to get along the best way they could; or an eccentric old bachelor, surly in his loneliness, might brood too deeply upon the fancied wrongs done him by others and have to be apprehended.

For these services we paid no taxes, and Dad and some of the other settlers felt that the time had come to assume more responsibility for local affairs. Hence their interest in the Improvement District already mentioned. At first this body, operating at the local level, concentrated upon the question of roads, and it was then that the homesteaders became conscious of road allowances as something more than mere abstractions. Some money was spent on improving the existing trails, but the aim of the planners was to see that any taxes or grants were used along the road allowances, which it was hoped would some day be proper roads.

Up to this time all roadwork had been voluntary and consisted of a settler doing enough along the road each way from his place to remove the trees which fell across it. The problem of mudholes was solved by using the trail until the wet hole became impassable, and then clearing a way around it. If such a detour was impracticable, a few of the neighbours turned out and laid logs across the wet place, so that wagon wheels would not cut further into the mud. This corduroy made the road passable, but boneshattering. In the new era of the Local Improvement District, with its insistence on using the road allowances, natural obstacles to a straight road had to be dealt with more sternly. Even at that, when the road was cut through the bush half a mile straight south from our corner, there were at first five places where it swung right or left around a slough. The road from our corner north was not straightened out finally until about 1925; at first the forest was too heavy to have a road cut straight through it, and the winding old trail to Donkelaar's and Mund's continued in use till after the First War. By that time the forest had nearly disappeared, and the trail was replaced by one along the road allowance. Even then there were two creeks to cross in going north along the west side of Section 21, and the new road looped around to cross them at favourable places. Finally, about 1925, the creeks were filled and bridged, and at last, after nearly twenty years, the King's Highway ran where it was intended that it should. Even in prosperous communities it was another twenty or thirty years before such roads were "high-graded" and partially gravelled.

Today, if it were necessary to build a road through the bush and sloughs as they were fifty years ago along the west side of the North-West of 16, a bulldozer would be sent out. It would rush and snort through the bush, slamming the trees right and left. Then, roaring "cats" and other earth-moving machinery would push and pull, and carry earth, until in a day or so they had built a highway fit for Cadillacs. But, in the pioneer days, passable trails were thrust through the trees and thrown over muskegs only by means of back-breaking human labour and by the harness-snapping struggles of horses.

About this time, another sign of civilization appeared. On the hilltop at Hazel Bluff rose the frame building of the Methodist church that for so long stood as a landmark on the left side of the road five miles west of Westlock. (The village of Westlock, of course, was unheard-of at the time; it did not come into existence until about 1913 when the railroad went through to the Peace River Country.) This is the church that was renovated in 1954. I'm glad that they rebuilt it instead of just tearing it down and building one of stucco in its place.

Many of our neighbours were Methodists and Baptists. Although they were too far away to attend services at Hazel Bluff Church, they found it invaluable for weddings or funerals. The MacGregors, while accustomed to repair to it on some of these occasions, were themselves far removed from worry over weddings, and fortunately were spared the sorrow of funerals. As a matter of fact, it was only the "Sassiety" weddings of the Eastburg Community that were held here—the kind where the groom shaved and the bride wore a white dress.

One of the early burials there was that of an old man who lived close to us. He was a nice old gentleman whom we will call Smith and who had some daughters and maybe a wife living in Edmonton. Word was sent to the family, out of deference to whom it was decided to bury him in the Hazel Bluff Cemetery.

He had died on the descending wave of a cold snap. While Dad worked away in the kitchen of our shack making the coffin, the trees outside snapped in the cold as the temperature dropped to forty below. The funeral was set for a Monday; meanwhile Joe Fowlie, Axel Clausen, Henry Paulson, and one or two more, went to Hazel Bluff to dig the grave. By Monday the weather was bitterly cold. Chappie and Charlie were hitched up, the body was put in the sleigh in its coffin, and Dad and these men, muffled to the ears, made their way to the church. In case of frost-bite, Henry Paulson took along what he called a "yug" of Hudson's Bay Whisky.

When they arrived at the cemetery no one else was in sight. They lit a roaring fire in the church and carried the coffin in. Soon they hung their sheepskin coats over the benches and sat around the heater sampling Henry's "yug." Presently the preacher arrived. As the afternoon wore on they decided that the drifted roads and the storm must have detained the family; for all anyone knew, they might still be in Edmonton. So they held the service in the church and carried the coffin out into the storm. A problem then arose: the coffin was too long for the grave. Dad and the others encouraged the preacher to go home, and with relief they witnessed his departure. Then Joe drove Chappie and Charlie to the nearest neighbours for a hand-saw. In short order they sawed six inches off the coffin, lowered it, threw the end on top, and filled in the grave, thus bringing to a rapid close the first of Eastburg's formal funerals.

If weddings and funerals were the only social gatherings in Eastburg, they were not the only topics of conversation, which ranged widely but somehow always came around to the subject of railways. Railroad surveys were a recurring feature of life in those days. Eastburg lay in a direct line between Edmonton and the Peace River Country; and to the north stretched vast timber berths. As a result, a year never went by without some party coming through the community on a reconnaissance survey. No stakes were actually put in, and no brush was cut, but these parties travelling through the forest, blazing trees, never realized what hopes they aroused in the farmers' breasts.

When we first settled on the homestead the nearest railway was at Edmonton. By the end of 1906, trains were running to Morinville. Riviere Qui Barre on the old trail out to the homestead had been an important stopping-place, but when the steel reached Morinville it was supplanted and Morinville blossomed into a town with two or three hotels. Any grain that the farmers had for sale could be drawn there, and this cut twenty miles off the haul. Nevertheless, many continued their trip to Edmonton, because, after all, it was only another twenty miles, and Edmonton had so many additional inducements. While year after year the surveys continued, for some years no steel was laid beyond Morinville.

At first these railroad surveys were taken very seriously. A neighbour would come over with a light in his eye and say: "Yup, they're stakin' the line through my place. I always figured they would. I've said to myself, 'They can't go round to the south on account of De Laurier's slough and they can't go north across Blake's hill, so she's bound to come through my place,' and she is. I reckon the station will be down past my barn. What you figure they'll pay me when they put the town on my place?" But then a new survey party would come swinging along and locate a line across McGinnis's and Paul Cantin's. Then we'd hear that another party "aimed to cross the river" down at Lockhart's place. These hopes for railways never materialized. About 1928 a railroad did build a spur line within five miles of our place, but it was on a new survey, and then it was not a line to Grande Prairie and the coast, but a spur line to Barrhead.

So, with many births and few deaths, much clearing and some roadwork, many surveys but no railways, the year 1909 wore away to October. That month was the third anniversary of our filing on the homestead.

Mother had long looked forward to the day when we should "prove up." Once, in 1906, Dad had striven to avert a barrage of criticism by promising that our sojourn in the wilderness would be for three years only. That is, until we proved up. Then, he had promised, we would sell the place and return to the Old Country. This promise had not worried Dad unduly. One of his maxims, and a good one too, was "It's time to shake hands with the Devil when you meet him." As October 1909 approached, however, it began to loom over him. Mother had set her heart upon leaving this wilderness to the wolves.

At this most inauspicious time a letter arrived from London. In 1902, when Dad had left the Scots Guards to return to Scotland, he had placed a hedge on his future by putting his name on the waiting-list of applicants who wanted to become Yeomen of the Guard. Old soldiers of the Guards, after their active service was over, were eligible, if they so wished. This job consisted of dressing up in the costume of a "beefeater" and becoming a half guard, half guide at the Tower of London. The pay was in the nature of added pension.

In October 1909, a very formal letter arrived at the Eastburg post office. It said that his name had come to the top of the list, and asked if he still wished to be taken on. Dad handed over the letter and grinned. Who that has tasted the freedom of the frontier wants to be a Yeoman of the Guard? Who that has caught fish in the Pembina wants to march solemnly day after day around the Tower of London? Who that has eaten moose, killed in his own meadow, wants to be a beefeater? Dad smiled at the memories of his old way of life.

Mother smiled too. Just at the right time this heaven-sent letter had arrived. First she would write to sister Dolly in London, and tell her that we were returning at last—returning after three years of privation, three years of coal-oil lamps, three years of howling coyotes. Then she would start packing. In the first burst of elation Mother sang as she cooked the supper. As soon as it was over, she hurried Bill and me off to bed, and sat down to begin her letter.

Dad was very thoughtful that night. In fact he was thoughtful for some time. The Devil was here in very truth, and was holding out his hand with a vengeance. Dad went out to talk the matter over with Chappie and Charlie.

Discussion filled the next few weeks. Mother was adamant. Dad's lightly-given promise had come home to roost. Slowly he began to find it binding, and sadly he took the preliminary steps to implement it. "Let's all take a trip to Edmonton," he said, "and we'll arrange to get our title and sell the place. Then we'll see what arrangements we can make for passage to Glasgow." So, getting someone to look after Bunty and Belinda, we set off in the old wagon for Edmonton.

Meanwhile Mother had been thinking too. When she reached Edmonton she found that it had grown amazingly. Some streets were now paved. Since she had seen it last, two years before, many new buildings and hundreds of homes had been erected. Now that they were at this fateful point in their career, she wondered if going back to England was the right thing to do. After all, the worst was over; and Dad was obviously depressed at the prospect. How he had loved his freedom—his homestead. In her Edmonton hotel room she found herself wondering how Bunty was faring, and what would become of Chappie and Charlie. "It doesn't matter," she thought. "We'll leave this god-forsaken, barbarous bush, and in a year or so we shall have forgotten all about it."

Then, one night, Dad came back with the news that he had found a man who might buy the homestead. "I'll see him in the morning," he said; but Mother, hiding her face behind a newspaper, said: "Jim—we're not going back to the Old Country. Tomorrow we'll go back to the farm."

Many years later, when in Hazel Bluff Cemetery Dad erected Mother's tombstone, it bore the simple inscription, "Ruth I-16." My readers will remember the words: "For whither thou goest, I will go . . ."

8

Bill's boil burst in February, 1910. Except for this excitement, the winter of 1909-10 passed drearily away. To say that Bill's boil burst is an understatement. You see, Pete Klasson popped it.

Along about February, when, physically and mentally, the tedious winter is taking its toll, when everybody is sick of the snow and ice and the short dark days, and when the shoulders sag from the weight of winter clothing, it takes very little added discouragement to bring everyone to the verge of a nervous breakdown. In February, of all times, Bill developed a boil on his bottom. It was a beauty—big, red, and radiant with pain. Young Bill toddled about in such a wobbly fashion that every few steps he toppled over. Now, when you fall on your fanny and jam all your weight squarely on top of a big, red boil glowing like a ripe strawberry—well, at any rate, Bill yelled every time, and for three or four days neither he nor the rest of us got any peace or much sleep. We were all desperate.

Then one afternoon, when the sun, low in the wintry sky, shone bleakly through the half inch of frost on the little kitchen window, Pete Klasson walked in. Bill was lying in reverse on Mother's lap, his boil shining like a sundog on a frosty day. Now Pete was a labouring man, who for some reason was taking a brief respite from the Cardiff Mines. His horny hands had the grip of a vice. Pete bent over to examine the boil. "Let me see," said he, caressing it gently with thumb and forefinger. "Ummm—it's a beeg von, yust like I had last vinter. The doctor, he fixed it," continued Pete, as his thumb and forefinger snapped closed, and like a pea popping out of a pod, the boil burst. "Yust like that," said Pete.

Bill's scream of anguish rattled the pans on the shelf above the stove. The pet weasel dozing under the eaves of the porch leaped to the ground and raced wildly across the snow. When Bill subsided, the boil was history, and in an hour he was asleep. Grateful to Pete? Why, from that day on Pete was welcome to anything we had. A boil is a strange thing with which to cement a lasting friendship; yet it's things like that that go into the making of community loyalties.

Speaking of the weasel—you see, Dad loved our forest and all the little creatures that sought their happiness in it. Edible animals and birds he killed, sparingly and with regret. After all, we had to eat. But even some of these became his friends and confidants. There was the family of bush partridges that hung about the yard. They must be fed and talked to, but never molested. You can't kill and eat a friend. So, when we shot partridges, it had to be done well away from the house to ensure that none of this particular family fell to the roasting-pan.

There was also the host of twittering swallows that found security under the eaves of the barn. They, too, were Dad's friends. Within a year or two they had built their wondrous mud nests under every available inch of eaves. There were hundreds of swallows, and of an evening the yard was full of them, dipping and skimming about after flies, and catching our enemies the mosquitoes. I don't think Dad was ever so cross as that evening when he and Mother came home and found Lloyd Johnstone, Henry Mund and me, with boyish cruelty, pelting these nests with stones and bringing them down by the dozen.

In summer, wrens, thrushes, bluebirds, humming-birds, and robins sought the sanctuary of our clearing. Their whistling, warbling, and singing filled our yard with joyful exultation. In winter, whisky-jacks, chickadees, and snowbirds, allied with us against the bitter cold, fed at our door or picked at meat, tallow, or bread tied to branches.

But all the little creatures were Dad's friends, even those that were each other's natural enemies. At various periods we harboured woodchucks. Two or three successive porcupines snuffed and clicked into and out of the yard at will. The occasion when I took the shovel and chopped into segments the pet garter-snake who, with her young, lived in the dust under the porch, was a bad one for me. Then the year after the weasel disappeared, we had a white snow-goose for a pet. I often think of that time.

In the early fall, when these noble white birds were sweeping south on their annual migration, one morning dawned bristly and storm-swept. A flock of snow-geese, in some uncertainty of purpose, circled back and forth over the clearing, swinging low in small groups, milling around and honking. Dad, with his ·22 rifle, shot at one of them and broke its wing. As it dropped out of the flock and fluttered down by the big spruce, remorse filled him and he ran to try to make amends. He caught it, patched its broken wing, and then clipped off its great feathers, so that it would not try to fly too soon. Now that the harm was done, though, he indulged in visions of roast goose for Christmas. Within a few days this big, white bird had made it quite clear that he was infinitely above the cringing barnyard fowl, and at times, even with us, he was a bit overbearing and truculent. As Christmas approached, my excited anticipation was tempered with sadness over his certain fate. One night I fed him, throwing wheat on the snow; the next morning a great plucked carcass reposed in the roasting-pan beside the stove. We were all a little depressed that day.

But I have wandered away from the weasel. He was a long, snowy-white fellow with a startling black tip on his tail. How he and the MacGregors ever teamed up is a mystery. But every time we opened our front door, there he was in the slab porch. Dad fed him; but while the weasel deigned to bestow on us a sort of distant recognition, this fell far short of affection. Mother avoided him, and I eyed him from a distance. He stayed around all winter, climbing around the eaves of the porch in the snow, a graceful, slender creature, quick as a coiled spring. He was a big weasel; his skin might have been worth a dollar, and in those days a dollar would have bought many things we needed. But when our friendship palled, he was allowed to slip away unmolested.

Every wild creature that found some advantage in attaching itself to us was encouraged to do so. Consequently, we always had some wild pet or other. Our domestic animals were also pets, and calves and colts were the favourites. I'm a bit vague about our first colt. Maybe that's because, whatever he may have been to everyone else, he was no friend of mine.

I never liked that colt. I don't remember how we came by him. We must have been keeping him for somebody else, because at the time our only horses were Chappie and Charlie, and by no trick of science could he have been related to them. Like all other creatures, he followed Dad around. On a spring day when the little east field was being ploughed, and Dad, with reins around his neck, was holding the plough handles, the colt walked up and down, right behind him in the furrow. Now, that was a place in the procession hitherto reserved for Sonny Jim, who was four years old and stubborn as a mule and who was apt to dispute this easy assumption of precedence on the part of the colt. After three or four furrows had been turned, the colt settled the question once and for all by kicking me. I was not really hurt, but was terribly shocked and mortified. I was wearing a pair of light-coloured cotton pants open at the knees. The shock of the kick caught me unprepared, and I messed myself. Then I stood up in the furrow and howled. Dad, coming back to see if I was hurt, quickly discovered my plight. Then he took my pants off, scraped them with a stick, turned them inside out, put them back on me and sent me howling home to Mother. Do you see why I never liked that colt?

After the spring ploughing and seeding were done and the June rains were nearly over, Charlie Rose came over one evening. With some hesitation he explained his problem. His two boys, Charlie and George, were living with him, while Mrs. Rose remained in Edmonton. The time had now come, announced Charlie, to introduce her to the homestead. Like Mother, she had no faith in homesteading, and hitherto she had resisted Charlie's persuasion. But at last she was coming, said Charlie, and he had arranged her transportation on Marshall's stage as far as Hazel Bluff. Now, would Dad hitch up Chappie and Charlie and meet her there and bring her home?

Charlie would have gone himself, he explained, but he wanted to have the kettle singing on the fire and everything shipshape when Mrs. Rose arrived. "First impressions, you know, Mac; first impressions are what count. So you meet the stage with that good team of yours, and I'll fix the place up." Charlie stayed for supper and we passed a very pleasant evening, while he talked of his experiences all over the world and of his years in the goldfields of Australia.

Then Charlie went home; and next day, when the stage pulled into Hazel Bluff, Dad met Mrs. Rose. You can imagine what sort of trip she had had on the stage from Morinville, up through

Clyde, and on west to Hazel Bluff. Well, our old lumber wagon was no bed of roses either.

While Dad had been waiting for the stage, some good Samaritan had produced a bottle; he was therefore in fine fettle when Mrs. Rose, bruised and battered and aching in every bone, descended from the stage. Dad was a cheerful chap anyway, and a few drinks but added to his geniality. Moreover, Charlie's words, "First impressions you know, Mac," rang in his ears. So he did his best to reassure Mrs. Rose, got her seated on the broad, flat board that rested on top of the wagon box and did duty in place of a spring seat, and started for home.

"How far is it?" asked Mrs. Rose suspiciously.

"Oh, not very far," replied Dad amicably. "Not very far; just down the road a bit and around a corner or two. We'll soon be there, and the wife will have a bite of supper ready. After that we'll go on to Charlie's."

The old lumber wagons, as I have said, were perfect shock-transmitters—not a suspicion of a spring or any give to them at all. But Dad felt he must try to justify his words, so on every reasonable stretch of the trail he encouraged Chappie and Charlie to run. Now, add seven or eight miles of that sort of travelling to a couple of days on the stage and two nights in bug-ridden stopping-places, and you know what Mrs. Rose suffered.

Mother had a good supper and a cup of hot tea ready. She and Liz were both from London, and that helped. The supper was the only bright spot in the whole trip. "Now, how much farther is it to Charlie's?" Mrs. Rose inquired darkly.

"Oh, not far. You're nearly home; just down through the bush and we'll be there in no time."

"How far is it?"

To a pointed question like that you can only temper the truth just a little. "About two miles."

"Two miles through this awful bush, over these trails, and you and Charlie call each other neighbours! What a god-forsaken place to live!"

"First impressions," whispered Charlie's words of last evening.

The road from Hazel Bluff to the farm was a sort of highway. Everyone used it, so that to some extent it had been "improved." The trail to Charlie's was different, for just last fall it had been cut straight through the bush. Dad wondered whether or not to take the older trail around by Graham's; but this new trail, if not so well worn, was much shorter, and just then a short trail was what Dad desired most. So in the summer twilight he and Liz resumed their journey.

You know where, about a quarter of a mile from our shack, the trail crossed the long slough before it climbed the hill through the great spruce trees. The corduroy over that slough was still green, except where the wagon wheels had knocked great strips of bark off it. And towards the far end, where the deeper water was, some of the logs tended to float away. That was always a bad place to cross. At best it was dangerous and jolty and rough. But Chappie and Charlie plunged ahead, while Liz, scared out of her wits, hung on for dear life. In fifteen jolting minutes they were over the corduroy and up the hill and over the corduroy of the next four sloughs. Just down the hill now and over the creek, along a bit and over the long slough beyond Allen's, and, thought Dad, that will be that.

You know how the wind blows the dead trees down, and how they break as they hit the ground. If they blow across the trail, someone throws a broken log off the road into the bush and the way is clear again. Well, if you are on your guard when you pass one of these places, you'll pull well over to one side to avoid the broken butt-end of the log. The road up the last half mile of the hill was dry, and comparatively good. "The house is just beyond that," said Dad, indicating a clump of poplars. The horses trotted, and here, as they neared the end of the journey, all appeared to be well. That is, it did until in the half-darkness Dad failed to see the end of the log sticking out through the red willows. It caught between the spokes of one hind wheel and lifted it in a great arc, just the way a pole-vaulter is lifted. Up and up went the side of the wagon. "Crack, crack," went the branches as the log up-ended. "Whoa!" shouted Dad. "My God!" screamed Liz, as the seat slipped from under her, and she and Dad fell off into the stumps.

Liz had a good deal more to say, when she had got her breath, and finally declared she'd walk the rest of the way. So, with Dad driving on ahead with the luggage, and Liz walking behind, they drew up to Charlie's welcoming arms.

Two days later Liz lit out for Edmonton, but she took with her some very definite memories of the farm. As for Charlie and Dad, for a couple of years a slight coolness clouded their friendship. "First impressions, you know, Mac."

. . . . . .

The approach of spring that year had brought a sense of doom to the older boys of the community. This was because down on the North-West of 9 a new frame building was going up—a school. Inevitably it would bring with it a loss of their freedom during all the lovely months of late spring, summer, and fall. They viewed its advent with alarm.

Cotswold School No. 1862 was opened in 1910. That this was the year I became old enough to go to school is not a coincidence. Dad was chairman of the board. Otis Johnstone, of course, was a member, and so was Charlie Rose. I cannot remember who was secretary, but most likely it was Dudley Graham or Elmer Kipp. Anyway, for years these five, in one combination or another, kept the school running. Dad also supplied the name for the school district, calling it after those hills in England which he had loved so much.

It had not been possible to get the school started earlier. The Cotswold School District took in the area we knew as Eastburg. Of those residents upon whom fell the burden of organizing the school, there were nineteen families with children of school age. Some homesteaders were childless or had families already grown up. They had nothing to gain by having a school. Neither did the twenty-four bachelors, although thirteen of them were destined to marry in the future. Many of the people who lived in the school district were but recent arrivals and they naturally dreaded any more taxes.

In due course the school disrict was set up and empowered to sell debentures; and finally the money was raised. The selection of a site came next. The best compromise was to locate the school on Paul Cantin's quarter. Paul, as I have said, was a bachelor; but he donated two acres for the school grounds. The building was largely a community effort—and a creditable one. It became a frame school and, except for the Kipps' home, it was the only frame building in the district. Fortunately Jim Allen, who lived just across the road, was a carpenter, and he guided its construction. Everyone chipped in to raise the walls and the roof. The only hired help was for the finishing carpentering and the plastering.

So in the spring of 1910, the pioneer children of Eastburg carried their first lunch pails to Cotswold School. For most of them this was the very first day at any such institution. Some, like the bigger Dodson boys, may have been six when they came to Eastburg; and now they were ten or eleven. Several who were even older than that had never been to school either, because of the lack of such an institution wherever they had come from. As a result, Cotswold School was for this first year a glorified Grade One containing pupils from five to fourteen years of age.

On the first morning most of the fathers took their children to school. Many of us did not know each other, but we soon got sorted out. Before the bell rang we wandered in and out of the new edifice, gasping as the magnificence of this frame building with its fir floors and smooth plaster. Most of us had never seen a building made of these materials. In due course Jesse Bell, the teacher, wearing a scout or police hat, rode up on a chestnut horse.

I have no idea whether Jesse Bell was a good teacher. I believe he was. Certainly we needed a male teacher to break in the free farm boys to the discipline of school. He seems to have performed this task without much difficulty. By the end of that first term—at Christmas time—we were all seat-broken at any rate, and ready for the lady teacher who followed him.

The Dodsons, who lived practically four miles away, had the furthest to come. Last summer I drove around Eastburg, and in doing so drove from Dodson's to the school. On the reasonably good roads which now run all over that district it took me seven minutes, and I did not speed. The Dodsons generally rode horses. Sometimes they came in a buggy, but when during seeding time and harvest time they had to walk, it took them nearly two hours. Except for the Allens, who lived across the road, we all arrived in the mornings in two contingents, one from the north and one from the south.

If the money held out and the teacher did not quit sooner, school usually ran from April until Christmas. (A few years later, when the roads got better, the school year was made to coincide with what we regard as the proper term.) The summer days of July and August were hot, and I doubt if we learned much during those months. Flies buzzed up and down the five or six large south windows through which the sun streamed. An occasional blue-bottle flew around, buzzing and bumping the ceiling with a sort of pop every few feet. Noon hour was a welcome relief from the boredom of the heat, the buzzing, and the multiplication table. We all ate lunch in the shade of the school, and then played pumbley-peg or prisoner's base.

After Jesse Bell had eaten his lunch it was his custom to lean on his desk, rest his head on his arms, and enjoy a short nap. As the sultriness of the summer increased, the duration of his slumbers lengthened. Afternoon classes did not start until he woke up. I doubt if any of us had watches, but we all knew and enjoyed the fact that·these siestas lasted far longer than they should have.

One day as we played indolently in the yard, a horse and rubber-tired buggy emerged from the bushes at the south edge of the school yard. The driver tied his horse to the hitching-rack and spoke to Floyd Dodson. "What are you doing out here?" he asked. We had no idea who this man was, but he was well-dressed and seemed like one in authority. Floyd wasn't sure what to answer, but the obvious thing to say was that we were playing. "Yes, I can see that," observed the man, "but where is the teacher?"

"He's inside asleep," snickered Floyd. More questioning brought from Floyd the fact that the teacher usually slept at noon and that we were accustomed to play until he woke up.

"So," said this man, whom we afterwards found out to be the school inspector. "Well." Pulling out his watch which indicated 2.15, and looking around at the hot, dusty playground, he said, "You children go in quietly now, one at a time, and get your caps and lunch buckets, and go home. No," he said, changing his mind, "I'll go in and hand them out to you. Now, above all, be quiet." He tiptoed in and came out with an armful of caps and some lunch pails. "Now go home quietly and be back tomorrow morning," he instructed. As we ran out towards the road, he re-entered the school.

What happened next, as we learned later, was that the inspector took a seat directly in front of Jesse Bell's desk and settled down with a book.

Shortly after this Jesse woke up, lifted his head off his arms, and nearly jumped out of his chair when he saw in front of him a strange man fast asleep. It was 2.30 P.M. and everything was quiet inside. Sizing up the situation, Jesse rose stealthily, sneaked out the door, and was soon astride his mare, galloping through the bush. What the inspector said when he awoke in the empty school-room is not on record, and it was years before anyone could understand why Jesse Bell got such a good inspector's report.

During the rainy season the road to the school was a sea of mud. Parts of the various corduroys were often afloat, and sometimes they were dangerous for a small child to cross alone. In the mornings, whenever the roads were like this, Mother would come with me. She was apprehensive of the effect of sitting in school all day in wet clothing. So, many and many a time she carried me over the floating sections of corduroy. If, coming home from school, I got wet, that did not matter so much, because then my clothes could be changed right away.

What great times we had, we who went to school from the north, with so many inviting sloughs to cross. In the spring these ponds were full of frogs, and floating about at the edges were great masses of jelly-like frog eggs. We'd fish out the masses of eggs and throw them at each other, catch tadpoles, and throw sticks at any luckless frog that showed its head. On the way home this would go on until some youngster—usually I—would slip from a half-submerged tree trunk that extended well out into the slough and have to be fished out, wet through and half drowned.

But fall was the glorious time. Then the road was dry and dusty, and the yellow leaves fluttering down littered it like a mosaic. Then the leaves of the cherry trees and the cranberry bushes were red. When the afternoon sun shone slanting through the trees, the bush was a golden paradise. Not only were the cranberry leaves red, but so were the juicy berries. They were tart, so we seldom ate them, but what fun we had with cranberry fights, squirting these berries at each other until we were dripping with red juice.

Not all the fun of school was on the road to or from it. Each year the men of the community sawed up and stacked a great pile of firewood blocks in the school yard. We divided into two factions and built houses and forts of this firewood. These were quite creditable structures, although at a moment's notice some sticks were apt to fall through the roof and give someone a black eye; but that was all part of the fun.

One hot day, when the teacher came out to call us in from afternoon recess, she found the school ground deserted. Not even the smallest child was in sight. She was dumbfounded. Then, from far away in the direction of what we called the Graham trail, she thought she heard voices. She walked a few hundred yards that way and soon was certain that she was on the right track, although she had to travel about a quarter of a mile before she arrived at the source of the shouting and the scene of the merriment. Just off the trail was a most inviting little pond, possibly two feet deep— a little gem cradled in the forest. As she parted the bushes, there, in the water, was her whole class, boys and girls, five-year-olds and twelve-year-olds, having a delightful time, stark naked.

When the news of this episode was carried to parents, there was intense indignation and some criticism of the teacher; but it was not her fault. Neither was it ours. The day was stifling; the pond was tantalizing. Not one of us, I am sure, had ever in his life given any thought to the impropriety of mixed bathing.

For many years now that pond has been broken up and has been growing grain.

If our school play was fun, our school lunches were not. All the farmers were hard up. There was little variety in their daily food, and less in the school lunch-baskets. When you run out of money you eat what food is left in the house, and gradually one thing after another gets eaten up. Then, when everything is gone, there is always some way out, even if you have to go shamefacedly to the store and for the time being charge up a little flour and tea. But the early settlers hated to do that. I remember one time, but I cannot remember how it came about or why, when the MacGregors lived on tapioca and milk for about three weeks. Don't ask me where such a large quantity of tapioca came from, because I don't know; I suppose that on some previous occasion we must have found a bargain and bought a big supply.

Beans were a staple food of the early days. You bought them by the pound, or by the sack; and a sackful of beans when eaten by one family seemed to last forever. Fortunately it is difficult to incorporate beans into a schoolboy's lunch pail. Onions, on the other hand, slice into nice flat rings and fit well into a sandwich. So, in many cases, a schoolboy's menu consisted of beans for supper, bean-cakes for breakfast, and onion sandwiches for lunch. On a blizzardy, winter day, when all the windows are tightly shut and the roaring heater circulates the odour of drying moccasins, a country school, packed with bean-fed, onion-flavoured boys is not all it might be.

Sandwiches for school lunches, however, quite often contained meat—beef, moose-meat or venison it might be, but usually it was pork. Every farm had pigs. Ideas about pigs and pork have changed during the last half-century. Nowadays a pig is stuffed with food and in a very few months attains the optimum weight of two hundred pounds. This, the connoisseurs say, makes the tastiest pork. In the early days of Cotswold School it seemed a shame to kill a little pig of only two hundred pounds. Most pigs grew to maturity and, when they weighed three hundred pounds or more, were fattened further and then killed. Pork, at least if my childhood memory is correct, was fat, very fat. Away over in one corner of a slice of pork you could find, if you were lucky, a small piece of lean. In the shade of Cotswold and hundreds of other school-houses, how many hundreds of pounds of fat have been torn from pork sandwiches and thrown away?

Eggs, too, were plentiful on pioneer farms. Morning, noon, and night we ate them—generally fried. As fried eggs they appeared in our school lunches: flat and greasy, oyster-like, they lay torpidly between two slices of buttered bread. Flat and saucer-like they too sailed over the school fence to fraternize with the fat pork. Those school lunches are now forty years in the past. For forty years I have eaten few eggs, and never a cold fried one. For forty years I have declined more than a minimum of pork.

During the fall, though, we had other fillings for our sandwiches. No one ever threw away the dark, tasty drumstick of prairie chicken or the white, lightly salted breast of bush partridge. Another happy memory is the tidbit at the bottom of the lunch pail. Here lay the jam sandwiches—blueberry, strawberry, dewberry, raspberry, currant, or saskatoon. As a variation from jam, there might be jelly—raspberry, currant, cranberry, or cherry. As I reflect upon these school lunches now, I think of the harried mothers who each morning were faced with the task of putting them up and of trying to include some tidbit that would relieve their monotony—if not a jam sandwich, then some bit of cake or a cookie, or maybe an apple, to surprise and please.

If we school children were hard to feed, we were harder to shoe. In winter, of course, we all wore moccasins; at least the boys did. What the girls wore, I have no idea, but they probably wore moccasins too. To the boys of Cotswold School, girls were a matter of complete indifference. In the cold, wet weather of March and April we wore boots; then came the glorious days of spring when we could go barefoot, and in spite of stubbed toes, we continued to do so all summer. I don't suppose a city boy, or even a modern farm boy, knows what a stubbed toe is. Maybe that's just as well, because they were most painful, and a half-healed stubbed toe just seemed to invite further stubbing. Every barefoot boy had at least one sore toe all summer.

With the frosty days of fall, bare feet had to be forgone for another year. When I was in Grade Two, Mother sent me off to school in a pair of shoes that almost fitted, were almost new, and were soft and shiny. They were warm and comfortable, and, until

I walked up the school steps, I gave them little thought. But schoolboys everywhere can be unconsciously cruel, and on that morning my friends were no exception.

"Look!" yelled someone, "look at Jim's shoes—he's wearing his mother's shoes—women's shoes—he's a sissy. Button shoes! Button shoes!"

It was a long, painful day, and that night at home I vowed that I would not wear these high buttoned shoes to school any more—that's all. Poor Mother! She felt it more keenly than I did. But what could we do? Next morning, fortified with some of her courage, I walked up the school steps in my buttoned shoes, and in a day or so the subject was forgotten in favour of some new excitement.

Now, don't get me wrong. None of us were poor; we were simply short of money. We had few conveniences and none of the modern luxuries; but poor—no! We were the happiest, most optimistic, most favoured people in Canada. There were some indigent families, but only two or three of them, and they were poor in spirit. They would be poverty-stricken today, surrounded by all Alberta's wealth and in a modern town or city, coddled by our modern legislation. They were poor then too; but the rest of us at Eastburg were just "hard up."

Our school soon became the centre of the community. And it was never more so than at Christmas time. I suppose they still have Christmas concerts in every country school. In fact, I know they do, because occasionally there is an item in one of the daily papers about one. But now the country schools are nearly all consolidated into central schools of many class-rooms, and now the Christmas tree is lit with electricity. The essence of the Christmas spirit is still there, but the little touches that meant so much forty years ago are all changed. Maybe it is just because I'm getting older, but it seems to me that there never has been, and never again can be, anything in this world so jolly and so genuine as the Christmas concerts in the old Cotswold School about the year 1912.

I feel sorry for the poor teachers. They were kindly mortals who plunged into the spirit of Christmas and worked their heads off, and worried themselves to the verge of a nervous breakdown. The teacher had to select the programme; she had to decide that little Millie So-and-so was to be an angel, that Muriel Somebody-else was to be a fairy, and that Mrs. Such-and-such's little girl would sing to the accompaniment of the old organ which Mrs. Allen usually played. She had to pick somebody to "say a piece." Then there would be the plays and the skits, all having some relation to Christmas time. It must have been quite a job. Everyone had to have a part, including the big boy who was pretty stupid and could not remember a poem two stanzas long; and she had to be so careful not to offend any of the parents. Talk about tact! Why, compared to the school teacher's task, the work of diplomats is child's play.

Whenever I recall those old Christmas concerts, the picture of Brother Bill making his début as an actor comes back. That Christmas he was to say a piece. For weeks Mother had coached him with care, until he was letter-perfect. I forget the poem now, but it was something about Bethlehem, stars, shepherds, and the Christ Child, compressed into six saccharine lines. Bill knew it well. Dad, whose soul sometimes rebelled at too much sweetness and who, on occasion, loved a practical joke, had taught Bill an altogether different poem. Bill enjoyed it, but his chuckles evoked from Mother only reproof for him and severe censure for Dad. Unfortunately this poem stuck in Bill's head when, in a crisis, all but it had fled.

The concert that year ground ruthlessly on. The room was full. Proud mothers beamed as their little ones recited, lisped, or sang. Bored fathers sought desperately for some relief to the tedium. Bill gave it to them. In his turn he marched out on the stage, red-faced and perspiring, his freckles aglow, and his wiry hair standing straight up. As he confronted the packed room, he stared aghast. His hands did not appear to hang at his sides so much as to be drawn towards the floor by an all-powerful magnet. He opened his mouth, but no words came. Mother fidgeted, the teacher prompted; half the class hissed, "Billy—'*Twas Christmas Eve in the stable!*" But it did no good. The open mouth was empty, until the wildly roving eyes encountered Dad's smile. Then inspiration filled Bill. He took a long breath and recited faultlessly:

> "Who took me from my warm, warm cot
> And put me on the cold, cold pot,
> Whether I wanted to go or not?"

Then pointing happily, he roared out the last line,

> "My mother."

The uproar was deafening. Never before had the roof of the school resounded to such applause. Mother, red-faced and humiliated, reserved her comments for Dad on the way home.

Not the least memorable thing about those Christmas concerts was the change that occurred during the day. In the morning we all went to school as usual, though the only work we did was to brush up on the parts we were to play in the coming concert. When we were dismissed at noon, as we invariably were, the school was its normal, drab self.

When we came back in the evening, however, a magic wand had swept over it. During the afternoon one or two of the men had gone over into Jim Allen's place, and there they had cut and triumphantly borne back a magnificent Christmas tree. During the afternoon, too, all the mothers in the community had dashed down to decorate the school and the tree. When we saw it again the school-room was an enchanted place. Usually it was cold outside and the windows were all frosted up. One by one the parents came in, taking off their heavy coats and hanging or piling them in the ante-room, and then, with eyes aglow, would walk into the magic they had helped to create.

Sitting in the audience they faced the platform of rough spruce boards knocked together that afternoon and covered with red and green crepe paper. At the right, occupying a third of the platform, was the Christmas tree. I suppose in those old days in Alberta at Christmas time there were well over four thousand of these school Christmas trees, and each one of them was radiant with magic. Ours was decked with tinsel streamers, draped from one branch to another, around and around the tree, and wrapped in the other direction with snowy ropes of strung popcorn, white and puffy and glowing in the lights. And the tree was alive with Christmas lights—little wax candles, red, blue, green, and white, each one placed so that it would not set fire to the branches above it, and each one flickering away, shining on the presents and the decorations of the tree. From the tips of the branches sticking out beyond the lights, and the red and green garlands, and the shiny tinsel, hung the lightest Christmas presents. Further into the tree, next to the trunk, were the presents that would balance there. Others were tied to the branches, and any spaces that were left were filled up with gaudy glass balls, the same type as we use today. But these alternated with walnuts, strung up I forget how, and with striped candy-canes and candied apples. And hung here and there between the Christmas stockings were gauze bags, red and blue and green and yellow, filled with walnuts, Brazil nuts, peanuts, and hazelnuts; filled with Mrs. Johnstone's popcorn, Mrs. Allen's white walnut fudge, and Mrs. Kipp's butterscotch. Oh, there simply wasn't enough room on the tree to hang all of these, so the rest were piled on the floor. Shining from the top of the tree would be some sort of star or an angel, or possibly good old Santa Claus himself. At its foot, piled high, were all the presents you could think of, packaged in red and blue paper—dolls and rocking horses and everything else that the parents could make or could afford or could buy from Eaton's catalogue. In good years the mound was four feet deep. For the children of parents who could not afford presents, a collection had been taken up in some mysterious way so as to assure that every child at the Christmas tree got one present, at least, with his name on it.

There was no suspicion in any little mind that this was not wholly the sorcery of Santa Claus. There was no knowledge that for months past mothers had been scrimping and saving, a nickel here, a dime there, putting them into the old crock well back on the top shelf of the cupboard. No excited, tousled head ever knew that on a night a month before, after bed-time, mother had turned up the coal-oil lamp as she sat poring over Eaton's catalogue, filling in an order blank, so that on this great night Santa might thrust into eager little hands a mouth-organ, a teddy-bear or a doll. No shining eyes, that on this night reflected all the expectancy of Christmas, had seen the tears fall on the order blank when item after item had to be scratched off the list and a fresh calculation made. Children knew nothing of the secret moonlight walk their mother had made to get the parcel from the post office and into the house and stowed away while they slept serenely. Nor did they know that night after night mother had knitted mitts, stockings, and toques, while father worked beside her, planing and sawing, rasping and sanding, so that there should be toys by the tree.

When the concert part of the evening was over, when the last boy had mumbled his lines, when the last gauzy angel had swept off the stage, one red flannelette pant-leg dropping below her filmy skirt, when the teacher had ceased prompting and perspiring, a hush silenced the chatter in the overheated room. It was then that Otis Johnstone came running down the road and turned in at the school gate, ringing his sleigh-bells like mad and galloping thrice around the school yelling, "Whoa, whoa," at his reindeer.

It was then that Joe Fowlie pounded and scraped at the outside of the windowless north wall, helping Santa's sleigh mount to the roof. All eyes turned from the tree to the trap door in the ceiling. Santa's red legs dropped through the hole. With his make-up smeared from the heat of the attic, he wriggled his way down, panting and puffing, tugging to bring his beard back from below his ear and patting back into place the pillow that formed his tummy, and which the narrow hole had jammed around his neck.

For a moment he beamed from the stage before explaining how he had been afraid he wouldn't make it through the drifts by Byvank's pasture. And then he would see Billie Hoogers and greet him, and Nellie Dodson and Alida Byvank, and Cecil James and Bessie Mason—why, he seemed to know them all! Of course they all knew him, for here once more was Santa Claus. Even when Brother Bill cried out, "Daddy! it's Daddy!" no one noticed or believed him.

Such a rustling of paper as presents were torn open, such blowing of horns and shouting, such happy prattle, such running and yelling you never heard before. Such a scene, such a happy throng as filled Cotswold Schoolhouse that night was never duplicated— except in four thousand other school-houses on the same night! It can never be repeated. You can't describe Christmas. Only in the heart, or in the shining eyes, or in the memory of a child is there a fit description of Christmas.

9

Christmas on the farm began with the concert and went on for many days. From the school it followed us home and hovered around till Christmas Eve. At three o'clock the next morning it resumed again. And when, before noon, we went to Otis Johnstone's with Chappie and Charlie hitched to the old sleigh, it followed us there. Christmas dinner at Johnstone's, with its loads of food, should have been enough to put it to sleep for another year, just as it put all of us children to sleep. But it didn't. Christmas was still around when the Johnstones came over to our shack on the North-West of 16 for New Year's Day. We'll get to all these things when I have set down just one more memory of those school concerts.

I remember one year when Dad, Mother, Bill, and I decided to walk the mile and a half to the school. There was a mere inch of fresh snow, and the evening was just cold enough to keep it from melting, so we four tramped expectantly along the old bush road. When the concert was over, the full white moon was riding high in the sky. Several neighbours offered us a ride, but the night was too beautiful to be hurried away by riding. After the last sleigh-load had passed us, we four had the night, the bush road and the moon to ourselves. Tired?—well maybe Mother was, but she would not admit it. If excitement tires, Bill and I were ready to drop, but at the moment we did not realize it. Mother and Dad walked along at an easy pace, while Bill and I marched ahead, blowing triumphantly on a mouth-organ and a tin bugle. There was no music to it, but what we lacked in music we made up in noise, while the bush road shuddered at the discord. What the old owl sitting in the twin-topped spruce thought, no one knew. What the whisky-jacks and rabbits thought, no one heeded. How startled were the partridges perched ten at a time in the great poplars, no one cared. It was Christmas, the concert was over and, surfeited with joy, we tootled our way home. I still remember turning now and then to wait for Dad and Mother, and seeing the white forms of rabbits crouched under brush piles, silent and still but watching and ready to bolt further into the woods. I can still remember the great gap through the trees that was the old trail. I can still see the snow-carpeted forest with the huge poplars swaying gently while, in their topmost branches, black round balls that in the morning would become partridges were silhouetted against the moon sliding silently past the clouds.

On the North-West of 16 with its combined English and Scots traditions, both Christmas and New Year's were savoured to the full. In those good old days a case of Scotch whisky cost only a few dollars. Whoever made the trip to Edmonton before Christmas brought back a case of whisky for Henry Paulson, one for Dad, one for Joe Fowlie, and perhaps for others. Now, a case of quarts—pre-First-War quarts of Teachers Highland Cream—represented a lot of alcohol and, if used wisely, a lot of merriment. The Christmas concert, I forgot to say, was usually on the last Friday night before Christmas. That usually left a few days of anticipation before Christmas Eve. Whoever brought out the Christmas cheer this particular year delivered our case during this interval.

December 24 dawned upon a light fall of fresh, fluffy snow. A good breakfast of fried moose liver and fried potatoes started us off to a proper enjoyment of the great day. No work, except the necessary chores, was done that day, although Joe and Dad opened the case of whisky and fortified themselves against possible frost-bite. Axel Clausen came over, and the three men communed together at one side of the big kitchen. Bill and I played about in the snow with Gyp, one of a long succession of dogs all named Gyp. As dusk began to gather, a dozen or so turkeys sought roosts on the roof of the henhouse, on the hay rack, and even in a tree or two. One of them, a huge gobbler, had been fattened with care. His flight to the top of the henhouse reminded Mother that it was time to kill him, so that he could hang till New Year's Day. Accordingly, she called upon the three men to go out and slay the gobbler, promising to have supper ready by the time they had done so. But one story led to another, and supper was ready before the deed was done.

"All right," said Mother, "right after supper, then."

After supper the men sallied forth to the woodpile for the axe, while Bill and I, hopping about in anticipation, ran ahead to point out the last roosting-place of the turkey gobbler on top of the henhouse.

But it was not just as simple as the men had planned. The gobbler, aroused by the hullabaloo, craned his long neck and tried to make out the reason for all this uproar. Five voices rose on the evening air, shouting at him to come down; for who could get at him there? A sixth voice awakened all the sleeping turkeys as Gyp joined in. The impressive bird gobbled in annoyance. From their posts high above the yard—from the hay rack, the trees, and the barn roof—lesser gobblers joined the medley, while turkey hens chattered nervously.

"Throw something at him," suggested Joe; and a rain of missiles clattered on the henhouse roof, all falling short but alarming the hens, so that they added their voices to the din. Chappie and Charlie, who had previously been dozing over at the straw-pile, were aroused and came galloping in to share the fun. Bunty, secure in the cow barn, raised her voice.

"Get your twenty-two and shoot him," suggested Axel.

"But I don't want to make holes in him," muttered Dad.

"Get a pole and wire, and snare him."

"Get a ladder and the pitchfork."

"Where's Jim's bow and arrow?"

The pole and the snare-wire seemed to be the best bet, but elbows that had bent all afternoon were not connected with steady hands and the wire only tickled the gobbler. Other turkeys left their perches and milled around the yard in alarm, but the prize of the flock refused to leave the safety of the henhouse.

"Let's go back to the kitchen and steady our nerves and talk things over while the turkeys settle down," said Joe. Since this was the most practical idea brought forward so far, it was adopted with only Bill and me and Gyp dissenting.

The consultation refreshed the men and they came out filled with new determination. This time they came brandishing Dad's salmon rod, complete with a hundred feet of fishing line and a lump of lead dangling at the end of it. They marched resolutely on the henhouse, but the gobbler had flown. He was soon located in the company of three disturbed turkey hens behind the straw-pile. As the chase was resumed, he registered annoyance and stamped on the ground. When three determined men rushed at him from three different directions, he neatly eluded them by flying to the top of the pile. Here he rocked with anger, pointing his out-thrust head down at his pursuers, while flaming away in the moonlight his red wattles swayed in time to his angry gobbling.

"Swish," went the salmon rod; "creak, creak," sang the reel; and "whack" went the lump of lead against his long wing feathers. The cast, intended to encircle his neck or legs, had missed. The challenging gobbler stopped abruptly as anger gave way to anxiety, and he flew down the other side of the pile and ran off.

The tempo of pursuit quickened as the gobbler, leading a dozen or so frightened hens, streaked around the barn and raced off through the trees. Axel led the attackers, with Joe right behind, while Dad, having difficulty getting the fishing rod through the trees, trailed slightly. And behind him came Gyp, two boys, and Chappie and Charlie. The gobbler flew to the top of the chicken-house, but Axel clattered so much when he tripped over the neck-yoke of the sleigh that the bird unwisely left this security and the mad rout started all over again. He flew to the top of the hay rack, and loomed against the bright sky like a vulture as he peered about anxiously.

"Try sneaking up on him," said Joe; "we'll wait here and you slip around into the shadow of the biffy. From there a good cast should get him." So, while we all watched tensely, Dad sneaked up on the vigilant gobbler. This time the lump of lead whirled around the gobbler's outstretched neck and we had him. The chase which had occupied a thrilling hour was over. Tranquillity settled over the yard. The moon cast stark shadows on the trampled snow. The rabbits ventured back to the woodpile. Reluctantly Bill and I heeded the summons to bed.

In the excitement we had forgotten that it was Christmas Eve. "Hurry up and go to sleep," said Mother, "for Santa Claus will be along any minute now; and you know what happens if he comes around and little boys are not asleep—he goes away again."

Go to sleep on Christmas Eve? When ideas of Christmas and of Santa raced after each other through a boy's head? Why, you might as well take him to a circus and tell him to go to sleep. If, for an hour, he has galloped about in the moonlight in all the excitement of capturing the turkey gobbler, that makes it all the more impossible. For what seemed like hours, Bill and I turned and tossed, afraid of offending Santa Claus and trying desperately to go to sleep.

Downstairs, as Mother worked in the kitchen, pots and pans rattled. Snatches of talk drifted up to us as Dad, Axel, and Joe reviewed parts of the recent chase. I became anxious, then angry, and marching to the head of the stairs I scolded all and sundry for keeping us awake, and for scaring Santa away. Mother came up to soothe our taut nerves, and just then from far down the road came the tinkling of Santa's sleigh-bells. Even Mother stood in the darkness and listened as the sound of the bells came nearer. Up the road they came; twice around the house they swung— then paused. Right out there in the moonlit yard, just beyond the blind which we dared not pull aside, Santa and his reindeer waited and listened, trying to find out if all in the house were sound asleep. We dared not look out, because at the least peek he would discover us and away he would go. But you can't fool Santa. In a moment, with a gentle tinkle, his reindeer started up, and we could hear the receding bells as they made off rapidly past the barn and over the fields towards Paulson's.

It was life's bitterest moment. Santa had come, heard the three men talking downstairs, and at the sound had passed us by. He would not return till next Christmas, if then. We had been tested and found wanting. If we were not asleep, it was not our fault; the blame lay on everybody else, on poor Mother, and especially on Dad, Axel, and Joe. Anger rose above our anguish. All the adults came in for bitter denunciation. That over, Bill and I lay down to sleep. The excitement of the hunt and the anticipation of Christmas had given way to despair.

What wakes boys so early on Christmas morning? When the first streaks of dawn breasted Tracy's hill, swept down over the east field and lighted the roof of the barn, Bill and I were awake, peering into the gloomy recesses of the room. There, at the foot of the bed, were two stockings fairly bulging with oranges, nuts, and toys. On either side of the bed were packages, a drum, a mechanical clown, books, and mittens, and moccasins. Santa Claus had relented, and the world was whole again. How were we to know that Santa had been very late making his rounds that night and that what we had heard was only Joe Fowlie running around ringing a set of sleigh-bells?

Christmas morning on the farm! You can't describe it. It's just a jumble of fleeting, gleeful moments as a boy's happiness jumps from this joy to that. Breakfast? Who wants breakfast, with nuts and oranges, apples and candy piled all over the place? Who has time for breakfast with drums to beat, clowns to wind, and books to read? Even Tabby the cat knows it's Christmas as with tail held straight aloft she stalks around, sniffing at teddy-bears, toying with wrapping-paper, or playing with a piece of string dangling from the large red Christmas bell in the centre of the room. Even Gyp, waiting outside, ever ready to welcome two boys emerging from the house, and keen to get into whatever deviltry seizes their attention—even Gyp knows it. And Bunty, as she turns her head to watch the milking, munching the while at an extra ration of oats, Bunty knows it's Christmas. Chappie and Charlie, chomping over extra bundles of greenfeed thrown down from the loft, know something is afoot as the barn door is opened to let them out to gallop and frisk and kick up their heels on the way to the water trough. Then, when you want to put them in the barn again to harness them, they pretend that they can't find the door. Inching slowly along, they stop to look in as if dimly they recognize it but are not quite sure. And then with a toss of the head and a flip of the tail, they swing off and gallop round and round the barn. But it's all part of the fun, for they too are going to Johnstone's for Christmas Day.

Going to Johnstone's! You can get in your airliners and fly to Hawaii for Christmas. You can motor to Los Angeles for Christmas and the Rose Bowl Game. You can assemble in Times Square and sway with the crowd as the New Year comes in. But for me— I would like to turn back the years and celebrate another Christmas Day at Johnstone's!

Let Dad hitch Chappie and Charlie to the sleigh. Let Mother bundle her boys up in coats and mitts and scarves. Let her fill the sleigh with straw, blankets, and cushions, and carry out two stones heated in the oven to keep their feet warm. Let her tuck everybody in. Let Dad, in his old sheepskin coat and moccasins and his moth-eaten old muskrat hat, flip the lines to the horses as they start. Let all hear the bob of the bunks, the swish of the runners over the packed snow, and the tinkle of the heel chains, as gaily we swing down the trail. For today we are going to Johnstone's for Christmas dinner.

In a hundred yards the trail left the farm behind, and for two

miles it picked its way between great trees of the forest. Soon
it passed the gnarled balm blasted by lightning the previous
August. Before that this majestic giant had towered beyond the
lesser trees, reaching far over their heads a huge, rough column
with tremendous arching branches bearing its dense, leafy canopy.
Now, bereft of leaves, stark against the heavens, riven from top
to roots, it loomed against the sky, twisted and terrifying. Then
the sleigh slipped on past the "Bear Tree," where three summers
before, as he had climbed the green poplar, a bear had left the
marks of his four claws on the soft bark—marks that since had
turned to black, witch-like scars. Then on through the forest past
the willow flat where the moose had been shot.

The sleigh track cut straight across the snowy whiteness of a
little meadow, scarcely a hundred yards across, surrounded with
a frieze of willows and backed with its wall of evergreens. Count-
less rabbit tracks, mere shaded dimples in the soft whiteness, criss-
crossed its powdery snow. On the fringe of willows and the spreading
alders the mystic tracery of hoar-frost clung undisturbed in the
breathless, sunny air, till the vibration of the passing sleigh shivered
it off in dripping cascades of starlight to find repose on the white
blanket. The meadow was still and silent. Motionless under every
snow-piled branch or log sat a snowy cotton-tail, its presence
revealed only by its black eyes, and nothing broke the silence till
the invasion of the swishing sleigh. In stillness and snowy whiteness
the rabbits celebrated their Christmas. For it was Christmas in the
cathedral of the forest.

Quickly we slipped along, and almost before we knew it we
emerged from the forest into Johnstone's field and swept on to the
warm welcome of Johnstone's hospitality.

Christmas dinner at Johnstone's! That was an experience never
to be forgotten—an experience, alas, no longer possible to duplicate.
Yet the recipe for it is simple. Take the hungry stomach of an
active farm boy that gnaws again an hour after any meal. Give it
a breakfast cut short by the excitement of new toys. Bundle stomach
and boy into heavy clothes, and whisk them in a farm sleigh two
miles through the crisp spruce-scented air. Let the boy run into
Mrs. Johnstone's kitchen. Let the aroma of roasting turkey fill his
nostrils and the crackling of the basting fat assail his ears. That is
your recipe.

Garnish, if you wish, by letting his eyes dart about the kitchen.
See—there on the shelf are six pies, two blueberry, two mince, and

two low-bush cranberry, still hot from the oven, their acrid smell blended with the odour of hot lard. On the stove, bubbling away in the big pot, is the Christmas pudding, its savoury steam competing in gusto with all the other smells. Let this boy stand looking through the doorway with his back to the crackling kitchen and before him the long log room (usually part dining-room, part sitting-room, but today all dining-room). Let his eyes take in the red Christmas bell in the centre, with its green paper streamers sweeping off to the corners of the room, and then the long table set for ten, and loaded with colourful, cheery Christmas goodies. Look at the piles of home-made crusty bread, the plates of cookies, plain or iced with red or green, and the red candles flickering their welcome. Look at the green of the cucumber pickles, the yellow of the mustard pickles and the glowing red of pickled beets. And there, on the sideboard, right there enthroned in the very centre— that is Mrs. Johnstone's chocolate cake. What a cake! Made as only Mrs. Johnstone can make it. Five inches high—two layers, chinked with jam and roofed with a quarter inch of chocolate icing. And there to keep it company stands the huge bowl filled with preserved wild strawberries and flanked by two piles each of five ruby glass dessert dishes, while tucked into every vacant space on the sideboard are bowls of nuts, oranges, apples and candy, a plate of jelly-roll and a pile of cinnamon buns. Over all presides Mrs. Johnstone, beaming with friendship and with Christmas time and with pride in her handiwork.

Let this boy walk slowly around the table and see all the side dishes—here a dish of low-bush cranberry jelly waiting for the turkey, there a jar of high-bush cranberry jelly, and there some spiced black currants. Finally the glistening bowls awaiting the arrival of potatoes and carrots, and, beside each of the ten white plates, flanking each knife and fork, red, yellow, and green Christmas crackers.

Then, amidst all these smells and sights, make him wait nearly an hour while the turkey roasts to its brownest crackling excellence. Then seat everybody. Otis Johnstone at the head, his face beaming and his bald head shining, while he whets away at the huge carving-knife made from a piece of scythe blade and hafted with deer horn. Next, a chair for Mother, still busy in the kitchen, and beside it, Bill's chair. Then Pearl Johnstone, placed so as to be able to tend both Bill and her younger brother Charlie. And so on around the table; Mrs. Johnstone and Dad and Lloyd, with me sitting beside him; then Charlie Rose with the iron-grey beard, and Grandfather Johnstone with his white one.

Then let Mrs. Johnstone carry in the turkey, while Mother brings bowls piled high with mashed potatoes, white and fluffy, and with rich golden carrots, and the steaming dark brown gravy. Have Otis stand up and, with deft strokes, lay bare the white meat of turkey breast and the dark meat of drumstick, and scoop out the dressing. Let no grim visage nor solemn discourse mar the pleasure of passing back for second helpings and then following these with cake and cookies, pies and strawberries. Finally, lay before Otis the steaming Christmas pudding with its blue brandy flames flickering and following each other round and round about.

There's your recipe for Christmas dinner at Johnstone's—a boy's unforgettable Christmas dinner.

For hours afterwards Mother and Mrs. Johnstone washed dishes, and before they were all dried Lloyd and I were eyeing oranges and cracking nuts with a hammer. Soon Mrs. Johnstone dug out the ice-cream freezer; and this luxury, strange to a farm boy, would fill in any chinks that had developed as his enormous dinner settled. Then, as the early dusk dimmed the room, old man Johnstone brought out his fiddle and all joined in singing the old favourite songs—"My Old Kentucky Home," "Sweet Genevieve," "Kathleen Mavourneen," "Killarney," and many more. All the while Otis played the accordion and Lloyd chimed in with his Jew's-harp.

Finally the coal-oil lamps were lit, and Mrs. Johnstone began to prepare supper. But who, except the children, could eat any more? The adults had a cup of tea or coffee, and, for courtesy's sake, nibbled at some Christmas cake. The children, of course, did not miss the chance to start again; but, alas, as Mrs. Johnstone said, their eyes were bigger than their bellies. Sighs of satisfaction succumbed to sighs of surfeit, while heavy eyelids testified to the toll taken by Christmas. It was time to go home.

Chappie and Charlie were soon hitched up to the sleigh, and amid repeated shouts of "See you at New Year's!" they picked their way along the trail, winding through the twisted birches and the stark tamaracks. Bill and I were soon settled down in the bottom of the sleigh-box, while Dad and Mother sat watching the trail ahead as it wound into the recesses of the forest.

Before long the little meadow was reached. On a winter forenoon it had been beautiful in the brightness of fresh snow. By moonlight a haze of mystery had dropped over it. Even Chappie and Charlie realized this, as to cross it they slowed to a walk. Horses, heel chains, even the sleigh itself, and its occupants, were hushed in the presence of the sleeping meadow. The very shadows of the great black spruces seemed to tiptoe across it. The darker hollows of the criss-cross rabbit tracks were now softened to blue shadowy traces running from brush piles to cavernous hollows under fallen logs. All around the edges of the meadow the bright moonlight outlined the snow-laden branches of willows, alders and spruce, each standing out clear and motionless as a mountain peak. Against the blue-blackness of their shadows, each snow-capped tuft of grass, each snow-capped hummock of moss, each snow-capped knee of spruce stood out. And yet you couldn't be certain if this one or that was merely a cap of snow or was in reality a rabbit hunched up and watching. The only way to tell was to throw a stick or to shout; but in this shrine of the forest, sticks and shouting would have been sacrilege. A whisper, maybe, was permissible, but no more. For tonight the whole silent forest, and this sacred circle in particular, worshipped.

And so the team and sleigh stole out of the little meadow and slipped along the trail, leaving the great trees to stand sentinel all through the night. Then out across the big meadow the horses trotted, swinging around the shadowy willows whose flaring branches were dotted with a dozen partridges huddled into balls, asleep—inky silhouettes against the streaming Northern Lights. The horses quickened their pace as they came to the rise that marked the ascent to our clearing. Their heel chains fairly rang now that they were in sight of the smokeless house and the shadowy barn, and in a moment we were home.

Dad sprang out of the sleigh to unhitch the horses, glad of the exercise to revive chilled limbs. Mother climbed down carefully, and she and her two boys, mumbling with sleepiness, bumbled their way into the darkness and the chill of the farmhouse whose wood fires had gone out hours ago. She groped for the lamp and lit it. Soon, paper and kindling were piled on the fleecy grey ashes of the old air-tight heater. For a moment the match flickered, then caught the paper, and in minutes the fire was roaring away. I don't think that there is any kind of heater which warms an ice-cold room so quickly as these old-time ones. With hands nearly numb with cold you stood around and the very roar of the fire catching on the spruce logs seemed to warm you. As soon as the fire was well established and roaring up the smoke-pipe, you partially closed the damper in that pipe. At the same time you burned your fingers as you screwed in the little damper low down on the front of the heater. The adjustment of these two dampers was always a delicate one, because if it was not done exactly right, the fire would start to puff like a locomotive, and billows of smoke and spurts of flame nearly rocked the heater off its legs. Glowing red spots soon appeared on the metal sides of the heater. Then it was time to take off your cap and coat, for soon the room would be too warm. A wonderful thing was an old air-tight heater.

Soon the chill was off the living-room of the MacGregor household, and before long it was time to go to bed. That takes a bit of courage too—leaving the fire and climbing into an ice-cold bed. For fifteen or twenty minutes the issue is uncertain. If you can stick it out long enough to warm the bed, you win, for the pile of blankets is a wonderful insulator; if you warm just that small part of the bed in contact with you, the blankets will keep the heat from escaping. Your face and nose, exposed to room temperature, may almost freeze, but never do. Soon you drop off to a blissful sleep.

Getting up on a winter morning is another matter. The fire downstairs has long since gone out. In the kitchen the milk pans will be frozen solid, the water pail by the kitchen stove will be nearly so. As you lie in bed you carefully raise one eye over the quilt and peek at the window. No comfort there. It's half an inch thick with frost. The beautiful designs etched by the frost crystals do not appeal to you. You sneak a look at the knotty spruce floor so hard and shiny and cold. Your bare feet curl and cringe at the very thought of it. You raise your head and listen in case some other member of the household is awake. If you hear any sign of life, oh joy, you snuggle down tight, for he may get up first and light the fire.

But at last you can't pretend any longer. You are hungry and can't seem to settle back to sleep any more. You reach out for your socks, great heavy wool ones, and as you lie in bed you pull them on till they reach far up your underwear towards your knees. Pyjamas? In a shack on the homestead you would freeze even as you stood on the cold floor exchanging them for ice-cold underwear. No! Far better to sleep in your underwear and to have its warmth cling to your body while you pull on your overalls and sweater and grope for your moccasins.

Then you fairly fly down the stairs. Noise? You make plenty of it. It announces your courage. For you above all others have dared to get up and to face the chilled house. It also eases the conscience of all the other members of the household. With a great clatter you lift the lid of the glorious air-tight heater and light it. Then you set a fire in the kitchen stove and put on the kettle. Soon the old heater begins to puff and smoke as the flames roar up the chimney. The roaring increases as the heater rejoices that it, too, has lived through another winter night. Smoke begins to ascend the chimney. Its clear, grey column, rising straight into the still air, announces to all who may see it that the MacGregor household is awake and ready to face another day.

With a rush, clad only in underwear and socks, the rest of the family fling themselves down the stairs and huddle around the heater as they put on the balance of their clothes. Next comes a quick dip in the wash basin. A hammer or a butcher knife will serve to break a hole through the ice of the water pail. The water beginning to boil in the kettle must be saved for tea and for cooking porridge. Anyway, ice-cold water is best for washing. Ice-cold water is challenging. It helps to brace you for the problems of the day. Equally bracing is the quick run through the snow to the two-holer beyond the woodpile. Dad always referred to this operation on a wintry morning as "making an exposure." Woe to him who had to make a time exposure!

But the day's work that followed these stern beginnings rarely failed to provide some pleasure and excitement for a boy. There was rail-cutting, for instance. Our quarter was enclosed by a fence of barbed wire, but all the fences across and around the yard were of rails. There were many of these fences, and they were neat ones, with three rails nailed to tamarack posts standing in line and erect as soldiers, and capped by another along the top. The rails were carefully selected for straightness and uniformity. Our fences may not have been as picturesque as some haphazardly built ones, but they served well, marching off as they did in a determined sort of way, erect and straight from henhouse to haystack and from barn to biffy.

The selecting and the cutting of these rails was most interesting. They grew down on the South-East of 17, which, because of its proximity to our place and because Dad had opened up trails to all its many inviting meadows, we always regarded as practically our own. On the great days when we set out to cut rails, Dad would hitch the horses to the sleigh, load Bill and me into it, throw in a bundle of greenfeed for Chappie and Charlie, and off to work we'd go. As we slipped along, the sleigh-runners sang as they went bump, bump, bump over the little inequalities in the snowy trail. The heel chains tinkled, and now and then the horses sneezed in contentment or snorted in pretended fright at a black upturned root which they had seen scores of times. Here and there a rabbit hopped across the trail, a partridge burst from the bushes and went roaring off into the deeper woods, or a squirrel challenged from a spruce bough high above. Going down into the bush on any excursion was fun, but going down on a frosty morning to cut rails was sheer enchantment.

After the trail had crossed the partridge meadow, skirted the grove of sentinel spruces, wound far along the beaver ditch, then over the little hummock at the edge of the Bear Tree meadow and was well on its way to the skunk meadow—here, just past the huge leaning poplar that ever threatened to fall across the road but never did so, the trail forked. The left fork ran two hundred yards to the stand of rails. This grove of slender spruces covered two acres or maybe three. On it stood rails, "thick as hair on a dog," as Dad said, growing about a foot apart—hundreds of young spruce trees all of an age, and that about twenty-five years. Straight as arrows they were, tall and slim, as each sought to outstretch its neighbour in reaching far into the sky for more than its share of sunshine. No undergrowth marred the symmetry of endless trees. No branch obscured the first thirty feet of the tapering trunks. Above that no sunlight could penetrate the wood, thickly thatched with swaying boughs and slender needles. In winter, silence prevailed as the soft snows muffled the moccasined tread. In summer, the yielding moss stifled the tramp of boots. In such a vale grew our rails.

In summer this mossy carpet, so soft, so cool, so velvety, was a favourite spot for ground-wasps to build their nests. These wasps brought a sudden end to one idyllic rail-cutting expedition. As usual, Bill and I accompanied Dad, but this time Bill brought along his little axe. While Dad was busy chopping, young George Washington proceeded to whack away at a nearby tree. As he laid into the tree, an earnest determination suffused his freckled face, while the effort he expended vibrated the legs of his little open-kneed cotton pants. The force of his blows likewise shook the tree and vibrated the moss around its roots. Suddenly the stillness was rent with a yell as Bill dropped his axe and slapped vainly at his pants. From the foot of the tree an angry buzzing arose, and from a hole in the moss, imperceptible till then, a snarling stream of ground-wasps ascended. This stream split into two columns, each one disappearing into a leg of Bill's pants and rejoining the other further up. Dad grabbed Bill and rolled him over in the moss and stripped shirt and pants off him, but not before a dozen or so wasps had stung him at various vital spots from his knees to his neck. Right then the rail-cutting ended.

But in winter, when we reached the rail patch, the horses were unhitched and munched contentedly at sheaves of greenfeed. Dad, first testing his axe with cautious thumb, swung deftly at the nearest spruce. Two or three blows from the axe, and a push, and the long, slender poem fell slowly to be cushioned in the snow. A few licks with the axe to remove the top and the uppermost branches, and there lay a rail tapering imperceptibly from four inches at the base to two and a half inches thirty feet away. Two or three hours' work would produce the rails for hundreds of feet of fence, and then Chappie and Charlie would whisk us home so that they might enjoy the shelter of the shadowy barn and the luxury of forksful of hay, while we repaired to the cheer of the kitchen stove and hot soup. Some other day a trip or two with the wide bunks on the sleigh would suffice to bring home our forest harvest as a long pile of slender rails.

I mentioned our line fences, our wire ones. What pleasure is there comparable to fencing-in your own quarter, your own 160 acres of land? Dad was a pretty good mathematician, a bit of a surveyor, and engineer. He enjoyed this fencing to the full. For a start, he had the surveyors' cutline which ran north and south along the west side of the quarter. As I have said, it was sixty-six feet—the width of the road allowance—west of our property line, but by using it as a guide he soon determined where our line ran. Many a happy day he spent cutting out this line. First he cut half a mile north of the survey mound, then half a mile east along the dividing line between Donkelaar's quarter and ours, until he reached the north-east corner of the quarter where our corner post touched Mrs. Cantin's place. Here half the joyful task was completed. Half a mile south to separate our land from Gordon Tracy's, and then half a mile west between Dudley Graham's and our place, brought this cutline for the future fence back to the point of commencement.

The winter before the fence was to be erected, Dad took me

far beyond my previous boundaries, three miles north-east down to the "swamp." Here, two miles wide and fringing the Pembina River for an unknown distance, lay a region of muskeg and marsh in which spiralled tamarack thrived. This swamp provided fence-posts for all the farmers of Eastburg; for the tamarack trees, while of all sizes, were mostly just right for fence-posts. One tree would cut into three or four posts.

It takes a lot of posts to enclose 160 acres, even if you don't "cross-fence" it, that is, build subsidiary fences inside it. It is two miles around a quarter-section, and, at a rod apart, this takes 640 posts. Usually all the neighbours co-operated in this fencing. In our community it was standard practice for each adjacent neighbour to fence half of the boundary between his place and yours. As a man stood on his quarter facing his neighbour, he fenced the half of the line on his left. If the neighbour did likewise, the half mile of line fence was completed by their joint effort. This meant that Dad had to cut posts and supply wire for only one and a quarter miles.

The sleigh trips to the swamp were memorable—up at dawn on a winter's morning and winding down the trail as the sun came up, and then coming home long after dark. Best of all was the break for lunch, when Dad would light a little fire to melt snow and boil water in the five-pound lard pail so that we might have hot tea. The sandwiches so carefully packed by Mother would be frozen by lunch time, but the toasting they received when jabbed on a stick and thrust into the flames to thaw them added a price-less zest to the day. Towards dusk we would load up the sleigh, throw a rope and a logging chain around the load and cinch it up tightly with a stick used in the same manner as a stick in a tourniquet. Then we would start out of the swamp. The smell of fresh-cut tamarack is sour but aromatic, and it clings to the memory of such days, along with the flaking bark that chipped off, the stickiness of gum, and the wisps of lichen that grew like Spanish moss on the tamarack trees.

After the posts were sawn into lengths, and piled, Dad worked for days sharpening them. While each post leaned more or less vertically against a tripod, its end was placed on a block. Then with a good sharp axe each was whittled to a pencil-like point. As the pile of sharpened posts grew, so did the pile of chips. Several times the block and the tripod had to be shifted to get away from the accumulation of bark and cuttings. All the next summer these chips provided Mother with ample kindling for her fires. Before the snow disappeared Dad and I distributed the stakes along our cutlines at one-rod intervals. When summer came and most of the sloughs dried up, George, Dudley, Gorodn, and he went to work to build the fence.

First the posts had to be placed in proper alignment, and Dad did this with care. Then followed days of man-killing work with the maul. Two men worked together at this, one driving the wagon alongside the post, while the other swung the maul to drive it well into the ground. Three or four men worked at stringing the wire. First of all the end of a spool of barbed wire was fastened to a well-braced corner post. Then, with a stick thrust through the hole in the spool, two men walked along the line unreeling it. Then it had to be tightened with our wire-stretchers (a simple block-and-tackle arrangement) until when you plucked it, it sang like a fiddle string. Later it could be stapled in place, and before many days the North-West of 16 was fenced in. Now it was plain for all the world to see where the MacGregor farm began and ended. It was plain to Bunty, too, that henceforth she was intended to stay within this light, three-strand fence.

It was obvious enough to Bunty, but it did not accord with her desires. The grass just beyond the fence was always greener, and Bunty became an adept at getting through between the wires. That is why I became acquainted with every slough and stream, with every creek and coulee for miles around, because for times innumerable I sought Bunty over half the length and breadth of Eastburg.

I don't want to be the Prime Minister of Canada, the President of the United States, the Emperor of all the Russias, or a Vanderbilt or a Carnegie. I just want to be a farm boy again on the homestead at Eastburg, going over to Johnstone's for Christmas, going down to the bush with Dad to cut rails, living over again the seasons as they sweep across the land. Only this time, for the winter mornings, let me have lots of hot, running water in a nice warm bathroom.

They called him Old Doc Phillips. No encomium could add to the lustre of the words "Old Doc." From the most remote shack thirty-five miles away in Neerlandia they came to him, galloping all through the night. From the edge of the great muskegs up Naples way they rushed to him. From Mellowdale, Paddle River, Lunnford, and Belvedere they sought his help for a loved one labouring long in childbirth or stricken with fever. Along the trails to Dunstable, Arvilla, and Picardville, Old Doc and his driving team fought their way for years through mud or storm to the bedside of a sick mother or a wasting child. Finally there came the Spanish 'flu of 1918. Far away in Swallowhurst or Sunniebend, through blizzard and snowdrift, Old Doc rode, dozing between calls, hastening to fight it. His very presence instilled a courage that often won the battle. And when it was all over and the 'flu masks were put away and services of thanksgiving filled the country schools and churches, Old Doc had a heart attack. Only he and his wife knew that till afterwards. But he fought that off too—for a while—till that day when he was attending a patient only three miles from home and they came galloping to take Mrs. Phillips to him. "I'm going, Carrie," was all he said; "Good-bye."

That was Old Doc Phillips—a gentleman, a profound scholar, a Christian and a lover of good horses—a short man with close-cropped grey hair, flashing eyes and the grim jaw of an Irish fighter.

Why he left a practice in Michigan; why, of all places, he came to Eastburg, why he filed on the South-East of 17, diagonally across from us, and the only quarter in the whole community considered useless, no one knows. In a pioneer community the better folk do not ask. The others, those who gossip and speculate, do not matter. That is, they didn't matter until they were stricken ill. Then they sent crying for Old Doc, and he cured them.

He must have had a Christian name, but I doubt if anyone knew it, except perhaps Dad, who was his closest neighbour and best friend. He was just Old Doc Phillips. To me he was a friend and a god. I don't think I ever had his professional help, but he did much for me. He had a library filling one side of his front room with books, and good ones. He allowed me the privilege of Scott, Dickens, Cooper, and Stevenson; and had I been able to understand them, he would have introduced me to Milton and Shakespeare, Walt Whitman and Thoreau. And ever he held before me the goal of high school some day, and perhaps even university. If he had lived, I know he would have helped financially; as it was, his inspiration, added to Mother's ardent desire and Dad's pocketbook and quiet advice, eventually gave me these advantages.

One spring evening he drove up in a new buggy and tied his smart horse to a tree. Homesteaders do not wait for the knock at the door but go out to welcome the visitor, so Dad and I met him on his way to the house. We saw a short, pleasant man, with grey hair and a close-cropped moustache. Actually he was only about forty-five, but looked much older.

It is hard for one in the city to understand the pleasure brought to a bush farmer and his family by the arrival of a polite stranger. If he will give in and stay all night, so much the greater is the boon bestowed.

That first evening with Old Doc flew by while he outlined his plans for settling amongst us.

Next morning when Dad and I walked with him through the thick bush of his quarter, he seemed more delighted than dismayed by its worthlessness. On a slight rise at the south edge of his land he decided to build his log house. He could have afforded a frame house, but something about the primitiveness of a large log house and barn appealed to him. I believe he was "getting away from it all." It was necessary to break fifteen acres within three years if he was to get title to the land. This he hired someone to do, but insisted that it be done at the corner diagonally opposite from and out of sight of his buildings. Around them only enough of the forest was despoiled to plant a small garden. He, too, loved the forest.

As soon as the house was far enough built so that one room could be lived in, Mrs. Phillips came. She was a woman of great charm and kindliness. Her rugs and furniture told of a fine home in the east. As much as Old Doc loved the place, she loathed it.

Before Doc Phillips arrived, many of the neighbours had brought their illnesses, their fractures, and their aching teeth to Dad. I guess an old soldier is supposed to know about these things. Maybe his discipline encourages trust. Yet Dad of all people had little faith in many phases of medicine. Patent medicines he despised. He swore by two remedies only—permanganate of potash for cuts, and Epsom salts for everything else. "Keep your mind easy and your bowels open," was his philosophy. With this philosophy he never spent a day in hospital in his life, except for that time when he was eighty and fell off the pig-house he was building and hurt his shoulder and head; and that time, a few years later, when the "old man's friend," pneumonia, carried him gently away.

Aching teeth were the worst plague of the pioneers. Of all ills, Dad hated them the most, for in the early days, in a moment of weakness, he had prevailed upon his friend Dr. Clare Darling, a dentist in Edmonton, to give him two pairs of forceps. Soon everyone in the country came to our place for relief from toothache, and went away spitting blood but once more looking the world in the face. When Old Doc came, Dad quietly packed the forceps away in a drawer and directed his former patients to him. Until Doc's death the forceps stayed in the drawer. By that time, however, there was a town of Westlock, and a dentist there. So I can remember only two occasions after that when these instruments were used. Mother was the patient on one of these occasions, but we will tell of that later.

The other patient was old man Shelley. Early one morning he came mumbling into the kitchen, holding his swollen face and desperately pointing far back into his cavernous mouth. The impression he conveyed was that he had not slept for two nights and was nearly demented. His face was too swollen for Dad to try the job, so, with a good slug of whisky, he sent Shelley the twelve miles to the qualified dentist in Westlock. At dusk Shelley returned, whipping his team up the road. His face was worse than ever. The dentist had absolutely refused to pull his tooth till the swelling went down. Anger and pain nearly stifled Shelley. "I don't give a damn about infection, Mac," he muttered. "You pull it. Even if I drop dead an instant later, it will be a blessing compared to this." So Dad pulled it. Shelley was too far gone in pain to mind Dad's amateurish probing. When it was out, he sat down on the steps and cried with relief. In an hour or so he set off for home, but not before the whisky he had swished around in his mouth (to kill the infection, of course) had further assuaged his pain.

In times past, many of the accident cases had been brought to Dad—or he went to them. As Doc's reputation began to spread, people from near and far came flocking to him. At first Doc's place was described as being near the MacGregor homestead, so at any hour of the day or night a man in frantic haste might gallop up to the old log shack, to be redirected along the trail past the Bear Tree. Before Doc came, men or women had been ill and had either died or got well without a physician.

One of Doc Phillips's earlier patients was Mother. At that time she was thin and desperately tired, but on a homestead you just could not give in. One day she walked down through the gap in the bush for a formal consultation with Doc. He checked her over carefully and prepared a tonic, one spoonful to be taken before each meal. Armed with her bottle of medicine, she started home, but felt so tired that soon she sat down on a roadside log. After resting a few minutes Mother went on again, but in two or three hundred yards sat down once more. This time, reasoning that, if a tonic were needed, she might as well start taking it now, she uncorked the bottle and sipped at the medicine. It was sweet, aromatic, and soothing. Almost unconsciously Mother sipped, until she was startled to discover that the bottle was drained. "Good heavens," she thought, "now I've probably killed myself." But on getting up to walk, she felt much better. She had lingered so long lapping up the tonic that Doc Phillips, who with his smart team of drivers was now on his way to make a call, overtook her. Haltingly she told him what had happened to her month's supply of tonic. At first he was incredulous. Then he slapped his leg and burst into laughter. "My goodness, woman—that stuff's full of alcohol. You're probably drunk, or soon will be." Then, reaching a spot in the trail where he could do so, he turned his team for home again. "Come on," he said, "we'll go back and get another bottle—but this time, take it with a spoon!" Then he drove her up to our old log shack.

As Doc's fame spread across the country north-west of Edmonton, his practice grew. It was noticeable, however, that his wealth did not keep pace with it. Backwoods patients have little money. The few of them that can do so, pay. Many cannot. Others never expect to pay anyway. Fortunately for Doc and the community, he had some money when he came to Eastburg. It was a good thing that his driving-horses cost little to feed, and that in those days medicines, of which he had a regular dispensary, were relatively simple and cheap; otherwise he would have gone broke. Even so, it soon became evident to Doc that he could serve better if he lived in Westlock, so he moved to town during the First War.

I'm not certain whether Doc ever took a drink of spirituous liquor in a social way. If he did drink, it was in a most abstemious manner. But he had an Irish intolerance for stupid restrictions. When, about 1917, like a black pall, prohibition lowered over the land, Doc was "agin" it.

During prohibition days the only legal way you could get a drink of whisky was by prescription from a physician. By that time doctors were becoming more common in the district, so that it was relatively easy to get a prescription—at two dollars a time, mind you. In Westlock, drug stores had half their space filled with patent medicines, while the other half was liquor. Now Old Doc, stubbornly truthful and even blunt soul that he was, declared that whisky had only an infinitesimal medicinal value. He believed, however, that, used with discretion, it had a great psychological and uplifting value, and for that reason he held stubbornly to the opinion that no man had a right to deny his neighbour the proper use of it.

Old Doc, like all other physicians, had his books of liquor prescriptions, and gave them out quite freely to those who asked for them honestly. But woe betide you if you came snivelling to him with a pretended illness, hoping to get one. Prescriptions were worth two dollars in the open market, but Doc, whose income did not exceed his expenses, in all those years of prohibition never charged for one that was honestly requested nor supplied one to any man who, in his opinion, was unfit to have it. Henry Paulson, not surprisingly, was one of his visitors. Being cautious and long-headed, Henry had laid in a stock of whisky before the plebiscite was held. "Yust in case," said he. But even that generous supply could not last for ever; eventually he had to hitch up Lars and Dagmar and set off for Westlock; and Doc, who was glad to see his old neighbour, did not have to ask what was on Henry's mind.

But Doc Phillips has taken me ahead of my story, and I must get back to our pre-war years on the North-West of 16, the good years, before modern inventions and their concomitant problems had got much grip on us. Dad threshed his first crop on the North-West of 16 with a flail. I'm tempted to say that he flailed for the fun of it—that he enjoyed farming the hard way—but I guess he had no alternative. The next year a proper threshing-machine came to our place. It was Racine's, if I remember correctly—Racine who was later killed when dynamiting stumps. I don't remember much about it, except that the motive power was two horses hitched to the end of a long pole. As hour after hour these horses travelled around in a circle, they turned a system of gears, which in turn operated the small separator. The internal-combustion engine was still in its infancy.

The threshing-machine that came the following year was a gaudy red thing. It also was run by horses, two big black ones, who, after being coaxed on to a treadmill, tramped away all afternoon and never got any further forward. Again, I suppose, some mysterious gears finally operated the separator. I remember feeling sorry for the horses.

In those days nearly all of us had small fields not exceeding twenty or thirty acres. Stook threshing was unheard-of, because it might be well into the winter before a machine could come along and thresh out the few bushels. For this reason, all the grain was stacked.

Our grain was always hauled in and stacked at the north side of the barn. After some neighbour with his binder had been hired to cut it, and after it had dried thoroughly in the stook, Chappie and Charlie were hitched to the lumbering hay-rack. Loading the rack with sheaves was simple. So was driving the load to the end of the barn. Even the first load or so that went into making the bottom of the stack did not present too much difficulty. After that, however, the fun began. Dad excelled in the skill and patience with which he made household furniture, and the deftness with which he could repair guns or make parts for them, but there were some crafts that he would not have learned had he lived to be two hundred. Stacking grain was one of them. Try as he would, he could never produce anything symmetrical. Now, a well-built stack silhouetted against the red of a fall sunset is a thing of beauty. From a small bottom, a stack expands as it rises to its waist. After

that, in graceful curves, the sides taper inwards, until finally the
cap itself is put in position and held there by a wooden stick. A
perfect stack looks much like a graceful pine cone standing on its
base.

Dad's stacks looked like nothing on earth, unless perhaps it was
the side view of a Christmas stocking, bulging here with an apple,
there with a fire-truck, and further up with an orange. Now, good
dry sheaves, if correctly placed, grip each other like iron bands and
knit themselves into a unit that wind and rain may buffet but never
disturb. These same sheaves, if incorrectly placed, invite the caresses
of wind and rain. Moreover, they are as slippery as the proverbial
banana-skin. When Dad stacked, everything would go smoothly
for a load or so, and then a lopsided bulge would appear at some
point in the pile. This was a bad sign. Dad would climb down and
look at it, scratch his head and go back and rearrange some of the
sheaves. Usually this did not help, for at the most unpropitious
moment there would be a swoosh and we would see Dad picking
himself up from the ground and emerging from sheaves scattered
half-way to the henhouse. This was no time for a boy to laugh, I
can tell you that. Eventually, teetering with every step, the stack
would rise in a faltering fashion until it reached its cap sheaf. Then,
gingerly, more exhausted from frustration than fatigue, Dad
would climb down. "That will be enough for today." I know he
scarcely dared to hope that the stack would still be standing to
greet the morning sunshine. Sometimes, however, it was.

In any event, we stacked our grain for years. Even when Ed
Hughes got his big steamer and threshed for settlers for a radius
of twenty miles, it was often February before he reached our place.

But what a thresher that was. It was huge. How Ed ever paid
for it, I don't know. Perhaps he never did. Why, the engine alone
was as big as a house. You could hear its whistle for miles; and
from our hilltop location you could see its great column of steam
nearly all the way across the township. Day by day you could
watch its progress by this column of steam. Day by day it got
nearer. Now it was at Charlie Caron's, next at Ritter's. Then it
moved over to Armstrong's and back to Byvank's and Mund's,
and then on to Donkelaar's. At last you could see the steam rising
above the winding trail, puffing across the creek. Hughes' steamer
was coming! What a gigantic thing! Its iron wheels were higher
than a tall man, taller than Henry Paulson. Their lugs gouged out
a track that marked the ground for months. The firebox alone

was nearly as big as our kitchen. The smokestack was higher than the henhouse. And, swaying along behind, lumbered the separator, a shiny metal thing nearly as long as the barn and higher than the hayrack—and wheels, why, wheels stuck out all over it.

While these two, the steamer and the separator, were the star performers, there was much more to the procession than that. Next in line and hooked on behind the separator was the caboose. Here was a new and tongue-tickling word, caboose. It was really a house on wheels, and the men of the crew slept in it. After it came the water tank, driven by George Brock. Then one of the Rogers boys drove the wood wagon loaded with blocks of spruce and poplar four feet long. Some of the crew rode on the water wagon, while others stood on the engine, talking to Ed Hughes. There were men all over. I have forgotten what they all did, but there were ten of them.

As the thresher pulled across the yard we stood open-mouthed, marvelling. Even Mother, wiping her hands on her apron, came out of the kitchen to stand and stare. So did Sofie Johnstone, for she had come over to help with the cooking, and with her came Pearl to peel potatoes. Those potatoes, they had to be cooked by the bushel; not to mention carrots and turnips and cabbage. And meat, why, it took half a steer to feed so many hungry men. Of the crew alone, there were ten; and Dad, Otis Johnstone, the inevitable Bill Bowman, Joe Fowlie, George Donkelaar, and Dudley Graham were all busy doing their part of the job of threshing—sixteen men to crowd into our little shack, sixteen hungry men, who for breakfast ate four or five eggs apiece, as well as pork chops and a bucketful of fried potatoes. How Mother and Sofie Johnstone ever cooked enough for them I don't know. How these two had the heart to face the pile of dirty dishes, I'll never know. But the threshers always liked to come to our place.

What a busy place is a farmyard during threshing! First the steamer advances on the four small stacks huddled in a group, dragging the separator around to the far side. Snorting and challenging, the engine backs well away into the yard, then charges head-on into the gap between the first and second stacks, and stops short. A logging chain is run through the narrow passageway and fastened to the truck of the separator. Then the steamer, with whirling pulleys and belching steam, drags the separator forward into position between the two rear stacks. Then the great black belt is tightened up and all is ready to begin. The

men take their places, one or two men on a stack on each side of
the feeder, two men with long, sharp knives and goggles, on
platforms beside the feeder. Somebody puts a wagon box under
the grain spout. The separator man, oil can in hand, stands on top
of the separator.

Then, at a wave of his arm, threshing commences. The engineer,
Ed Hughes, bends to his throttle, and slowly the big belt begins
to run, slapping together and whizzing by, until with a whirr
of wheels and a roar of shakers the separator is brought up to
speed. All eyes are on the separator man. Finally when the whirring
and rattling reaches an even, full-throated roar, he signals again,
swinging one hand down and around to the feeder. From each
stack a sheaf slams down to the feeding platform. The goggle men,
they with the long knives, cut the binder twine and spread the
sheaves evenly across the feeder, which seizes the grain and drags
it inexorably into the growling maw of the cylinder. You can look
in and see its shiny teeth whirling and beating the heads, and watch
the sheaf disappearing into the roaring innards of the separator.
What happens inside is all darkness and mystery, but along each
side of the separator, pulleys whirl and belts race in fantastic patterns. Some of them speed straight back and forth. Others run
round and round three pulleys, while one seems to coil like a
giant snake around five or six of them.

The separator man opens this flap or that, peering and oiling.
Then he walks back to the huge pipe, which with a twist of the
wheel he can direct up or down, to right or left. There's a bang
and a rattle. Then out of the end of the blower pipe shoots the
straw, to be flung fifty feet. What an improvement this is, compared
to carrying the straw away or forking it back! Far overhead, with
a bang, the weigh scales trip and half a bushel of golden wheat
gushes out of the pipe into the wagon box. The first grain has
been threshed. And so the machinery goes, banging and roaring
all day long; while now and then the separator man idles over to
the steamer to loaf with Ed Hughes.

The steam rushes up the great funnel. Far above the barn it
shines white and clear in the sunlight and the frosty air. If the men
on the stacks, the goggle-eyed feeders, and the men in the grain
wagon are busy, so are the water men and the wood men. Weeks
before, word has been passed along that for every stack of grain
there must be so much dry wood cut into four-foot lengths and
piled near the stacks. The wood man's job is to pile this beside

the engine and to feed its craving maw with these logs, three or four at a time. And, if the farmer has not provided enough, the wood man has to hustle more. The water-wagon man's job is not so simple. He has to drive to a creek or slough, break the ice and pump his tank wagon full, so that it can take its tribute of water to the steamer.

Where is the water man? The engineer looks at his glass, scowls, looks down the trail and fidgets. His water is getting low. It is at this point that we unravel the mystery of all the whistles that we have heard these many days past—the two toots, the three toots, and the long and short toot. The engineer, scowling, pulls a cord. Three bursts of white steam shoot out from a different place on the steamer, and "Whoo, whoo, whoo," goes the whistle. "Water, water, water," it shouts. Then again in a minute or so, "Water, water, water." This is the signal for the water man, rolling a cigarette down by the creek, to get the lead out of his pants and whip up his horses. The great god, the steamer, is demanding more water, and its high priest, Ed Hughes, is mad.

The steam engine was an exacting master. For days we had heard it whistling and tooting, and now we learned that these imperious toots meant business. Three toots for water; two toots made the wood man bend to his labours; one toot repeated at short intervals meant hurry up and get the grain wagon back here, or else this mighty monster would spill the golden treasure on the ground, for nothing must delay or hold up THE THRESHER. One long blast—not angry or staccato, but mellow and happy— meant meal time. Near dinner time everyone worked with one eye on Ed Hughes and one ear cocked for the whistle. At its first note men dropped their forks, the grain-wagon man straightened his stiffening back, the bundle-cutters yanked off their goggles. In a few seconds every man was off the stacks, the feeding platform and the separator. The high pitch of the spinning wheels, the whine of the flying cylinder teeth, dropped to a lower note. In a minute the wheels stopped turning. The straw, streaming from the blower, dribbled to a stop. The great black belt slapped together convulsively, slowed, and shivered to a stop. Silence, so noticeable it stunned you, fell over the yard. Then the excited, hungry voices could be heard as the men talked and laughed on the way to the kitchen for lunch.

In less than an hour the steamer gave two long peremptory shouts. It champed at its idleness. Hurry up, it said, and get back

to work. So the long afternoon grind began; but on such a little
farm as ours, four puny stacks soon disappeared into the insatiable
throat of the great machine. In almost no time the pitchers were
standing on the ground throwing sheaves up to the feeder. One
by one the sheaves forming the bases of the stack were thrown up,
while scores of mice, who had so far found the stack a haven for
the winter, began to scamper desperately away, running wildly
from disturbed nests—running out over the snow in all directions
to escape destruction—running from the quick death of a blow
by a pitchfork to the slower death of starvation and freezing. The
best laid plans of mice gang aft agley, in Alberta as elsewhere.

Soon the machine was stilled again, and the silence that flooded
the yard was broken only by the great steamer leading its convoy
down the road. How a boy hated to see it go! With the passing
of the steamer, the crowd of men and the roar of the separator,
the place seemed empty and lonely. Even the bright, clean straw-
pile, only relic of the thresher's passing, seemed to add to the
emptiness of the yard. But it had its fascination too. What a joy
it was, this straw-pile, to lie on, to climb up and to slide down.

The sense of emptiness gave way to a sense of peace and fulfilment.
The labour of the summer was over. The reward of that labour
now lay dry and flinty in the grain bin. Let winter come. Let it
snow now—let it freeze and blow. We were ready for it. The
log shack was warm. In the granary lay the wheat that would
buy food and winter clothing. In the barn were the cows and horses,
and in the hay loft, feed for them. Let winter come.

So the days of late fall passed away in a round of small chores—
milking Bunty, feeding the pigs and cutting enough wood for
one day and night. The late-rising sun endorsed sleeping in of a
morning. The short day, when the sun set about four in the afternoon, meant long evenings by the heater and the yellow glow of
coal-oil lamps. In this phase of life on the farm, Mother still would
not allow playing-cards in the house; but, if we lacked this relaxa-
tion, we had one far more valuable. We had a good-sized birch
bookcase which Dad had made and stained a mahogany red. In
this were a few choice books, and these, added to those we could
borrow from Doc Phillips, made an interesting library. After the
dishes of an early supper were washed and put away, we all took
up our favourite positions around the heater—Mother in the
rocking-chair knitting, Bill and I on the couch or sitting on the
floor, Dad, with the lamp pulled close to his shoulder, reading

aloud to us—*Ivanhoe, Rob Roy,* Dickens, Macaulay and Ancient Rome, *Uncle Tom's Cabin,* and much of the world's great poetry.

As Bill dozed on the floor and Mother's needles clicked, I sat straight and tense while Ivanhoe entered the lists at Ashby-de-la-Zouche. Dad's voice would get hoarse, but it was no use. "Read another chapter!" Those were the happy evenings as, huddled in our little clearing, we went with Caesar to Gaul, or with Richard the Lion Heart on the crusades, or repulsed Sennacherib at the very gates of Jerusalem.

So the winter closed in on us, not as a friend nor yet as an enemy —rather as one of those physical facts of life that one accepts with resignation if not with pleasure. That it was not a pleasure, we were reminded by an annual ritual of Dad's. On the morning of December 22, for forty years, he never failed to voice the feeling of all dwellers in Canada's winter. As he came down to breakfast, and before any of us had realized what day it was, he would sing out, "Well, Mother, the days are getting longer." Two months of the severity of a northern winter lay before us; but we, and our ally the sun, were winning the battle. The longest night was past.

II

Twice every week Gerry Hoogers delivered the mail. Early every Tuesday and Friday morning Gerry hitched up his horses and drove to Hazel Bluff to meet the stage which pulled in there after lunch. About four o'clock in the afternoon he arrived at Eastburg Post Office with his sacks. Twice a week for years and years Gerry faithfully performed his trust. In winter, with icicles clinging to his moustache and with hands numb with cold, he would come in fumbling with the mail bags. A cup of tea and a few minutes beside the hot stove and he was ready to turn his team homeward once more.

And thereby hangs a tale. Whether Gerry was a Liberal or a Conservative, I don't know. Whichever it was, at that time Dad was an adherent of the opposite party; but what does a boy know of politics? For that matter, what did Gerry or Dad know? Each was a newcomer to Canada and no inherited politics had descended on either of them. Neither one had a grandfather who voted for the grand old Grits or Tories and whose shade in consequence demanded that they do the same. It is probable that each of them, Gerry and Dad, had voted for a Conservative or a Liberal at one election and had reversed his allegiance before the next one. All I can say for certain is that it was not till 1921 that both Dad and Gerry were definitely behind any party, and that was the United Farmers of Alberta.

At any rate, it soon became evident that one of the facts of life in Alberta was that the location of the post office and the tenure of office of the postmaster depended upon which political party held sway. For some years we had run it; but one year as winter came on it appeared that our political faith proved conclusively that we were no longer fitted to keep the post office. Gerry Hoogers, it seemed, possessed the necessary political fitness. Then the battle was on.

The job of postmaster in those days in the bush meant a clear gain of ten or twelve dollars a year, unless you counted the labour you expended on it. That, of course, was providing you did not make an error in the change when selling a postal note, and providing you didn't pay the postage-due charges on letters out of your own pocket, and providing you did not give away a stamp or two to someone for whom you wrote a letter and who had no change just at the moment. In any event, the emolument was not great; and, viewed in that light, it mattered little who kept the post office. But as a question of pride, now, it mattered a lot. Dad wanted the post office. Gerry wanted the post office. In a day or so it became a matter of community pride also, and the community was divided. One half sent in a petition saying that Dad was unfitted to be a postmaster, that the road to our place was a poor one, that—well, I have forgotten what all the arguments were, but the petition proved conclusively that we lacked every accomplishment necessary to run a post office, whereas Gerry, it seemed, had all of these. Our side immediately sent in a counter-petition which demonstrated beyond question, by reference to the roads, the lay of the land, the flow of the creeks, and the direction of the prevailing winds, that no place was so ideally suited to a post office as the North-West of 16.

The score so far was tied. The battle swayed back and forth, and something was needed to break the deadlock. There was no country store in Eastburg. If either Dad or Gerry ran a store, that would be the deciding factor; both sides realized that. Then one day when the advisory committee, consisting of Dad, Henry Paulson, Axel Clausen, and Doc Phillips, assembled for a cup of tea in our kitchen, the grapevine brought the news that Gerry was going to start a store. It was Tuesday now, and the grapevine said that right after Gerry delivered the mail next Friday afternoon he planned to start for Morinville to purchase a stock for his store. In that way he would travel Friday night and would have Saturday and Sunday and Monday before he had to be back to carry the mail on Tuesday.

The advisory committee were flabbergasted. In heavy silence they sipped their tea. But pioneers fighting a cause are resilient and resourceful. "Okay, Mac," said Henry Paulson, "you'll have to start a store."

"But I can't lay my hands on more than ten dollars," said Dad dolefully.

"All right," said Henry, "I'll put up a hundred dollars."

"And I'm good for fifty," said Axel, shoving his hand into his pocket and bringing out the money.

"I'll put up the rest," said Doc Phillips. "I'll put in anything else you want, up to five hundred."

"Yes, but where would I put a store?"

"Well, you've got a lot of lumber, haven't you, and you're going to build a new house, aren't you? Make it larger and put the store in half of it. In the meantime, put it in the kitchen and move into the other room."

A few minutes after this decision had been made, Gerry arrived with the mail; and, as he drank his usual cup of tea, he found the committee all smiles and secrecy. Meanwhile, Chappie and Charlie were munching away at an extra and unexpected ration of oats, all unaware of the race that lay before them.

In a few minutes Gerry untied his team and set off for home. As soon as he was out of sight around the bend, Dad headed for the barn, and Chappie and Charlie, annoyed and blinking, were hitched to the cutter. Dad, armed with his own ten dollars and Axel's fifty, started out. Henry Paulson rode with him as far as his place, where Dad was to pick up Henry's contribution. Then Chappie and Charlie were to swing into their long stride and travel through the night to Morinville, where it was hoped to acquire a stock sufficient to start a store. Thus, in the space of an hour or so, Dad embarked upon a new career, that of a merchant.

On Wednesday, while Dad was gone, Mother and Bill and I set to work on the two upstairs rooms. Some chapters back, I explained that when the house was built in 1907 the gable ends were of logs right to the roof, and that dividing the house in two was a log partition running along the short axis of the building. This partition, like the gable ends, had been continued up to the roof. In the intervening period the two upper rooms had been floored. Other than that, nothing much had been done to them and they were cluttered with trunks, boxes, and other impedimenta. Standing dispirited against the far wall reposed the Sunbeam bicycle, a picture of desolation with its tyres flat as pancakes.

"First," said Mother, "we'll take that thing out to the hay loft. Then we'll paper the walls." She had never liked the bicycle.

The walls were logs, very roughly hewn, whose interstices had been chinked with moss and then plastered. They were a knotty, cheerless sight. Fortunately we had lots of paper. Those copies of the Edmonton *Capital* not used for lighting the fire and not carried out to the W.C. had been folded and piled upstairs. With these we papered the walls. Fortunately we also had a good supply of shingle nails and roofing caps. In case you have never seen roofing caps, they were nearly flat disks of tinned metal about an inch in diameter. When a nail was driven through them, they held the roofing material or paper so that it would not tear off the nails. I haven't seen such things for many years. Possibly they are not made any longer. Since, however, I lay in bed night after night, staring at copies of the Edmonton *Capital* nailed to the walls with these, it may be that even if I never see any more of them I have seen my share.

The papering was finished and our belongings rearranged well before noon on Friday. The activity of interior-decorating had left us little time to speculate upon Dad's progress to and from Morinville. After lunch on Friday, however, we spent an anxious hour or two, worrying about whether or not he would get back in time. It was necessary that he get back before Gerry came with the mail. If he didn't, the plot would fail, because we knew that Gerry planned to set out for Morinville just as soon as he had delivered the sackful of letters. As the hands of the clock raced around the dial we were on tenterhooks. Many times we went out into the yard to peer down the trail or to stand and listen for the tinkle of heel chains.

Finally, with a burst of speed, Chappie and Charlie arrived, pulling the jumper which was piled high with goods. Dad carried the merchandise in and set up the store on a hastily improvised shelf extending along the west wall from the stove to the post-office corner. We were in business. There on the shelf, or standing on the floor, displayed for all to see, was our new stock. There may have been a few minor items which I do not remember, but our opening stock consisted mainly of the following:

    1 caddy of Macdonald's plug smoking tobacco.

    1 caddy of Macdonald's chewing tobacco.

    12 packages of Old Chum tobacco (in its red-and-yellow sacks).

12 packages of Bull Durham (in little white sacks).

1 box of Ziz-Zag Cigarette Papers.

6 tins of Copenhagen Snuff (Henry Paulson's "snoose.")

3 100-lb. sacks of Strong Baker's Flour.

3 20-lb. sacks of Sugar.

3 10-lb. sacks of Rolled Oats.

1 case of Salt (in 1-lb. sacks).

1 box of Dried Apples.

1 box of Dried Prunes.

6 tins of Axle Grease. (These might have waited till summer!)

1 sack of Beans.

Several cartons of Matches.

Some assorted Candies.

By the time we had got the shelf up, Joe Fowlie appeared, and he helped put the finishing touches to our display. Then he and Dad and Mother sat down to a cup of tea, while they waited the arrival of Gerry Hoogers. That day the mail must have been late in getting to Hazel Bluff, for it was about five o'clock when Gerry drew up outside and came hurrying in with the mail sack, anxious to get rid of it and to get away, so as to start for Morinville for his stock. Hustling from the outer darkness into the glow of the coal-oil lamp, he pulled icicles off his moustache and rubbed a cold hand over his frosty cheeks. He dropped the mail sack and hurried over to sit by the stove to get some of the chill out of his bones. Mother handed him a cup of tea which was sipped appreciatively. His back was to our store, and each time Gerry rocked he nearly bumped it. This was too much for Joe. Trying to be casual, he said, "What do you think of Mac's store?"

Gerry jumped. "Huh?" he said.

Joe, with a wave of his arm, said: "Mac's started a store."

Gerry turned in his chair to see what Joe was pointing at. His face fell. He simply stared. "So," he said. "So-o-o, so-o-o."

That's how the news of our store was broken to Gerry. That's how we kept the post office many more years and how Dad, twenty-four years a soldier and five years a farmer, became a merchant. We nearly went bankrupt as a result, but that is another story stretching over the next five years.

In addition to all this, Dad was usually kept busy with a variety of civic duties. He was a councillor in the old Local Improvement District, and in the Municipal District of Lockerbie; he was game guardian, school trustee, commissioner for oaths, official auditor; and he generally helped in other minor offices that no one else would take on, including that of Justice of the Peace. It was the exercise of this function that Bill and I liked most. Not that he went around fining people or sending them to jail; though we did have a case of arson, which the Mounted Police very promptly solved. Wherever possible, Dad tried to smooth out disputes between neighbour and neighbour. Most of the time he was successful, and sent the opposing parties home with some of the bitterness removed from their hearts.

There are people, of course, who always fight with all their neighbours. There are those, too, who are long on their rights but short on their responsibilities. Then there were those who were hell-bent for "getting the law" on someone. They all came to the North-West of 16 overflowing with grievances. There was the time, for instance, when a man came to complain that his crabby neighbour had frightened his daughter, waving a hammer over her head and threatening to "knock the —— out of her." Dad was able to smooth that out, although privately we all thought that the neighbour would have been a community benefactor if he had carried out his threat.

Pigs got into gardens, pigs crossed line fences, pigs got into crops, pigs mysteriously disappeared. The Justice of the Peace became an expert on "pigicial jurisprudence." Bulls strayed, either in an absent-minded or an amorous manner, and Dad had to deal with fist-waving farmers. Husbands sometimes strayed too. These cases were generally sordid and misery laden, but Dad's advice was given, for whatever good it could do. Many other problems also were brought to him. For instance, there was the lady from the far side of the township whose frustrations invented alleged advances on the part of one neighbour man and then another. Dad, in commenting on her case to one of his friends, expressed the absurdity of the complaints in a few well-chosen words. "Who could possibly take an interest in her?" he asked. "She has a face like a festered fig."

There were, however, cases in which the alleged attentions were not imaginary. A remote neighbour and his wife came to Dad in great agitation one day about their daughter, who had evidently been more generous than prudent in her response. "It's that young scoundrel . . ." they said, naming a neighbour lad whom we will call Tommy. "Well," said Dad, "will he marry her?" "Yes, he's willing," said the mother, "but we won't let him near the place; we want him put behind bars."

Now Dad could never bring himself to regard sexual aberration as one of the cardinal sins. It was true that any society must set up certain rules. But it was equally true that nature had a way with young people that sometimes set these rules at naught. Dad looked out of the window and sighed just a little as he thought of it. He pointed out that Tommy was a nice young lad, clean, decent, and a good worker. True, the girl may have been slightly under age, but it was too late now to think of that. Tommy was willing, even glad, to marry the girl. Why not let them get married? In six or seven months the community would shake its heads and wag its tongues; but six months after that the world would still be rolling along, too busy to remember. Just a few years back—a very few, when Eastburg was young—couples could not always go through a formal ceremony, so they took each other, and when the next preacher came along their union was formalized.

Dad even cited a recent case over at Manola, where a man and a woman had, in one day, participated in three solemn rites: The first ceremony had formalized their marriage. They had then had their first child baptized; and after that they had buried their infant second son. Yet they were a fine couple and none but the malicious thought any the less of them. "He that is without sin among you, let him first cast a stone at her."

"Never mind that," said the over-wrought mother. "I want to see the young scoundrel behind bars." Dad advised them to go home and think it over. They did not heed his advice, and the next we heard of them they were represented by legal talent. This drove Tommy to similar action. In court his lawyer produced several other youths who in the fine language of the Bible "had known" this girl, so that the case was thrown out. Tommy has long since married someone else. I have lost track of the girl, but the last I heard of her she was still unwed.

As I have said, January and February were the hard months to get through in those days. The cold seemed to settle down over the house and the barn as mud settled in a glass of water. The windows, already thick with frost, became even more dim as more frost was added during a new cold snap. Every time the door was opened a cloud of steam filled the little porch as the moist air from the kitchen condensed. The metal ends of the door hinges visible in the kitchen were coated with frost. Frost built up along cracks between the logs if they were improperly chinked. The very logs of the house and barn seemed to shrink in the appalling cold and cried out with a loud crack when they could no longer endure the stress. The surrounding trees snapped and cracked in the cold. Any water spilled at the well froze instantly, and a mound of ice built up around it. The pump, never too robust and complaining bitterly at being used in such weather, shivered and rattled. As like as not, it would give one final shudder and the flow of water would cease. Then Chappie and Charlie and Bunty and her progeny would stand at the water trough and stare at the pumper. Bunty, with her tongue reversing as it alternately dived up one nostril then hastily switched to the other, eyed one reproachfully because the water trough was empty. Why is it that on a bitterly cold day, as you stand working frantically on the wind-swept pump platform, that is the time when each cow apparently drinks twice as much as she does ordinarily? Why is it that every last one of the cattle chooses that time to come straggling along to tank up? Any other time you could never find all the cattle at one place.

If the pump rods parted on such a day, they had to be pulled out and fixed. Since our well was eighty feet deep, length after length of dripping rods and pipe had to be hauled up and disjoined. Where did the rod come disconnected? Certainly not near the top where, by enduring the bitter cold for an hour, one could fix it. No, not there, but right down at the cylinder so that, for hours, pump rods and wrenches had to be handled with icy mitts. Then, just at the critical moment, a wrench would let go its grip on the pipe and jerk itself away and with a clatter go shuddering down the well, never to be recovered.

Yet our very battle against this bitter cold drew us together into a greater family loyalty. With all the doors closed tightly and the lantern swinging from a nail, we did the milking and the other chores. After a final good night to the horses we closed the barn doors and set out along a path bordered waist-high with snow. There through the picket gate lay the house, its snow-piled roof silvery in the moonlight, while a column of smoke rose slowly as if reluctant to leave the comfort of the shack. The feeble light through the frosted window beckoned and hinted of the coziness of the room behind it. There, with chores safely past, with caps, mackinaws, and mitts hanging in a row by the door, with another cup of tea to remove the last trace of chill—there we could spend a long winter evening with Ivanhoe.

Beyond a momentary freezing of cheeks, nose, fingers, or toes, the MacGregors never suffered permanent damage at the hands of winter. Once or twice our neighbours did, and from away back in some of the other communities came tales of old men frozen to death, or of children perishing in a storm. For all of us, until the end of February, winter was something that had to be endured. If one lived till then, a glimmer of hope emerged from the darkness. It flickered and grew and finally became the certain knowledge that spring would come again. Like a reward after a long and difficult task, like freedom after imprisonment, spring finally triumphed over ice and snow; spring burst over the land.

There came a day, a great day, when Dad had to go to Edmonton for something and decided to take me with him. I was about eight then and hadn't seen the city since 1909, four years before. Neither had Mother, but then farm women were not expected to go gallivanting off sixty miles to the city every few years.

By this time the railway had pushed on from Morinville towards Athabasca Landing, so that Clyde, twenty-three miles away, became our nearest station. This had re-oriented our system of roads. Whereas the old road to Edmonton wandered off south and east through Independence, Riviere Qui Barre and St. Albert, we now used a road taking us north and east to Clyde. For several years the top chord of Township 59 running east for miles had been used as a road by the settlers in Swallowhurst, Hazel Bluff, and Rossington. Somehow or other, erroneously, this came to be called "the Base Line," and we all referred to it as that, although in reality the nearest base line was six miles further north. When the railroad reached Clyde, this line began to have work done on it, and soon became quite an important road. By this time Rogers' Stage and Marshall's Stage ran between Clyde and all points west, including Rossington, Freedom, Manola, Barrhead, and their adjoining communities.

So one summer morning, with Chappie and Charlie hitched to the lumber wagon, Joe Fowlie drove Dad and me up to "Agnew's Corner" on the base line to catch Marshall's Stage, which took us the remaining eighteen miles to Clyde. All I can recall about Clyde is the hotel. There we had our supper, and I remember it only because of two things new in my experience. The idea of people preparing meals and selling them for money was a novel thought. We had eaten meals at all our neighbours' homes and they had eaten at our place. So had a great variety of travellers and overnight visitors, but never before had I heard of anyone paying for a meal. The other thing new in my experience was that at this hotel they served preserved pears for dessert. This was something entirely delightful. After all, maybe such delicacies called for payment in money.

But the hotel, the meal, and even the pears were only incidental, for the train was expected to arrive at any moment. This was the first train that I can remember. Undoubtedly I was excited, but strangely enough all I can recall now is the plush seats and the terrific speed at which trees and stumps, grass and sloughs sped by. The land seemed to be nearly all lakes and sloughs, and each one of them seemed literally filled with ducks. I don't remember arriving in Edmonton or going to an hotel; possibly I was so sleepy that I merely stumbled along beside Dad.

We stayed at the St. James (now St. Regis) Hotel, diagonally across First Street from the old C.N.R. Station. When we awoke next morning the city was a hive of activity. Our window faced on what is now 104th Avenue, with the C.N.R. Yards north of it, and to our left, running north over the railway tracks, was First Street. Trains puffed and shunted back and forth. People hurried by, and the street was full of vehicles of all descriptions. The drays and vans, the wagons and carts, the buggies and democrats, the milk and bread wagons were of great variety, and there were more of them than I could have believed existed. There was the scrawny old nag with the broken harness hitched to the little delivery van, thin, dispirited, and bedraggled. There were the high-stepping teams pulling smart buggies, their harness polished and shining and their heads held high. But my choice fell on the sleek black Belgians and the huge splay-footed Clydesdales that in their might and pride drew the great drays piled high with merchandise or beer kegs. I could understand them and appreciate them, as with their great heads, arched necks, and broad chests decked out with brass or nickel trimming, and bright celluloid trimming on the leather, they moved the heavy loads over the rough block paving.

The main lobby of the hotel was no less fascinating. At one side was the desk with its push-bell, its broad old register, and a set of pigeon-holes holding room keys and mail. Around the other three sides were huge stuffed chairs in black leather. These, compared to the hard, straight-backed, home-made chairs of the North-West of 16, were the last word in elegance and comfort. It was wonderful just to sit in them and to sink into their softness. At least it was at first, for then I didn't know how well I was to become acquainted with chairs of this type during the next three or four days. The rotunda was bustling with activity. People came and went in a ceaseless stream. Some walked upstairs to their rooms, others sat around and talked, while still others passed through the lobby to a mysterious inner room from which, for some reason I did not understand, I was excluded.

After breakfast Dad and I set out to explore the city. The front door of the hotel faced on First Street, so we started south along it. This was the great city of Edmonton, the city of forty thousand, of which Mother had tried to tell me. Even this, she had said, was a mere outpost village compared to her native London. But what do population figures mean to a boy; what do descriptions or even pictures tell? Here, right outside the door of the hotel, was the busy city itself.

Who can describe a city as seen for the first time by a farm boy? Nothing has prepared him for the many and varied sights. A stormy fall afternoon, filled with scudding clouds and with successive flights of geese a hundred at a time; the wheeling of hundreds of blackbirds, screeching and milling about—such sights have given him some idea of multitudes; but only the erratic scurrying of thousands of ants when the plough crashes through an anthill could have given him any conception of the crowds of a city street. And it's not only the crowds but the multitudes of other sights that fascinate, attract or repel him. For there, jammed hard against their neighbours in long rows, the buildings tower over the street two or three storeys high, and even brick and stone buildings of six storeys. Whoever imagined so many buildings, or such variety? And the signs advertising their owners' business, painted in large letters, some illuminated and all overhanging the street in bewildering confusion, why, they make your head swim! And there was the wooden horse, nearly life-size, standing by the door of the saddlery shop. There were the great jars filled with coloured liquids in the windows of the drug stores, and the barbers' revolving poles—fascinating to a boy. Then, down the street, open to the summer day, was the shoe-shine stand, where also hats were cleaned and blocked, and over it hung the picture of the long-nosed Dr. Chapeau, L.D. (lid doctor). But it was only after dark that the king of the signs stood out in all its glory over the Selkirk Hotel. This one, done in many light-bulbs, showed by successive combinations a man pouring a glass of beer, lifting it to his lips, and then quaffing the liquor. If I had seen nothing else in all the city, this would have been enough.

On nearly every street corner was a red mail-box, a marvellous thing where you could mail letters without having to wait until Tuesday or Friday when Gerry Hoogers came to start them on their way to the rest of the world. And in almost every block, left over from the hazards of railway construction, sat a legless man selling laces and pencils. The city was indeed full of the strangest sights!

And sounds! A country boy's ears, that can distinguish the distant murmur of the creek from the sough of the breeze in the trees, were assailed with all sorts of new sounds—the surge of the crowd, the clumping of horses' feet on the pavement, the rattle of street cars, the roar of the riveters as they piled storey after storey on new buildings in every block. But there were other and gentler sounds. For instance, there was the persistent ring of the telephone bell in the hotel lobby when no one attended to it. A marvellous invention it was, by means of which one could talk to someone blocks or miles away. Then, the cries of the paper boys—"Read all about it! Latest e-e-edition!"

But maybe it's the smells of the city that will haunt a boy's memory, especially if that memory is connected to an active little stomach—the scent of freshly ground coffee beans, the spicy smell from the grocery shops and the hungry smell from the popcorn stand. The drug stores with their scent of soaps and perfumes were entrancing. Around the hotels hung the aroma of cigars, while the streets, even at that early day, held the unmistakable smell of exhaust fumes from the very few cars.

After walking up and down the streets, gazing in at all the windows, we entered a few stores. There was James Ramsay's, with the long aisles and the rows of tables piled high with clothes and scents and soaps; and hard by, Woolworth's, just full of five-cent and ten-cent and fifteen-cent gadgets. Most of these stores had a system of cords and pulleys and pipes. The girl would take your money and put it in a little box and something would go "fftt" and then up in the air and along the wires would whiz the box, away down the aisle, across to the corner and up through a hole in the ceiling. In a minute or so it would retrace its course and land on the desk with a plop, as much as to say, "There's your change; count it." Oh, I tell you, they had great things in the city. And some of the stores were filled with fruits we never saw on the farm—pears and plums, oranges even, and bananas!

It was all incredibly wondrous, the first morning, as we wandered hither and yon. But you can have too much of a good thing—too many miracles and too much of hard, hot, paved sidewalks. Towards noon we wandered down to watch them building the Macdonald Hotel. As Dad stood gazing up at the men aloft my eyes roamed, and there, away below, lay the cool, green, flowing waters of the Saskatchewan River. "Oh, look Dad, look at the river, look at the water!" For the moment I had had my fill of the city. I don't think I said so. I don't think I mentioned my hot feet and parched tongue, but Dad understood.

As a result, we walked two or three blocks to the most marvellous place I had ever seen, the American Dairy Lunch. We had opened the screen door and started to descend a flight of steps when, half-way down, we saw a whole counter spread with pieces of pie and cakes and puddings and baked apples. Even Mrs. Johnstone's table at Christmas time was nothing compared to this. From somewhere Dad produced two trays and soon they were loaded with food, but that was only half of the miracle. As we turned around to walk to a table, there was a pool of water and a hill sticking out of it and real green grass growing on the hill, and swimming around in the pool were dozens of goldfish. It was like Aladdin's Cave and Grimm's Fairy Tales, and I don't know what else. And beyond it was this inexhaustible supply of pies, for as fast as a customer took one, they filled its place with another.

As we walked on towards the table I noticed the little gargoyle men, some done out in outlandish costumes while some wore only a barrel, pushing away with all their strength to hold up the ceiling beams. And the daylight shone right down on our table, away down there in the cellar. We were sitting under the very sidewalk, and people went tripping or clumping along over the glass that was set into it. The other wonders of the city were as nothing compared to this American Dairy Lunch, not even the noisy indoor W.C. at the hotel where you sat on a smooth round seat and where paper, soft paper, unwound off a roll, and where you twiddled a lever and with a roar and a swoosh the W.C. was ready for the next visitor.

For the next two or three days Dad took me with him to stores and offices and, in fact, almost everywhere he went. While he transacted his business I sat and talked shyly with someone in the office. Dad, as I have said, was a friendly sort of chap and not all of his visits were on business. We would start out of the door of the hotel, and in a few steps he would meet someone he knew. They would talk for a minute and then the three of us would set off down the street, and before I knew it we would be in one of those rooms with the large leather chairs. "You just sit there, sonny," Dad would say, and disappear with his friend while I settled into one of the big black seats. Now, as you first settle into them, these chairs are soft and yielding, but in ten minutes a boy gets restless. In twenty minutes of fidgeting the chair becomes hard and tiresome, and at the end of half an hour I'd wish I had never seen it. About the time it began to get unendurable, Dad would reappear, smiling broadly, and we would be off again. During our stay in Edmonton we seemed to repeat this process almost every block, and I described my experiences very fully to Mother when we got home. She questioned me minutely about the frequency of these sojourns in the rooms with the big black leather chairs, and when Dad came in after doing chores she "gave him a piece of her mind." It seems that leading off these hotel lobbies were iniquitous places called saloons, and from my description of our trip to Edmonton, Mother gathered that Dad had not missed a single one of them.

Mother rarely rose to the heights of what I am forced to admit was generally righteous wrath. When she did, Dad did as he was told. It was some time before Mother forgot these visits to the pubs. Each time she thought of them she "hauled Dad over the coals." And finally she came out with this directive. "All right; if you have money enough and time enough to spend in saloons you can start building the new house that you have been promising us these last few years. You have lots of lumber drying in the yard. Now get to work. The store is growing and crowding us right out of this shack."

So, the new house was started. It was a big eight-roomed, three-storeyed house with a large basement. As soon as it neared completion, the store was moved into it and occupied half of the ground floor. It was the largest house in the township; and for that matter,

I believe it still is. What it lacked in fine carpentering, it made up in strength. The only imported lumber was that in the windows and doors, the shingles, and the fir floor. The rest was lumber cut on the farm. The floor in Mother's bedroom was birch, the same splendid birch that had grown on the very site of the house.

Joe Fowlie, after he left us and filed on a quarter further south, had been in the habit of working on his land all summer and then going out to labour at railway construction during the winter. That fall—it was 1913—he went out, but could not get work; so he returned and spent some weeks at our place. Joe was a favourite with all of us and was always welcome. He set to work finishing the building of the house, and then began to enlarge the basement. We spent a busy and a happy winter. And after the cramped quarters of the shack, the roominess of the new house was wonderful. The old shack that had served us so well for five or six years became a blacksmith shop and granary. Later, as befitted the changing times, it served for some years as a garage, and then, sometime during the thirties, it was torn down.

12

Dad enjoyed his new rôle of merchant. It permitted him to go to Edmonton and Clyde, and later on to Westlock, to buy his merchandise. It also provided a further outlet for his natural talent of orderliness; he took pleasure in making shelves, counters, drawers, and other fittings to accommodate the stock, and between making fixtures for the business and furniture for the new house he spent three or four happy years.

The profit from the store, the pension from the Army, the partridges from the bush, and the produce from the farm somehow or other combined to keep us fed and clothed until 1916. Then, when Dad went overseas, Mother sold the business. After paying off the wholesalers and settling other business debts, she found that she had about two hundred dollars left in cash. There was, it is true, over a thousand in accounts receivable, but if in the succeeding years we collected any more than fifty dollars of that amount, we did well.

The balance sheet of the store over the years had not in fact been very favourable. By exercising the utmost economy, we had lived. By extending credit we had materially helped many others to live. We had had some fun out of it, and in the end we appeared to be ahead two hundred dollars. Place all this on the credit side; then look at the debit side. Mother and Dad had worked long hours in the store. Moreover, Dad could not look after it and farm too, so the breaking of new land had ceased after our fields had spread to eighteen acres. During this time our neighbours had been vigorously clearing up their quarters. When, during the war, the price of wheat began to soar, the MacGregors had little land on which to sow it.

When I say we obtained our living from the store perhaps I should modify that. Dad was of the old school. The motto of the people of the Maritimes fitted him well: "Eat it up, wear it out, make it do"—in other words, no waste, and no frills. Canned foods he held in low esteem; and housewives who used them, in the lowest esteem. Although we sold these foods in the store, Dad's good opinion of housewives varied inversely as the size of the pile of empty cans in their kitchen dumps. He held the view that farmers did not need to have food shipped to them in cans. Of course, there were exceptions. One had to buy axle grease. Cane syrup was not obtainable locally. Cocoa and Keen's mustard both had to come in cans. But canned fruits, jams, vegetables and meats he held to be wasteful. So the groceries we transferred from the store to our kitchen were largely restricted to flour, rolled oats, sugar, salt, and tea. Occasionally Mother might be forgiven if, for variety, she stewed up some dried apples, prunes, or even dried apricots. But canned food—never! In those days tomatoes had not been developed to the stage where Eastburg farmers could grow them, but on the North-West of 16 the use of a can of tomatoes was rank heresy. Mother and Bill and I discovered that, if we were to indulge in a can of tomatoes, it had to be while Dad was away, and all of the contents had to be eaten up right then and the empty can secreted in the bottom of the old dry well.

If the store did not provide us with canned luxuries, and if in the end it did not lay up for us any treasures on earth, it did give us an insight into human nature. All our neighbours, except possibly half a dozen, found it convenient or even necessary at times to charge up what they needed until the crop was threshed in the fall. Then they would rally round and pay up and would remain on a cash basis for some months. When the store was sold I don't think the people of Eastburg owed us more than possibly fifty dollars, but the fame of the store had spread to Fawn Lake, High-ridge, and Manola, and we had many customers in those communities. On the whole, the people in those parts were trustworthy enough, but after we had been in business a year or so we began to observe the phenomenon so well known to country storekeepers. The less trustworthy and the poorer in soul would come along during spring and summer with grievous tales of their poverty and of their children's hunger. Could we carry them till fall?

Why, certainly. Their last purchase in the fall would be for supplies to feed the threshers. Then, strangely enough, we would not see them again for months, sometimes not until the next spring, when with woebegone faces, and with tears ready to burst forth or already flowing copiously, they would ask for more credit. Dad, torn between our own lack of money and the picture of their hungry children, would generally weaken and their bill would mount still higher. What these people did when they threshed was to go to Westlock, where they had to pay cash and where they probably did get their goods a mite cheaper. Now many of them could go to Westlock only by the trail which passed the front of the store. In the cool of the morning we would see them taking a load of grain into Westlock, but in the dark of evening they slipped stealthily by on their way home. Then some of them would have the effrontery to come over again for more credit the following spring.

It was easy to distinguish sheer laziness or untrustworthiness from real hardship or bad luck, but still it was difficult to turn down importunities. Mother, in going over the Accounts Receivable ledger, would fret, but Dad was inclined to be philosophical. He agreed that "the Lord tempereth the wind to the shorn lamb," and felt that perhaps he had some responsibility to help the Lord with the tempering.

There were also, among our customers, one or two who were neither improvident nor unlucky, but simply mean. Dad usually let them get away with their haggling and their tedious little tricks, but he would turn to me when one of them had gone and say, "Son, if ever there's a silly beggar in the country, I'm sure to be bothered with him."

This was a favourite expression of Dad's, provoked also by itinerant preachers and others who came with flaring nostrils, prophesying hell-fire or the imminent end of the world. Usually Dad listened quite patiently and then deflected them down the road to the next neighbour. As they walked away carrying their tracts or their hell-fire with them, Dad would shake his head reflectively, and out it would come: "If ever there's a silly . . ."

From about 1910 till the end of the First War we seemed to go through a phase when every second stranger tramping in the dust of the road turned out to be some sort of Bible-puncher. Maybe it was the times, for unknown to us a depression was under way and was putting many men out of work. Or maybe it was just that pioneer communities are subject to such visitations. These men who straggled through our community snatching souls from the burning, and snaring meals while they snatched, invariably arrived at our place. I'm sure that many a neighbour with a sense of humour passed them along to Dad, just as he in turn recommended them to the tender mercies of some of his cronies. I'm equally certain, however, that many a pious pioneer sent such men to the North-West of 16 in the sincere hope that, after all, good would ultimately prevail over evil in the struggle for Dad's soul.

These visitors fell mainly into two classes. Some snorted brimstone, grimacing and flailing their arms while they talked. These Dad dealt with gently, convinced that they were destined for a mental institution. Others were sad of face and oily of speech; broken-down insurance peddlers, Dad said, destined for jail. But not all were like these. Some were sincere and sensible enough; and they got a courteous hearing, a bite to eat, even a bed, and went on their way in the morning, disappointed perhaps, but not disheartened. In many cases these evangelists travelled in pairs, and Dad would often say, "That little one—he'll bear watching."

There were Bible meetings in the school, baptisms at the brook, and camp meetings in the clearing; but before long the effect of the baptisms blew off. Little in the way of tangible results remained in the community, except a slight increase in the population during the following spring.

Of many active pairs of proselyters, one achieved marked success. I forget what branch of religion they advocated, but they held frequent and fervent meetings. Soon, at least one-third of the Eastburg community was attending these meetings; and news got about that So-and-so and Somebody-else had enlisted in the new ranks. Henceforth, according to rumour, So-and-so was to be known as Saint So-and-so. That religion took firm hold and did good in the community for years.

One day Henry Paulson wandered over with the little wrinkles around his eyes that meant that he had something to tell.

"Mac," he said, "if you had to choose the most confirmed scoundrel in the area—the biggest liar, the sharpest skinflint and the crookedest old cuss in the country, who would you pick?"

Only a moment's reflection was necessary before Dad answered, "Old Lem . . ."

"Then you're wrong," Henry grinned, "because he's now St.

Lemuel; and he's a saint one degree higher than the rest of them."

"Well, I'll be damned," spluttered Dad. "The old hypocrite!"

Dad had been brought up in the Presbyterian faith. His years of knocking around the world had undoubtedly removed the ritual and the finer observances of that faith, but its essence remained. He had seen various religions in many lands and thought them all good, but saw little to choose between them. He felt that, while your religion was like your wife—your personal affair, not to be discussed with others—there were, nevertheless, half a dozen or so stable varieties: Presbyterian, Anglican, Catholic, Baptist, Lutheran, and maybe one or two others. He looked a little askance at all other sects, especially if they tried to cram religion into him. He had slight regard for those who changed their beliefs with every passing preacher.

While Dad would not discuss religion, he did welcome the visits of well-educated priests or ministers. Many of these men, black-robed, clerical-collared, or with no distinguishing garb save the mantle of an educated tongue, turned aside to visit us. How glad Dad was to see them and to talk with them a whole evening is beyond estimate, and I believe they were just as glad to retreat to our fireside for an evening's flow of ideas. Someone has said wisely that great minds discuss ideas, mediocre minds discuss events, and small minds discuss personalities.

One of these occasional wayfarers was the Reverend Mr. Dallas, a young Anglican who before the First War ministered to his people in Paddle River, Lunnford, and Lac la Nonne. He was of the finest type, and, like so many others of that stripe, hastened to serve the troops in the First War. Early in the war he was killed as he went into No Man's Land to minister to a dying soldier. His memory is still green in the minds of many an old-timer in those districts. Perhaps it is a compliment to the broadmindedness of the man that his name is commemorated in that of a hotel in Barrhead—The Dallas. Some day perhaps a more fitting or more permanent memorial may be erected to him.

But we have strayed from the store and its problems. One of these was eggs. Many of our customers were hard up and most of them tried desperately to pay their way. Farm prices were very low. Everyone had to eat less and work harder, and that philosophy seemed to have been impressed on the hens too. If eggs sold for five cents a dozen, where formerly they had been worth ten cents, then, to keep even, the hens had to double their production. Worthily they responded to the cause. As times got harder and prices went lower, they first doubled their production, then doubled it again.

We had always dealt in eggs. There were many bachelors who did not bother to keep cows or chickens, and once a week they came to the store for eggs. Many of our customers would make a purchase and then say, "Oh, the wife sent along some hen-fruit, two dozen, I think," and then would go out to the wagon and bring in a pail of eggs packed in oats. Dad was glad to take these in trade so as to supply his other customers. Everyone was happy. The farmer's wife got some revenue from her hens, Dad probably made a cent or so on the deal, and the bachelors got their supplies. All was well with the world.

But when times got tough and the hens quadrupled their output, our bachelor market became glutted. Very well, then, Dad would just have to export the eggs. Next time he went to Westlock for supplies he'd take eggs along and sell them. From somewhere he got crates, and Bill and I sat in the basement packing eggs in them. In a few days we had crates piled all over the place, and every farmer who came to the store came bearing eggs. He would set the box on the floor and state that there were six dozen or ten dozen or fifteen dozen in the box. And be it said to every farmer's credit, there were always six or ten or fifteen dozen as he said. No matter how it strained the resources of a farmer's henhouse to achieve exactly so many dozen, no one stooped to half dozens. If necessary, an extra search was made in order to complete the last dozen. In some cases it must have been quite a search.

I suppose you all know about modern methods of producing eggs. The poultry people keep hens in buildings with rows and rows of windows, one row a hen-storey above another. From the time someone decides (I don't know who or how) that a chicken is a female and, therefore, a potential hen, this female, poor creature, is cooped up and set to work laying. She sits in her place in a long line of hens and starts on her career, dropping one egg a day on the spot designated and at the time appointed. This makes it easy to gather the eggs, which I understand travel about on a conveyor belt. Whether or not the hen puts a number on each one so that someone can check up on her afterwards, I'm not sure. When she is not laying eggs, she is thinking about them. You see, she has nothing else to think about; and it would not do her any good to escape to the yard even if there was one, because they don't allow a rooster anywhere on the same quarter-section.

How different it was in my day on the farm! There was generally a place called a henhouse and some of the more melancholy biddies settled there. Over in one corner there was usually some straw and these mopey hens laid on it. The more venturesome females, however, wandered about the yard singing happily and running losing races with roosters; and then if they had any spare time they spent it in the hay loft, the straw-pile, the cow barn, or the pig pen. And whenever they got in the mood they laid an egg, generally on something soft, but now and then on a beam in the barn or on the floor of the manger. That removed any suggestion of boredom from the hen and added zest to the farm boy's search. When the motherhood mood assailed a hen, she became coy and secretive and disappeared for days at a time. After three or four weeks, if a cow had not stepped on the nest and the coyotes had not gobbled her, she usually came forth into the yard some morning at the head of about a dozen or so chicks. But even the most expectant mother had to have a break; she had to get off her nest for a few minutes to feed. If, at such times, a farm boy in his search came upon her nest, he hit the jackpot. Here were eggs, plenty of them, a dozen or maybe fifteen or eighteen— and a dozen eggs over at MacGregors store were worth five cents. With no thought for the hen's sorrow or the consumer's surprise, they would be whisked away.

When you bought eggs forty years ago you were certainly gambling. You inspected them carefully, using what tests experience had taught you. Whatever other tests you may have applied to them, there were two or three, involving hands, ears, and eyes, that you always used. You hefted the egg and tested it for balance. That told you something—I'm not sure what. You held it up to the light. I always did that, but it never told me anything—I couldn't see through it anyway. But the telling test was to grasp the egg, hold it close to the ear, and shake it vigorously. Ah, that told you something! If there was no sound other than the swish of your elbow as it cut through the air, you smiled, nodded contentedly and placed that one in the bag. If any sound came from the egg, you shook it again to be certain. If there was a gurgling sound like the wash of the sea on the rocks, you grinned, said "Aha!" and shook it beside your friend's ear, nodding the while, and saying, "Rotten." If a pumping sound came from the egg, you repeated the grin and the nod and said, "Half hatched." In either case you rejected it and carefully put it back in the bowl to test the expertness of the next customer.

Well, it was our job, Bill's and mine, to try to detect these varieties as we packed the farmers' eggs in cases to be taken to Westlock. After a few days when crates filled the basement and overflowed to the verandah, and even began to obstruct the entrance to the store and to interfere with the progress of more farmers bringing more eggs, Dad got desperate. First he cut the price to three cents a dozen. That laid him open to vicious attacks as a profiteer—one who ground the faces of the poor. When cutting the prices did not reduce the procession of eggs, he refused to buy any more. This promoted him from a paltry profiteer to a condemned capitalist. He became a robber, a skinflint, a money-baron. But he was adamant. No more eggs! He even offered to give away the cases he had bought, but there were no takers.

The upshot of it all was that early one morning he loaded the wagon with eggs, and he and Chappie and Charlie set out for Westlock. It was a hot summer's morning. Chappie and Charlie were frisky. The roads, especially those sections with corduroy and chuck-holes, were rough. His load was poorly packed. A slimy liquid soon began to coat the floor of the wagon box. As this increased in depth, it attracted flies, wasps, and other insects. Chappie and Charlie became uneasy, and at a most inauspicious moment they shied at something and lurched forward. Dad, even though he had a firm hold on the reins, slipped backwards off the seat into a jumble of boxes, shells and eggs without shells. It was his further misfortune to land upon two or three eggs that Bill and I had missed—the kind that swished when you shook them. When he got the team stopped and examined the seat of his pants, it dripped. Not only did it drip, but it smelled—that unforgettable smell of ripe eggs.

Dad drove the team off the road into a thicket. There, with all the strength of a frustrated and angry man, he hurled case after case of Eastburg eggs into the bushes. Then he drove on to a little stream where he washed his pants and the wagon box before continuing his trip to Westlock. Arriving there he made straightway for Bill Hergott's hotel. He was a good customer of Bill's and this day Bill could see that Dad needed the good offices of "mine host." Thenceforth, any business involving the barter of eggs for groceries was firmly and not always politely declined.

Westlock was just beginning in those days. The Edmonton, Dunvegan, and British Columbia Railway (the E.D. & B.C.) was being pushed through the forest and muskeg from Edmonton to the Peace River Country. About 1913 its two uneven rails wiggled across the road we called the Base Line and, warped and heaving, lay on the surface of the ground through the old homesteads of two farmers, Westgate and Lockhart, former members of the Edgson community. Dad, on his frequent trips to Clyde for supplies for the store, kept us informed of the progress of the new railway. It was important to us, because as soon as a station should be built on Westgate's or Lockhart's quarter, the surrounding hamlet would serve as our shopping centre. The round trip to Clyde was forty-six miles—a two-day return trip. This new town would cut the round trip to twenty-four miles, which could be accomplished in one easy day. So it was with great satisfaction that Dad watched the rails wiggling along the new-made grade. There was some satisfaction in just watching these rails and thereby recalling the progress which the country had made since 1906. That year the end of the railway was Edmonton. In the intervening years it had moved north, ever closer to the North-West of 16. First it had been extended to Morinville, forty miles away, then, a few years later to Clyde, twenty-three miles away, and now to West-lock, only twelve miles away from us.

Once the townsite was laid out and a railway station built, Westlock sprang into being almost overnight. What do you need to make a town? A railway station, a hotel, a Chinese café, a livery barn, one or two stores, and a bank. Bill Hergott supplied the hotel. I forget the name of the long-suffering Chinaman who ran the first café, but in the history of Westlock his name should not be forgotten. Marshall started the first huge livery barn, while the Stanton brothers moved to town and started their store there. At the same time, McTavish started his general store. Almost as soon as the townsite dried out enough so you could see by the furrows in the mud where the main street was going to be, the Bank of Montreal opened its doors. Beside the tracks rose the big red U.G.G. grain elevator, where for so many years Lorne Campbell bought grain. Montpellier opened the first blacksmith shop. Tice, an old-timer in the country, started the first drug store. Across the street Grosse set up his barber chair in a corner from which he could supervise his pool tables, while Mr. Roc started a little bakery around the corner.

So it was a great day for us when, only twelve miles away, Westlock sprang into being. Dad could now take a load of butter and a roll of cash to town, and return that evening with a wagon-load of supplies for the store. I guess I forgot to tell you about the butter. We also bought that commodity, or rather, we let the surrounding farm women exchange it for groceries.

Now, for a country storekeeper, butter, like eggs, had its own problems. An egg is an egg no matter which hen lays it—no matter what that hen's nationality, colour, or housekeeping ability may be; it's delivered just as it comes from the hand of God, with all of what the modern advertisers call its "sealed-in goodness." Butter on the other hand comes from the hand of the housewife, and this unfortunately makes it subject to human errors and frailties. Nowadays most of our supply comes from Alberta's creameries. Since they are amongst the best in the world, creamery butter is a highly specialized product of uniform colour, flavour, and goodness.

Dairy butter of forty years ago, however, varied in all these respects as much as did the farm wives who brought it to the store. With a little practice you could soon pick out each woman's product as easily as you could distinguish that woman from all the others. Each woman varied in her colouring, cleanliness, texture, taste, weight, and quality. So did the produce of her churn. Butter, unless it is dyed, varies from a sickly, lardy white in winter to a rich yellow in early summer. Some women dyed their butter. Some did not. Some women kept spotless kitchens. Some did not. Some women kept their milk pails, pans, churns, and other butter-making vessels scrupulously clean. You could depend on the butter they offered you. It would be clean, properly churned, well washed and worked, so as to remove all the milk and all surplus water. When they presented it to you, it would be firm and cool, even in texture and colouring, sweet and wholesome. Other women's varied all up and down the scale of all these values. Butter was put up in one-pound packages by means of a wooden form into which exactly one pound was pressed. This mould, however, was capable of adjustment by the housewife. While most women's packages weighed a full pound, others somehow failed to tip the scales at this weight.

The flavour of the butter, which was its most essential quality, was also the most difficult to keep constant. It could be spoiled by so many things. In part, the cow was to blame. If she ate even one mouthful of stinkweed, that batch of cream would stink to high heaven. And you couldn't remove the smell by diluting it, because if it were added to good cream, it tainted that as well. There was only one thing to do with it—throw it away, or feed it to calves or pigs. There is no such thing as slightly tainted cream. Stinkweed is like pregnancy in that respect; you can't be just a little pregnant.

If the cow produced sweet wholesome cream, after that it was up to the housewife. She could spoil the flavour of her butter by lack of cleanliness or by laziness. Even if she succeeded and churned an excellent product, her troubles were not over. How or where she stored it was the next factor. Butter seems to reach out and pick up foreign odours. If stored near onions, turnips, or coal-oil, it soon tastes like these. Most women stored theirs in an ice-house, suspended it down the well, or packed it away in a cellar, although some of them just left it around to pick up odours and to soften in the heat of a summer kitchen. Most farm cellars were merely holes dug in the ground and were not even lined with boards. These cellars also contained rows and rows of jams, jellies, and preserved fruits or vegetables, as well as piles of stored potatoes, carrots, parsnips, cabbage, or turnips. Eventually these unlined cellars acquired a variety of smells, some of them tantalizing, some of them not. All were communicated to the butter.

So you see, a country storekeeper had many varieties of butter presented to him. It was one of his worst headaches. Some women, like Sofie Johnstone and Mrs. ter Horst, and possibly four or five others in Eastburg, prided themselves on their product and brought in premium butter. All of the bachelors soon got to know this and asked us to save it for them. Such other butter as we had (and we sometimes had hundreds of pounds of it) we had to dispose of by hauling it to Westlock.

But each woman naturally swore by her own product and was quick to detect any look, sniff, or inflection of voice that might cast aspersion on it. Poor Dad! He had a terrible time trying to be tactful about the quality of the butter, trying to pay less for it than he had paid Sofie Johnstone, or trying to decline it. What? Question a woman's butter? You might more safely question her chastity.

In winter time with its low temperatures, nearly all butter was passable. Then, moreover, the amount we were asked to take in trade was at a minimum. In spring, when lush green rippled in the meadows, the output of butter soared. So did the temperatures and the spoilage. As summer advanced and the hot weather came, the stream of butter to the MacGregor store rose daily until poor

Dad, not having a proper place to store it, had boxes of it piled all over the place. He tried taking it to Westlock, but everyone there had a surplus too. In the end we hauled hundreds of pounds of it down into the bush and threw it away. There was no profit in butter or eggs. There was nothing but loss in all directions— loss of money, loss of friends, loss of face.

You may think that eggs and butter were our chief commodities. Far from it. We had a well-stocked country store. We had a full line of groceries, including the pain-killing medicines of the frontier, and hardware, harness, and clothing. We carried neck yokes and needles; files and fiddle strings; barbed wire and baking powder; binder twine and Beecham's Pills. We had tobacco in all its forms; overalls, moccasins, shoe-packs, lumbermen's socks and felt insoles; grub hoes, axes, mattocks, and scythes, both hay and brush. We sold weasel traps, school slates, airtight heaters, and blankets. We had, in short, almost everything.

Our dried fruits, tapioca, rice, and macaroni were kept in carefully-made drawers, because Dad prided himself on his store fixtures and was always at work with saw and plane to improve and perfect them. These drawers were designed to make the bulk items readily accessible while at the same time excluding dust, and above all, mice. Nevertheless, it was a "sleekit cow'rin' tim'rous beastie" that brought to a head the hard feelings between Mrs. X and Dad. Once, Mother thought she had seen a mouse scurrying out of the apple drawer. And more than once Dad had found some kernels cozily cuddled amongst the rice grains. So he set traps in the rice bin and in the drawers of dried apples and tapioca. "Now Mother," he warned, "be careful. Remember these traps."

Well, that very afternoon, in came Mrs. X. She wandered about the store examining this and criticizing that, and after an hour had not bought anything. Dad did not like her, and she liked him less and took every opportunity to show it and to disparage him and his store. About this time two or three sleigh-loads of neighbours drew up outside and the store was flooded with customers. Mother and Dad flew about filling their orders and wrapping them up. This was the opportunity Mrs. X wanted. "Oh, Mac," she sang out, "you've got mice in your rice. I found some droppings in that last half pound I bought."

"Oh, surely not, Mrs. X!" said Dad, as he hurried around filling orders for dried apples and beans. "Surely not; why, we haven't a mouse in the house."

Now, we had scoops which were used for dipping in the various drawers. There was one scoop for each four or five drawers, and after use it was simply dropped into whichever bin had been opened. As a result, when it was needed again, no one could ever be sure which bin concealed it.

"And what else will you have, Mrs. Sallee?" said Dad as he picked a sack of rolled oats from the shelf.

"Three pounds of beans, please," said little Mrs. Sallee meekly.

"Oh yes, beans," said Dad, opening the bean drawer and feeling for the scoop which was not there.

"Be careful the mice haven't been in the beans," said Mrs. X.

"No mice in my store," said Dad, looking daggers at Mrs. X while he sought the scoop, groping behind him into the rice drawer. "We're very particular about mice, Mrs. X."

"Be careful, Dad," warned Mother.

"Wham!" went the trap and "Bang!" went Dad's temper, while the laughter of the store drowned out his muttered imprecations on himself, traps, women customers, and storekeeping. That round went to Mrs. X. Dad never liked her anyway.

Well, as I have said, the store gave us much fun if little profit. It brought in many charge accounts, if little cash. It gave us a lifelong knowledge of eggs and butter, and an interesting insight into the varying characteristics of country folk. Long afterwards, and very aptly I thought, Dad summed up its profitableness with the old Scots saying:

"Muckle skirl for mickle woo',
     As the Deil said when he clippet the soo,"

which being interpreted means, "Lots of squealing for little wool, as the Devil said when he sheared the sow."

And he did manage a little farming on the side. He became interested in alfalfa, and was one of the first to grow it anywhere in our area. When people began to realize how good it was, he sold seed for a dollar a pound for many a year. Once in a while he would get fed up with the store and then he would take an axe and clear up some more land. He enjoyed clearing, especially the burning of huge brush-piles. Sitting on a log, he spent many a philosophical moment watching the flames or looking out over the clearing as dusk was falling and the aroma of willow smoke drifted along on the evening breeze.

.   .   .   .   .   .

The North-West of 16 was visited by its first car in 1912 or 1913. How the car ever got to our place is a mystery, but it came by way of Clyde and the Base Line. By carrying planks and by dint of the utmost patience on the part of the occupants, and perseverance on the driver's part, it was steered between the stumps that studded the trail through East's old place and Chatten's place. It was a year or so later before enough cars came into use in the Westlock country so that there was any risk of meeting one on the road. Horses were naturally aghast at these smelling, clattering contraptions. Chappie and Charlie, always ready for a lark, reared and capered if they and Dad met a car. Both would rear up; first Charlie would try to climb over Chappie and then with one accord they would leap for the bush at the side of the road, stopping only when they were brought up short by a tree stump.

At this time Mother was very nervous. She had never really enjoyed an outing with Chappie and Charlie, and now she went along with Dad only if there was no alternative. She was never so relieved or astounded as when, upon returning safe and sound, she climbed down from the wagon. She knew that her fears were somewhat exaggerated, but that knowledge did nothing to allay them. She was with Dad on the second or third occasion that Chappie and Charlie met a car. They were skittish, and Dad was doing his best to make them meet and pass the car in an orderly fashion. Mother was terrified. "Whoa, Dad," she said. "Whoa— let me get off—wait, I'll jump!" and much more in the same vein. Dad, with one eye on the horses and the other on Mother, had a few busy moments. The driver of the car was courteous. He stopped fifty feet away and walked up to the horses' heads, saying, "Shall I lead them past the car?" "No," Dad blurted out. "You just lead the wife past; I'll take care of the horses."

On summer Sundays we shut the store, hitched up Chappie and Charlie and went down to the Pembina, three or four miles away, to fish. These were gala occasions. Sometimes we went alone and sometimes with the Johnstones. Dad was a skilled, patient fisherman and we generally came home with a dozen or so jackfish, a few pickerel, and some goldeyes. We did not care for the goldeyes, because they were so soft. If fried right at the river, they were delicious; but if kept a few hours before cooking, they became mushy. By this time the Pembina had been fished so much that a jack weighing more than five pounds was rare. As soon as I was thought capable of handling a fishing rod, Dad bought me a good bamboo one. Although I have not used it these last ten years, I think I still have it around.

In the same way, when Dad deemed me big enough and sensible enough to carry a gun, he bought me a ·22 rifle for my very own. It was the best in the country, a Winchester Automatic that would hold eleven shells. For a long time he drilled me in its care and its use, and taught me the elements of safety with guns. He had been one of the best shots in the British Army, had shot at Bisley many times, and for years had been a musketry instructor. He had seen too many men maimed or killed by the careless handling of fire-arms, and his training was very strict. It was a good job that it was; every year, some man or boy in one of the communities adjacent to ours was injured or killed by his own or someone else's carelessness.

This ·22 opened up to me some of the most delightful hours of my life. At first Dad and I used to hunt together. We tramped miles through the bush on Dr. Phillips's place and on John ter Horst's quarter, taking turns at shooting partridges with the little rifle or creeping up on ducks in the various sloughs, while Dad shot them with his shotgun. Eventually I was permitted to hunt alone. The game regulations said that no one under sixteen was to carry a gun. I was nine when the First War broke out, but some some time before that I had wielded the Winchester ·22.

To a boy with a rifle, a forest filled with partridge or a field full of prairie chicken was paradise. In those days, pin-tailed grouse, which we called prairie chicken, were plentiful. On a fall day they were always to be seen roosting on the trees at all edges of every little field. They seemed to be in family groups of fifteen or so, some sitting in the trees in one corner while others chose the trees a hundred yards along, and still others claimed more distant poplar clumps. During the afternoon they took possession of the stooks, and every other stook within a radius of a hundred yards had one or two prairie chickens feeding on it. After the stacking was done, they simply moved over to feed on the stacks, and all a boy had to do to get three or four was to sneak up under some cover and pot them off. Two or three could be killed before the rest became alarmed enough to fly. After the stacks were threshed, they fed on the straw-piles, or, before it got too deep, they picked about in the snow of the field.

Dad had always been an advocate of clover. In the first year or so he sowed White Dutch in spots around the yard. He took a handful of seed with him any time he walked through the drier meadows and scattered it in them. Within four or five years white clover had claimed every path or meadow. Every open glade or edge of field grew green and luxuriant with clover. Bunty and the other cattle, along with Chappie and Charlie, revelled in it, so that it was always cropped close, and in many places resembled a well-kept lawn. You know what it's like when the frosty nights of October arrive but the snow stays off. The days are usually warm—even hot—but at night ice forms over all the pools and sloughs. Each day it thickens till you can skate on the firm ice near the edges, and finally it becomes strong enough all over to support a venturesome boy. It is then that the rat houses sticking out of the ice become rimmed with frost, and white streaks appear under the ice—the bubbly pathways of muskrats going to and fro. Well, when these frosty days arrive, that is the time to shoot prairie chicken. Early in the morning before the sunshine has become too strong, and when a coating of white frost gives a hoary touch to the close-cropped clover, when each rock picked from the field and rolled out to its clover-strewn edge steams as the sun strikes its hoar frost, that is the time to go shooting prairie chicken. For then they are still huddled deep in their feathers, warming their toes in the sun. Then they are torn between sleepy curiosity, fear of the intruder, and a nodding need for just forty more winks.

But bush partridges—the evening was the time to get them. You took your trusty .22 and stole off through the shadows of the hay trail until you came to the big meadow. It was a fascinating place. Around its edges and scattered in clumps here and there over its twenty-five acres were giant willows growing to a height of thirty feet. The main trunks of these willows were eight inches thick and in the fall their branches were a favourite feeding place of bush partridges. Every evening just before dusk they flew out of the recesses of the forest to feed on the willow buds. Each willow had a spread of possibly thirty feet, and next to it was a clear space of about the same diameter; and at its edge was another willow. There were hundreds of these spreading trees and each one had at least one partridge feeding in it but more often had as many as a dozen.

Partridges are trusting souls. A boy could shoot them one by one; and so long as he took care to shoot the bottom one each time, the rest would remain there. Maybe this is not sport in the more technical sense; but when I was a boy of nine or ten, and particularly when the requirements of the larder called for four partridges each day, this was fun, and useful fun. All fall, from the beginning of September, when the partridges were full grown, Dad or I went down to the meadow and shot four of them each night. We could have killed fifty or a hundred, but four was what we needed. These would hang a day and be used for supper forty-eight hours later. Next evening four more would be shot, and so on until Christmas. During the breeding and growing season, from Christmas to the following September, Dad would not let us kill them. Shooting them for many years at the rate we did made no appreciable difference in their numbers. I believe that it was not shooting but disease, or destruction of their feeding grounds, that finally made them scarce.

The Manola Picnic was the big event in our summers, although since Manola was outside of Eastburg, we regarded it as being somewhat beyond the pale—a lesser place. Of course that is what we thought of Fawn Lake, Dusseldorf, Lunnford, or Highridge. What they thought of Eastburg is not on record, but there was one thing we had to admit about Manola. Over there they certainly could play baseball. Manola had been settled by Americans from the Wild Western States. This alone set it apart from Eastburg, which had few Americans but many British. By tradition, by a disregard for legal niceties, and by a hatred of England and the English, they differed from us. We British, backed by a thousand years of history and heroism, we who had been friends of one nation in one war and foes of it in another, could feel but could not understand their hatred which appeared to be officially nurtured in American schools and history books. We did not realize then that the American Founding Fathers and their successors had been forced to weld a heterogeneous mass of Americans into some sort of unity and to give them a mission in life, and that the quickest way to do this was to give them someone to hate.

Eastburg had been settled via the trail from Riviere Qui Barre to Picardville. Manola had been settled by way of the Fort Assiniboine Trail, which the pioneers had followed as far as Dunstable before striking out north to their new community of Manola. This, too, gave them loyalties and connections that differed from ours. Even their name, Manola, had been distinctive. Its very strangeness made you remember it. Something Spanish, was it not?

Few realized that it had been named by Albert McFee after his daughter.

What I recall most vividly about one of these Manola picnics is not the baseball games, thrilling though they were, but the refreshment booth out under the trees. In it hung the most peculiar greenish-yellow thing. It seemed to branch out and downward into rings that were made up of objects as yellow as a ripe marrow, as thick as a pitchfork handle and as long as a fair-sized cucumber. Every now and then people came up to the man in the booth and bought some, which the man cut off and handed to them. They stood around and peeled them and ate with evident relish. Bill sought out Dad and asked him about these; and even I, with my greater experience of the world, had had no idea bananas grew like that.

The summer days of 1914 sped pleasantly away, marred only by Bill's accident. In the matter of accidents, he was less fortunate than most boys. One night I was chopping an extra supply of kindling for Mother, and Bill was carrying it to the box in the kitchen. On a farm or in the bush you learn to be careful with axes, scythes, and other cutting instruments, but this time either I was careless or both of us were, for just as the axe descended on a slab, I saw Bill's fingers reach for it. The axe crashed across the fingers of his left hand, nearly severing the two middle ones and damaging the others. Fortunately Dad was in the house and he rendered first aid, and then down the old trail through the bush we rushed Bill to Doc Phillips. He sewed the dangling fingers back together, but it was many months before Bill could do much with that hand.

Meanwhile Dad and Mother had been following the alarming developments in world affairs. They had discussed them with some of our more interested neighbours, but very few cared or had any idea of what was going on in the outside world. Except for Henry Paulson and a handful of others, no one who in the past had not had some connection with Britain's armed services, paid much attention. Bill and I, of course, had no inkling of what was going on. It surprised me, therefore, one August evening a day or so after the war had actually started, when Henry Paulson came walking into the kitchen, while we were having supper, and announced, "The bombshell's burst." Dad and Mother looked grave. I did not understand what he meant.

When the war broke out, Dad, the
old soldier, could not rest. He knew that his regiment, the Scots
Guards, would march off to France the first day. In a week or so
the Edmonton papers told of the retreat at Mons, and reported
that the Guards Brigade had been almost wiped out. A month
later our *Glasgow Herald* confirmed this, giving a list of casualties.
Dad went to Edmonton to enlist, but at forty-nine he was too old.
He knew the regulations, but could not believe that they applied
to him. Sure, he was forty-nine; but wasn't he in robust health,
with twenty-four years of soldiering and two campaigns behind
him? He wrote Ottawa, the British War Office, and his old-time
colonel, the Duke of Connaught, who then was Governor-General
of Canada. All of these replied, regretting their inability to do
anything. And while Dad read the papers and fumed, the time
ran on. It was 1916 before they would let him enlist.

Within a week or so most of Eastburg's pioneers of English and
Scottish birth had so disposed their affairs that they were ready to
join the army. By Christmas all those of British extraction, who
were physically fit, had joined up—all save one. Dad said this man
was like a mule, having no pride of ancestry, and he fervently
hoped that, like a mule, he would have no prospect of progeny.
Many young men in Eastburg and the surrounding communities
hastened to return to England to join the British Army. In the
first few months of the war a few young Canadians and Americans
seeking adventure joined up, but to the majority of those to whom
this continent had been a homeland for some generations, the war
seemed very remote. The war was England's affair, and such were

their prejudices that they would not have been sorry to see England "licked," as the Americans called it. When the desperate days of 1915 and 1916 came, they were to change their minds; and this change in outlook was the dawn of Canada's nationhood.

Many of the younger men of Dutch, German, Danish, and Swedish extraction were torn between two loyalties. Since some of them, like Hendricksen, the R.N.W.M.P. constable who patrolled our area, had been officers in continental armies and were still on reserve strength, they returned to their homelands to do what they felt was their duty. Hendricksen was a good friend of ours, and when, some weeks later, we read in the newspaper that he had gone down with the *Lusitania*, it brought the war very close to us. Others were subject to call by the Dutch and German armies. If they refused to answer this call, they felt that they were forever cutting themselves off from the Old Land. Most of these took the difficult step of choosing their new land; and, having taken it, they never looked back.

As the war progressed and its gravity increased, many of those of continental European extraction fell under suspicion of disloyalty to Canada. Some of the Germans in the early days of the war had talked stupidly and heedlessly of their hopes, or their certainty, that Germany would win. As the months went by they found themselves in an embarrassing position. Some settlers from Sweden, which by tradition was friendly to Germany, were in a difficult spot, but were very discreet. Henry Paulson, for instance, disliked England. He was accused of being pro-German. Since he was a bachelor, and bachelors are queer anyway, he was suspect. Since he was well educated, and had accumulated some money, he was even more open to suspicion. With a knowledge of mathematics and a house full of financial charts and Lord knows what else, some of our neighbours asked "What would he be doing here if he were not a German spy, placed here many years ago by the German secret service? How many years ago? Why, nine. My, my, didn't the secret service plan a long way ahead—nine years!" A pioneer community simply had to suspect someone of something. Maybe, for that matter, this is true of any community.

Those who stayed away from the war started feverishly to clear land and get as much as possible of it into wheat while the bonanza lasted, for the price was going up and up. As more land was cleared and more grain had to be hauled to market, better roads were demanded—straight highways, along the road allowances. The sloughs that before had been too costly to cross were now cleared out and graded up into passable roads. Hills that had been too steep to breast were now graded down and new and better tracks followed all but the worst road allowances. As the fields were cleared, the aspect of the whole country changed. We became able to see each other's houses. A sense of coming together, a sense of community interest began to spring up.

One afternoon in the late fall of 1914, Joe Fowlie, all shaved up and in his best suit, dropped into the store. He and Dad talked all afternoon and then he had supper with us and stayed all night. After a late breakfast Joe and Dad went out into the yard and looked around for a while, and then the two of them walked a few hundred yards down the north trail. Dad came back alone and announced that Joe was on his way to enlist. "What?" said Mother. "And he never told me or said good-bye! Call him back; we'll never see him again." A new gravity settled over the house. Eventually she heard from Joe. He had joined the 49th Battalion, and his young brother Albert was also in that regiment.

Not long afterwards, Charlie Rose dropped in. A few days before, young Charlie had decided to go into Edmonton, and, said Charlie, "The young beggar, he's joined the 49th. They shouldn't have let him in. He lied about his age. He's only seventeen—not much more than a baby."

"Well," said Dad, "how old did you say you were when you lit out for Australia? Sixteen, didn't you tell me?"

But Charlie, although worried, was proud too.

So it went. Every week or so someone would come into the store with the news—that the Ellis brothers had gone; that one of the Peters boys had joined up—and then Joe Fowlie sent us a picture of himself and Albert in uniform. Young Charlie also sent us one. Some time early in 1915, the 49th Battalion went overseas. Not long after that, it went into action. Mother had a letter from her sister Dolly in London, telling her that her brother George had been killed, and that Bill Pallet, Dad's old fellow-sergeant, had managed to get in as an instructor.

The harvest of 1915 was gathered in, and the geese flew over in echelons ages old, unmindful of wars or rumours of wars. Christmas of 1915 came, with its usual festivities, plus parcels for Red Cross and for the soldiers. The school scribblers began to come out with covers depicting Michael O'Leary, V.C. and recounting his deeds, portraying the flags of all the Allies, and showing aeroplanes diving

on the enemy. Aeroplanes; imagine that! Then, with the Allies'
outlook becoming ever darker, the replies to Dad's letters became
a little less brusque. There might still be a chance to get in. Late
in March of 1916 it arrived, a letter saying that Dad could report
to the 192nd Battalion in Calgary. They were taking on many
miners from Crowsnest Pass and even a company of Japanese from
the coast. They needed an experienced regimental sergeant-major.

Dad was off to war again. Mother watched him ride down the
road and then came in and cried. She knew the colour and glory
and the music of war, but she knew too that these only hid the
other aspects. Still, this enlisting was Dad's wish and his duty.

Mother did not sit around weeping. For nearly ten years she had
been a pioneer's wife. For that period she had been irked by our
lack of progress; now she made a mental inventory of our resources.
She thought of the format of the auction-sale bills that were always
being posted in the store and post office, wherein the auctioneer
described the merits of the farm, the stock, and the implements
for sale. Mother's inventory turned out something like this:

ONE FARM: Clear title, 161 acres, fenced and cross-fenced;
18 acres under cultivation, three being in alfalfa, one in
timothy, eight fall-ploughed and six summerfallowed; the
remainder of the land is heavy bush, most of it killed off by
the fire of eight years ago, while patches of a few acres here
and there are nothing more than thick brush. The buildings
consist of one eight-roomed house, one log barn and other
outbuildings. The place boasts a good well eighty feet deep.

LIVE STOCK: *Horses:* Two (Chappie and Charlie), light in
weight, long in years, indifferent to work.

Cattle: Bunty; of doubtful age and ancestry. Her progeny;
two or three of different sizes, sexes, and sires.

Pigs: Half a dozen, various breeds, one fattening, others
razor-backed.

Poultry: Two dozen hens, a few turkeys, two geese.

MACHINERY: One wagon, sturdy in frame, wobbly in
wheels; one set of sleighs; one jumper; one 12-inch walking
stubble-plough; one 12-inch walking breaking-plough, one
set of disks and one set of harrows, one seed drill, assorted
axes, hoes, rakes, and scythes.

MISCELLANEOUS: One country store; one country post
office; one boy, aged eleven, tall for his age; one boy, aged
eight, short and freckled, but optimistic.

OTHER ASSETS: Army separation of $35·00 per month. Plus what pay Dad sends home. Good health and spirits.

LIABILITIES: None, unless the store should prove so.

As Mother sized up the situation there appeared places where improvements could be made. First, the store must go. Second, Bunty and her brood should be replaced with Holstein cattle. Third, Chappie and Charlie, friendly servitors though they were, must be replaced by a team of what Mother called real horses. Fourth, more land must be cleared and broken.

It was April now, and seeding time. Here Mother came face to face with what she considered her inadequacy. She could not drive the horses and work the land with them. She wanted to and tried to, but could not overcome her timidity. Other women worked in the fields all day long, and Mother envied them their nerve and capability, but could not equal it. What might not she be able to accomplish during Dad's absence if only she, too, could drive the horses?

Last year's summerfallow, before it could be seeded, had to be disked; so with Mother's help I hitched Chappie and Charlie to the disk, and on a glorious spring morning tried my hand at farming. I took several turns around the field, adjusting the disk levers this way and that, but had little to show for my efforts. If I set the disks too deeply, the horses could not pull for any distance. When I set them less deeply, they made little impression on the weeds. Somehow Dad had been able to cultivate these fields with these two horses and the disk. Whatever his knack had been, I could not duplicate it. Next day I tried again, but with no better success. It became sadly manifest that I could not put the crop in either, so Mother arranged with C. B. Smith to put it in as soon as he had finished his work. When harvest time came the horses and I were equally ineffective, although Mother and Bill and I did manage the stooking. We were also able to cut hay and to get it in, Mother and I taking turns with the scythe.

Long before fall Mother sold the store to Ad Geddes, who ran a similar establishment six miles north at Rossington. When it was sold and our creditors were paid off, we had—as already recounted—two hundred dollars left. Ad Geddes, I believe, gave us a fair price for our stock and such fixtures as he took over, although Mother had expected that the winding up of the affairs of the store would give us well over a thousand dollars with which to start out on our new farming programme. In any event, with the selling of the store, Item One of the new programme had been effected.

Mother next turned her attention to the cattle, and before long Bunty and most of her progeny were trotting smartly down the road as the property of the local cattle-buyer. Where the Holstein cow and other cattle came from I'm not sure; but henceforth, our pastures were dotted with sleek black-and-white kine. Item Two!

Now that the store was gone, Mother was free to clear some land. She could get some done nearly every day, and when we were not at school, she and Bill and I worked together. About this time the Cotswold School fell in line with the schools in the rest of Alberta, and set its term from the first of September to the end of the following June. The roads were better now. There were more children going to school, so it was thought reasonable to have them attend all winter and take their two months' holidays in the summer. This left Bill and me free to work on the farm during the summer months. I'm afraid we cannot claim to have accomplished much; but at least, under Mother's direction and with her encouragement, we made some progress.

The old trail still crossed our place to avoid clearing out a new road through the bush at the west side of the quarter. Down the trail about half-way to the north line-fence, the fires had done a reasonable job of clearing out a patch of about five acres. All of the big trees had been killed, and in the eight years since the fire, many of them had blown over. This patch was the easiest part of the quarter to clear. If Mother could not drive horses and work the land, she could compensate by the labour of clearing, so all three of us set to with a will.

God knows clearing was back-breaking work, with its repetitious swinging of the axe, its tugging at roots, its dragging of logs to the brush pile. It was also discouraging work, because after a day's sweat and toil, a pitifully small area had been cleared. But with every swing of your axe you had removed another antagonist or revealed another of nature's secrets. Here, hidden till now, was a clump of bluebells, and there, "born to blush unseen," was a white ladyslipper, or a vine of honeysuckle. Here, at the mercy of the axe, was the tiny nest of thrush or wren, fortunately seen in time to be spared. There, unsuspected, were the hidden runways of rodents busy about their own business and, until now, happy in their seclusion. All of these secrets fell to the lot of him who cleared land.

We had little thought of these pleasures, however, when we started out to clear the new north field. We did so with grim determination to carry out one more of Mother's projects for converting the homestead to a farm. Soon we enlarged our patch to ten acres; and Mother hired a man to break it. As it turned out, he did a rotten job.

It was this same man who, before we got wise to him, helped Mother carry out her fourth objective, and in this, too, he tricked her. She mentioned the fact that she would like to sell Chappie and Charlie and get a good team of heavier work-horses, preferably mares—a steady team. It appeared that he had just such a team, but he explained that Chappie and Charlie, of course, would not be worth much in any trade. Wait until the breaking was finished and he would bring his horses around for Mother's inspection. If they satisfied her, maybe they could make a deal.

When he drove them up into the yard we were pleasantly surprised. Both were mares and both were in good shape. The one named Molly looked a little old, but Diamond was a fine-looking horse, not too old, and quiet and gentle. He hitched this team to the wagon and took us for a ride. They were just what we wanted, so the deal was made. The new horses were put into the barn and Chappie and Charlie were hitched to his wagon and driven away.

We were all very pleased with ourselves and with the new team. For several days we fed them and led them out to water. After a while we let them loose in the yard, and eventually turned them into the pasture. We liked Molly and she reacted favourably to our kind treatment, but Diamond did not seem to trust us. As a result, we were kind to her but circumspect in her presence. Then, one day, when we proposed to take Mother to the store for groceries, Bill and I harnessed the new team and hitched them to the wagon. Diamond stood quietly while we hitched her up but, as soon as we started off, all the devil in her broke loose. I can't describe it. Diamond moaned and bucked. She reared up and kicked. She bounced about as if her belly were full of bed-springs. Her bowels and bladder moved jointly and severally but vigorously. She leaped into the air and came down astraddle the pole of the wagon. At the next leap she fell sideways, all the while snorting and squealing, showing the whites of her eyes, and kicking. Mother scrambled down out of the wagon, terrified. I was terrified too. Then, Diamond, squealing all the while, started galloping about the yard, dragging the wagon and Molly and me with her, until we smashed into something and the double-trees broke. Eventually I got her quieted down and unhitched and put into the barn. We had been sold a balky horse. Good, faithful Chappie and Charlie were gone; and so was the man who had taken them—at least we were never able to get in touch with him again. Item Four in the programme had been a mistake, a failure.

I don't know what was wrong with Diamond. If she had been a human we would have described her conduct as recurring spells of insanity. The next time I hitched her up she drove quietly enough; but then the following time she acted up again. We could not depend on her. Mother wondered if it was because of my inexperience with horses, but some of the sympathetic neighbours tried to drive her and they met with the same results. Clearly, she was untrustworthy and dangerous; but what was Mother to do? She kept her, knowing that we could not sell her to anyone for more than a few dollars and feeling that, if we did, and then bought another horse, we might get cheated again. At times Diamond let us work her, so she was kept until Dad came home. Even he, the friend of all animals, could do nothing with her. Eventually George Donkelaar bought her for next to nothing, vowing that, if he could not make her work, he would kill her and feed her to his hogs. When we saw George next and asked him how Diamond was, "The hogs et her" was all he would say.

So much, then, for Mother's farming accomplishments. On three out of four counts she was successful, and this is a good average. Furthermore, encouraged by the sight of the new breaking, we all set to and cleared more land. That piece of new breaking was the real start of our career as farmers. After that, clearing and breaking became an annual event, and in a little over six years the whole quarter was under cultivation.

Over and above Mother's extra efforts to develop the homestead into a farm, she had her hands full with the minor cares and duties of the place, as well as getting us off to school. She still had to tend the post office, although ordinarily this took little of her time. There were, however, those extraordinary occasions when Mother set out on foot to the home of a neighbour. There was no telephone communication with the outside world, although the telegraph office of the E.D. & B.C. Railway was only twelve miles away at Westlock. This distance sometimes took three days for a telegram to span. Telegrams could be flashed to Westlock from Ottawa or even England in a matter of minutes, but when they arrived at Westlock they were typed out and put into the mail. Thus it was that Mother became a bearer of telegrams. And not one of them brought good news. Each Tuesday and Friday, when Gerry Hoogers delivered the mail sack, Mother first searched it for telegrams, and then breathed more easily if there were none. She was not worried about Dad because, try as he would, he could not get from England to France. Telegrams arrived only for those with boys or husbands at the Front. Mother felt that she could not let a neighbour woman come over for the mail and then, along with seed catalogues and circulars, hand her one of these dread telegrams. Consequently, she opened each one (I suppose that was strictly against the regulations), read its message, had a cup of tea, and then, telling us to get our own supper, started down the road.

I believe the first one was addressed to the next-of-kin of Albert Fowlie. That was old Mrs. Fowlie. Just after the war started she had decided to come out from Scotland to live with one of her six boys, all of whom were in Western Canada. Shortly after Joe enlisted, his brother Bill came down from the Yukon and joined a Vancouver regiment, but was soon discharged as medically unfit. Then he came to Eastburg to farm Joe's place and old Mrs. Fowlie came to live with him. The first wire was for her; Albert was slightly wounded. Well, that wasn't too bad, and Mother walked the four miles over to Joe's old place with it.

I think the next wire was also for Mrs. Fowlie and concerned one of the other boys that we did not know. Certainly the third wire was for her. Mother tore it open and read the usual preamble, and then sat down in a chair and cried. This time it was Joe, killed at St. Eloi; Joe, who but such a little while before had walked gaily down the road without saying good-bye; Joe, our best friend, who at times had lived with us; Joe, the first to lend some cheer to the loneliness of the forest when in 1907 his happy song had reached us through the bush. He was Eastburg's first casualty. With a heavy heart, Mother plodded over to tell Mrs. Fowlie.

Only a few days later a wire came for Charlie Rose—young Charlie, killed. Charlie, the boy who should have been in high school.

With these and other casualties, the war was brought home to Eastburg and the neighbouring communities. A new patriotism began to sweep over the area, and with it a hatred for Germans and a suspicion of everyone of German extraction or German name, no matter how well beloved that person had been before. In the previous months a few Germans here and there had been interned, but these were mostly from the settlement of Dusseldorf. These Germans were torn between a natural loyalty to the Fatherland which they had left only five years before, and a love of this new land. It was a difficult time for them. In the hysteria of the war it was decided to forget the old community name of Dusseldorf, and it was officially changed to Freedom.

But, if feeling rose high against those of German extraction, that rise was as nothing compared to the rise in the price of wheat and all grains. Prosperity had reached the backwoods. Unfortunately, as it always does, it brought inflation with it. If wheat rose in price to nearly three dollars a bushel, the farmers found that the price of flour soared more in proportion. That was not so bad, because many of us had long been accustomed to having our own wheat gristed into flour. But other things also rose in price. Sugar, clothing, and tools also went up. The old bogey of supply and demand was operating. During the First War, unlike the period of World War Two, little scarcity was experienced on farms. A few items were hard to get. Grocers were asked to dole out the available supplies, so as to make them all go round, but I don't remember any ration books or anything of that sort. Sugar was scarce, but there appeared to be plenty of corn syrup and honey. There was no real inconvenience.

And there was a profusion of wild fruit. First in every way were strawberries, two varieties of them—first in the spring, first in flavour, and first in our affection. Wild srawberries are small and hard to pick, but perhaps the rewards of this life are directly proportional to effort. Mother picked quarts of them. Following hard on their heels came dewberries. I suppose there must be many of this generation who have never heard of a dewberry, let alone tasted one. It is a berry resembling a raspberry but growing on a little bush four or five inches high. There were two varieties of dewberries also, and each had a delicious flavour. I rarely see dewberries any more. They seem to have identified themselves with the cause of the forest on whose floor they grew. When the forest was swept away, dewberries likewise disappeared.

Raspberries, of course, everyone knows. Three or four years after any fire swept through the forest, raspberries sprang up to cover the black nakedness of the desolation. On our farm, or our neighbours' farms, we picked them at the rate of as much as a hundred pounds a day. All winter they were the mainstay of our fruit closet.

Then, on the chalky white soils bordering the muskegs, blueberries grew profusely. Hard by in the mossy places grew low-bush cranberries; and then there were the high-bush cranberries growing as individual berries on shrubs five or six feet high, filled with red sour juice. These, too, made good tart jelly. There were other berries—Pembina berries—which we also called high-bush cranberries and distinguished them from the ordinary kind by saying "high-bush cranberries, you know, from down by the river." Yellow in the early fall and turning to an apple-red later, they hung from the branches of trees up to ten feet high, in clusters that filled a man's outstretched hand.

By every creek, on every hillside, on every open glade, grew saskatoons. Their beautiful flowers bedecked the landscape in spring, and in the early fall their clusters of juicy ripe berries filled a boy's craving for sweets. They were unequalled when eaten raw, but, for some reason or other, were quite flat when preserved. So were the two varieties of cherries, the red pincherry and the black chokecherry. If you were patient enough, these made good jelly and added to the variety of the country desserts. If chokecherries were not highly regarded for preserving, they were esteemed for wine-making. At times we made wine, and it was good. It was so good that Bill once got high on it; but that was later on.

The wild red currants were very much the same as the tame varieties, but the wild black currants, of which there were two quite distinct varieties, were as different from tame currants as they were from turnips. No one can describe a taste; but nobody can forget one. Neither can I forget the taste of Mother's black currant jelly and jam. Dad liked these so well that he transplanted black currant bushes to the borders of all our garden paths, and from them for many years we picked our whole winter's supply.

But in describing these bounties of nature I have wandered away from the shortages brought on by the First War. By 1916 the papers were full of the idea of saving food. Culinary experts thought up recipes by the score for eggless cakes, butterless buns, flavourless flapjacks, and what have you. The idea was that you substituted something else for the items that were supposed to be scarce. In the proper season this wave of substitution washed over

Eastburg. It reached its zenith one day when the Women's Club held their meeting at the home of Mrs. R. She really went all out. The tea was served without sugar, the sandwiches were spread without butter, the cookies were made without eggs, and the culmination of culinary invention was reached by Mrs. R's cake. It was an eggless, butterless, sugarless cake. It went even further than this—it was nearly flourless. In a large measure, potatoes had been substituted for flour. Did ever patriotism flourish or damn-foolishness triumph more grandly? Eggs—we could not sell them. Butter—it melted on the pantry shelves and had to be thrown away. Flour—our granaries were full of it.

The cake was a sodden failure. But although the thought may have been feeble, the spirit was the spirit that wins wars and clears forests. Let no one deny that. For it was this spirit that did incalculable good in the contribution of the women's clubs to the war effort, and time and time again filled the demands of the Red Cross.

I remember one meeting of the Women's Club at our house. Mother was the president at the time, and a call had come through for the club to sew pyjamas. I believe the Red Cross provided the material and sent out patterns, but I'm not certain. If the Red Cross needed pyjamas, why, the Eastburg Women's Club would make them, although many of its members had to be very discreet in order to find out, without exposing their ignorance, what pyjamas were. They were impractical on the farm, and many a good soul grew to old age and died full of years and grace without ever having seen a pair. That day at our house the patterns were placed, the scissors plied, and parts of many pyjamas prepared. All that had to be done now was to stitch them together, sew on buttons, and make buttonholes. It was then that Liz sidled up to Mother and whispered. Mother looked up with a puzzled expression and shook her head. "Bless me, I don't know! Ask Dora Allen over there." But Dora did not know either. It turned out that no one knew. It was most vexing, this problem of buttonholes. Did they run up and down, or did they run horizontally? The pattern did not give the answer. All it showed was a non-committal + where each buttonhole was to go. The president thought they should be horizontal. The vice-president was sure they should be vertical. The secretary chipped in, followed by the treasurer, and then the other ranks became embroiled.

No more sewing was done that day. The executive resigned

and the club disbanded. Mrs. A, who had brought Mrs. B in her buggy, drove home without her, vowing never to darken her door again, while Mrs. B walked home with Mrs. C, stating that, if she never saw Mrs. A again, that would be too soon. All the pent-up animosities of years found relief in the great battle of the button-holes. Next week they all met at Mrs. D's, re-appointed the same executive, and plied their needles in harmony, while they discussed the pending arrival of young Mrs. E's baby—you know, she used to be Miss F, and wasn't she married only last April? Let's see, May, June, July . . .

The Women's Club also put on concerts to raise money, and in one of these the main event was a play. This play started with one director, but after the first rehearsal it turned out that all except timid little Miss T were directors. That made things difficult, but in spite of a slight coolness between Mrs. A, who had advocated vertical buttonholes, and Mrs. B, who had held out for horizontal ones, the play battered its way along until the final night. There were two heroines. (In country concerts you often have to have two or more heroines. People in the back rows can rarely hear what they say anyway, so you can take your choice.) The night of the concert, when the curtain had been dragged aside by Lloyd Johnstone and Billy Byvank, the play got away to a good start. The cordiality of tone called for in the part where Mrs. A and Mrs. B (the two heroines) met each other, seemed a bit strained, but this was relieved by the brightness of Mabel Allen's hair and her white apron when, taking the part of a maid, she came out to stand by the little table. All country plays have tables and white-aproned maids; but, for my money, give me Mabel Allen with her red hair. She was young and fresh-looking. Just having her standing there helped you forget the grim realities of the concert and the play.

Everything went well until Mrs. B had to mince over and address Mrs. A. The dialogue then went something like this:

"Have you seen Priscilla since the morning?" chirped Mrs. B.

Mrs. A's face fell. "Huh?" she asked.

Mrs. B, taken aback, repeated, "Have you seen Priscilla since the morning?"

"That isn't your next line," said Mrs. A.

"Oh yes it is," flared Mrs. B. "And now *you* say . . ."

"Oh, no, I don't!" shouted Mrs. A.

The schoolmistress was busy prompting from the wings, but the heroines never heard her. The other actors stood around highly embarrassed. Finally Mrs. B was beaten down. She put her hands to her face and fled crying as the curtain was closed. Mrs. A, however, marched right to the edge of the stage, in front of the curtain. "She's crazy," she announced. "She should have said 'I have a question to ask you,' and then I could have said 'Oh? What is it?', and *then* she'd say . . ."

You see, we did not lack for excitement in Eastburg, as with eggless cakes and flourless cookies, sewing circles and concerts, 1916 drew to a close.

14

It was during the last years of the First War that the number of horses in Alberta rose to its maximum of over eight hundred thousand. Those were the days when a man's prosperity depended upon good horses and could be assessed by a study of his steeds. Henry Paulson had excellent draught horses. When he did not stride about the country with his long legs or slip along beside the trails on his long skis, he drove sedately with his fine cream-coloured mares. And as an old man living in Edmonton he would sit for hours talking of the "good old days" when he and his horses had worked hard and understood each other perfectly.

Once, he said, some years after building his new frame house and while still using the old shack as a storage shed, he had gone in there for something and had forgotten to close the door. From the shack he had walked nearly half a mile to the north edge of his quarter and was burning brush on top of the hill that looked down over his farm buildings. His horses had been turned loose in the yard to graze on the rich Alsike clover. Towards noon, hearing a distant neigh, he looked down at his yard and could see there only three of the four horses. Rags and Dagmar were near the shack. Inga was nowhere to be seen. But Lars, with head held high, was stretching his neck over the north fence of the yard, neighing for Henry. For a moment or so Henry waved his arms above his head, then stood still, watching and wondering what was the matter. Lars, seeing the sign of recognition, turned and raced back to the other two horses. Then all three of them ran to the fence, looked towards Henry, and neighed. As he ran down the hill they went back and forth between the old shack and the fence. As he crawled through the fence they nickered at him in a relieved way and followed him, as much as to say, "It will be all right now." When Henry got to the shack he found that Inga had entered its shade to escape flies and had broken through the rotting floor into the old cellar hole and was now stuck there. Henry, in telling about it, said with affection in his voice, "Inga, the old fool, she was trapped, and I wouldn't have found out if Lars hadn't called to me to come and get them out of trouble."

Whereas we hauled our grain to Westlock, Henry preferred taking his to Picardville. That twenty-two-mile return trip to the elevator was long and lonesome, unless you talked to your horses and they talked to you by nickering, turning first one ear back and then the other, and finally both, to listen to what you had to say, and now and then looking back at you without the hindrance of blinkers on their bridles. In the morning, as Henry fed his horses, he always told them what he and they were to do that day. "We're going to seed the north field today," or "We're going to harrow the new breaking." On those mornings when Henry was going to haul grain to Picardville, he would walk into the stable and say: "We're going to Picardville today," and the horses would all look around expectantly and then look at each other, as much as to ask: "Which of us will he take this time?" "I'd keep them guessing for a while," Henry explained, "and then I'd say, 'I'm taking Lars and Dagmar today,' and then these two would look around, pleased as punch."

After Henry got them hitched up they would turn left at the gate and right at the intersection of the roads, and they'd be away. It was many miles before the lone elevator at Picardville came into sight, but when it did, the horses would prick up their ears and Henry would say: "See, I told you—Picardville." So, over the years, Picardville became synonymous with hauling grain to the elevator. Then a branch railway-line was constructed and the station of Highridge was built only six miles away. Henry decided to haul his grain there, but how to explain all this to his horses was a problem beyond Henry's ability. So, when it came time to haul grain, he went to the barn and said: "Lars and Dagmar, we're going to Picardville today."

When, however, they reached the gate and Henry turned them right instead of left, they stopped in their tracks and looked at him. "Are you crazy?" their looks said. But Henry talked to them and they went to the right, one mile west and then two miles south. In those days you could not see the Highridge elevator until you were almost upon it. So when Lars and Dagmar, shaking their heads dubiously, turned the last corner and the elevator showed up right in front of them, it took them by surprise. They turned to look at Henry while he said: "See, I told you so, Picardville," and then they understood and strode along to the elevator. From then on, they accepted these changed circumstances and ever afterwards when Henry said "We're going to Picardville," they turned right at the gate.

"Oh yes," said Henry, "you bet horses know what you're saying. They know much more than most men give them credit for."

While Henry hauled grain to Picardville, we hauled grain to Westlock. Our first real crop after Dad went overseas was harvested in the fall of 1917. That winter Lloyd Johnstone and I joined forces and hauled our grain and the Johnstones'. At 8.30 each morning we would hear the deep tone of Lloyd's sleigh-bells coming down the hill on the bush road and in a few minutes he would drive up to the house with his load of grain. I would be ready with our own team and load, and together we would set off down the north trail towards Westlock.

Lloyd and I enjoyed ourselves hauling grain. We hauled day after day, returning in time for a late supper. I don't remember how cold it had to get before we considered that it was too cold; I believe we drew the line at about twenty-five below. For most of the way the horses did not need to be driven, so that he and I could sit together on whichever load was ahead, and the other team would follow along behind. In this way, at a speed of from three to four miles an hour, we travelled the twelve miles to Westlock. In the first four and a half miles to Agnew's Corner we would probably fall in with half a dozen neighbours on a similar errand. It was there at Agnew's Corner that we became part of the great throng of Alberta farmers taking grain in to the elevator, for hauling grain was then a great winter institution, and on the larger farms in those days it took up most of a farmer's time for the whole winter.

As we turned Agnew's Corner we could look north up the rise towards Rossington, and east up the three-mile rise towards Hazel Bluff. What a sight that was! Each way there were grain teams spaced a hundred yards or less apart as far as we could see. By this time the main roads had been graded up so that they were straight and wide enough for two teams to pass each other. They had to be, for there were as many teams returning as there were going towards town. In no time at all, after each fresh fall of snow, the sliding steel-shod runners of the sleighs had levelled off the new snow and packed it into a smooth, icy coat. The runners slipped along easily. We all hoped for frequent light snowfalls, because in a day or so the road, which started out a glistening white streak of snow, became four brown strands where the offerings of thousands of well-fed horses accumulated in four long lines converging on Westlock in the distance.

When Lloyd and I reached Agnew's Corner and pulled into the long line of teams heading east, we became part of the procession. Sometimes we met old friends among the men and boys in the line-up and discussed the latest topics of the community. At other times the adjacent teams were total strangers, but we soon got to know them. There were Germans from Dusseldorf, or Freedom as we call it now, Italians from Naples, Dutch from Neerlandia, and all had difficulty pronouncing the English language. There were bearded Buffalo Bills from Manola, dyspeptic New Englanders, soft-spoken Southerners wondering why they had ever left "Plum Tree Down in Tennessee." There were Down-Easters, and Englishmen; both Cockneys and Oxford men. There were Scots and Irish and French. And each, according to his outlook on life, grumbled or whined, laughed or "joshed," but most were of the latter type and were happy and companionable, for were not all of us reaping the harvest in crisp green bills? Were we not all realizing the reward of months and years of work on the old homestead?

Eventually our team would reach the top of the hill at the Hazel Bluff Church. There we could look back along the way we had come and look forward down the long slope to the Wabash, and beyond it to Westlock. It used to be an impressive sight, this five-mile stretch, with possibly a hundred loaded teams heading for Westlock, and a hundred on the other side of the road returning. In cold weather it was a long five miles. The elevator was in plain sight, but at this snail's pace it took an hour and a half to reach it. (You do this stretch of the road now in a truck in five minutes.) If it was not too cold you huddled into your mackinaw or your sheepskin coat, but in really cold weather you preferred to walk on the left side of the load, keeping within reach of the front of the sleigh in case you had to swing on in a hurry to drive the horses. Upon arriving at the elevator, you found possibly twenty teams ahead, waiting to unload; and this waiting, chattering in the cold, and inching forward in the line-up, seemed the longest part of the trip. It seemed as if you would not be able to stand it until your turn came. But it came finally, and with a rush the horses scrambled up the cleats of the runway, and in a moment Lorne Campbell would weigh the load. The exercise of untying the bags and dumping them through the grating in the elevator floor helped to warm you. In a couple of minutes that was over, and with the grain cheque shoved well into a shirt pocket, you were on your way up town. The horses trotted across the tracks west of the station, then swung down Main Street, passed Murfitt's butcher shop, McTavish's store, and the "Chink" restaurant, and swished around to the left to Marshall's barn. In a minute or two the teams were stabled and busy lapping up oats and chomping at the sweet hay in the stalls.

Westlock in those days was booming and crude. Buildings were going up everywhere as more and more merchants recognized the possibilities of the riches that came pouring from farms as far distant as forty miles. Hergott's Hotel stood on the corner that the new and bigger hotel occupies today. Across the main street was the little Bank of Montreal. Between it and the railway station a block and a half away were various little buildings, chiefly Walker's Jewellery and Watch Repair, and Grosse's Poolroom and Barber Shop. On the west side of the street, between the hotel and Tice's Drug Store at the far corner of the block, there was a store or two, and the empty lots were piled high with lumber and timbers. Egar Stanton's Grocery was around the corner, while his rival, McTavish, was north across the side street from Tice's. I forget now who ran the hardware, but it was a fascinating place for farm boys.

But of all these places, the Chinese restaurant appealed most. Ten or perhaps twelve stools lined the counter, and three or four booths took up all the north wall, while the centre was filled with the roaring heater. Pies, cookies, and buns were piled on the shelf in front of the long mirror, alternating with plates, cups, and cutlery. By the time you had stood around the stove for a minute or two, thawed out your aching hands a bit, unbuckled your sheepskin, and hung it on the nail on the wall, Lee (I think that was his name) had set a place at the counter and confronted you with a bowl of hot soup. Menu? There was no menu. "What will you have?" chirped Lee. "Loast beef? Cold beef? Steak?

Liva onions? Steak an' onions?" Prices? It didn't matter, except
that the steak as big as a scoop shovel was ten cents extra. For
thirty-five cents you could eat all that a hungry boy could put
away; and that was even after the prices had been forced up by
the war. Dessert? Canned pears, peaches, applesauce or pies.
"Apple, laison, clanbelly and bluebelly—bluebelly and clanbelly
all gone, you have apple? Good," said Lee. And good it was, even
the second helping.

After our meal, Lloyd and I usually had half an hour on our
hands while waiting for the horses to finish feeding. This gave us
a chance to see the town, and to buy what groceries were needed.
Then we went back to Marshall's. What fascinating places those
old livery barns were! They were the great meeting-places of the
countryside, abounding in news, gossip, and politics. There used
to be one or two of them in every block, built big enough for a
row of stalls along each side and a broad passageway down the
middle, and long enough to hold a hundred teams. The hay loft
was overhead, on the second storey. The smells were captivating:
there was the prevailing ammonia smell always associated with
horse barns and not unpleasant to those who lived and worked
with horses. Mingled with this, but in a minor key, was the scent
of well-cured hay, and the smell of iodine or of creoline pervaded
the place.

It was usually run by a sharp-witted man with a handlebar
moustache, an eye skilled in the judgment of horses, a hand practised in the mysteries of poker, and a nose oriented to the sources
of illicit liquor. For those commercial travellers who had calls to
make in the surrounding country, the livery barn kept a few good
driving-teams. The hostler, if in the West we dare use that term,
was invariably a character. There seem to have been only three
names for such men—Scotty, Frenchy, and Bill. No one knew
or cared whether they had any other name. Many a yarn one or
another of them told Lloyd Johnstone and me as we waited for
the horses to feed. Older men went and talked to the mayor of
the town or to the great lawyer, or even to the M.L.A., but Lloyd
and I were on surer ground at the livery barn. We had the inside
track, there, with old Bill, Scotty, and Frenchy.

By the time we got the horses hitched up and turned their heads
west towards the railway tracks, the winter afternoon was drawing
in. The horses, eager to get home, trotted most of the way. In
order that we could sit together and talk, we used to tie the second

team to the back of the first sleigh, and then, huddled down in the box out of the wind, discuss the events of the day. As darkness settled in, especially if there was a breeze, it was very cold squatting there, and one night we hit upon a great idea. We resolved that on the next trip we should take along a small unused air-tight heater, so that for the cold, dark trip home we could be cheered by its warmth and glow. Wood to keep it burning could be picked up along the road, and two lengths of stovepipe would carry the smoke clear of the sleigh-box. With the heater we could enjoy those long rides home in the darkness.

Ahead and also behind we could hear, and sometimes see, other sleighs like ours, homeward bound on the long road. Overhead reigned the stars, myriads of them, distinct and close. There, high in the sky, was the Big Dipper pointing out the North Star. Low in the south-east was Orion with his belt and the seven stars of the sheath of his dagger, while directly across the Pole Star from the Big Dipper sat Cassiopea in her chair. We looked up at the stars and speculated about them. We gazed at them and spoke of the future that stretched so far ahead of us. Both of us were going to escape from the farm. I was going to be a soldier like Dad, and Lloyd was to be a locomotive engineer. How far away those days and dreams are now!

Eventually Lloyd and I would reach Agnew's Corner and turn south, and usually this put the wind behind us. For two miles south the sleighs would slip along past Renton's and Yeoman's and the light in old man Holden's shack. After turning west we passed the glow of George Armstrong's lantern hanging in the barn while he did his chores, and then, nearly a mile further on, when we saw Ritter's light, it was time to turn south again. From this corner it was only a mile and a half to a warm welcome and a hot supper. The horses broke into a spirited trot and soon Byvank's light appeared, and Axel Clausen's across the road. These two disappeared behind us as we swung around the curves through the bush, up past Donkelaar's old place, and finally dashed through the gate that marked the north boundary of the North-West of 16. In a few minutes we could see the lamp that Mother always set in the kitchen window. In no time at all we were home and, while both teams were feeding in the barn, Mother spread a steaming supper before us.

Lloyd and I finished hauling grain early in February, and, as a reward, Mother gave us enough cash to spend four or five days in Edmonton. Lloyd's father drove us to Picardville to catch the train. While Picardville had no real railway station, there was a shanty about the size and shape of a box-car, in which anyone waiting for the train could seek shelter. It contained a heater and a pile of wood, so that we could keep ourselves warm while we waited. The train was due at noon, but since it was the E.D. & B.C. on its way down from Grande Prairie through four hundred miles of bush and muskeg, the wait was apt to be long. Lloyd and I, and two or three other passengers, kept watch for the train all through the afternoon and night, and just as dawn was breaking on a blizzardy February morning, it arrived. It was eighteen hours overdue, but the E.D. & B.C. had often been known to be nearly a week late. We considered ourselves lucky on this occasion—and we were indeed very fortunate, for just a few years before there had been no railway at all.

In those days the train stopped at the Dunvegan Yards, and passengers had to take a bus from there into the city. My memory may be faulty as to the motive power of this bus, but I am almost certain that it was drawn with horses. Lloyd and I made our way to the Richelieu Hotel, and from there we set out to enjoy the city.

The Edmonton of 1918, though so young in years, was dingy, dirty, and shabby. To Lloyd and me, however, it was fairyland. We tramped up and down this street and that, entered all the big stores, rode back and forth in the street cars, and saw movies. Edmonton must have had five or six picture shows in those days, from the Dreamland in the east end to the better ones near First Street. The Pantages, playing vaudeville, was the most attractive, but it did not matter what kind of show it was, we went to two a day for five days. There were no movies any nearer to the farm than Edmonton, and these, the old silent ones, were the first either of us had ever seen. Two other places fascinated us. One of course, was the American Dairy Lunch, while the other was the waffle shop which was on the south side of Jasper, about where the new Macdonald Hotel is. We were frequent patrons. We had only one serious purpose in coming to the city, and that was to buy me my first suit. And not only that, but a suit having long pants.

We had wanted Mother to come to Edmonton, partly because she would enjoy it, but also to relieve us of the decision involved in buying a suit. She would not come. Had she not been to Edmonton twice since we had homesteaded, once in 1909, and once quite recently when she took Bill and me down to visit Dad at Sarcee Camp in Calgary? Travel was not to be regarded lightly, and she had had her trip for this decade. Most of the other wives had not been to Edmonton since they first set foot on the farm ten or more years previously.

When we were in Edmonton we saw many automobiles, but the city, like the country, was still run by the willingness of horses. Once in a while Lloyd and I would get lonesome for our own teams and would walk over and pat and talk to one standing at the curb. Even now, when the only horses left are those of the milkman, I cannot resist walking over to talk things over with the milkman's horse.

Lloyd and I left Edmonton broke but happy. From that day on, each of us was resolved to leave the backwoods and the toil and the dullness of the farm. As soon as we grew up we would come back to the city—the glittering, crowded city. For a year or so past we had all noticed that on certain dark nights when the clouds were just right, we could see a glow in the sky far off to the southeast. That, we knew, was the reflection of the lights of Edmonton, fifty miles away in a straight line. For many a night after I had returned to the farm, I used to go outside after dark, hoping to see this glow in the sky.

Meanwhile, in England, Dad had been champing at the bit. His battalion had been broken up, and while the old sergeant-major was held back, his men were sent over to France. He kept trying to go too, but without success. Once he nearly made it when he was promised that he could go if he could get by the medical officer. In the days when a man received one or, at most, two medals for each war, Dad's row of medal ribbons covered much of his broad chest. They were his undoing, for the M.O. was an old soldier too. He immediately spotted the Soudan ribbon, which went back to 1884, and refused to proceed with the inspection. "Too old," he said. "I'm sorry."

That blow, I am glad to say, was more than made up for at a later time. In 1939, when King George and Queen Elizabeth visited Edmonton, an invitation was sent out to old soldiers and Dad, who by then was seventy-three, secured a place at the foot of the steps of the Legislative Building to watch them go by. As Dad and all the other veterans stood at the salute, the Queen noticed the old man with the D.C.M. and the chestful of medals dating back fifty-five years. She drew the King's attention to him and the two of them came over to talk to the old Guardsman. Actions like that can bring greater happiness than all the riches of the world.

But in the spring of 1918 Dad was feeling pretty sore. If he could not get into the fight, what was the use of hanging around in England? So, after a few months' twirling of army red-tape, we got word that we might expect his return.

By that time Mother was managing very capably. She realized that we had a promising farm, and that cash would convert that promise into earning-capacity. When Dad came home he would have received deferred pay of one sort and another, and Mother planned to add this to our other resources so that the farm could get away to a fresh start. Unfortunately, Dad returned by way of New York and was delayed there for some days. The combination of New York and of newly made friends was expensive. When Dad again set foot on the North-West of 16, after catching a ride from Westlock with a neighbour, he walked in with his haversack, a bag of candy, and thirty-five cents. Mother's plans vanished like the candies in the bag.

Today, if anything happens in any part of the world, someone in another part who cares enough to turn on his radio can hear all about it a few minutes after it happens. How different it was in Eastburg in 1918! The Edmonton paper we received kept us abreast of all news up to the date it had been printed, that is, up to three or four days before the mail man brought it to the post office. We knew in October that the end of the war was approaching. We did not hear of it until November 13, two days after the Armistice had been signed. That day Bill and I, riding in the wagon towards Rossington, met a neighbour who said he thought the war had ended. Two miles further on we met a man who was certain. He had met someone from Westlock who had seen a paper, and there was no doubt about it. We went on to Rossington, completed our business there as quickly as possible, and hurried home with the news.

The war was over. We had escaped from its tyranny. We had been delivered. Never again would there be another war. Henceforth, common sense and Christian charity would rule the world. Henceforth, peace and goodwill would prevail.

15

Dad found that he had come home to a changed country and a transformed farm. His old bush had been swept away, Bunty had been booted down the road, and the store had been sold. The old homestead would never be the same again. Neither would the country, which now depended on farming for a livelihood. The price of wheat, the principal product, was good; and the price of cattle was not to be sneezed at. This new Eastburg, which had been given its first real stimulus by the war's demand for its products, found itself needing services and wealthy enough to afford them. The old winding trails, for instance, would no longer suffice. They were inefficient, and the farmers wanted to break the land over which they ran. Even the North-West of 16 insisted that the old trail through the middle of the shiny new north field should be relegated to the sloughs and the bush of the road allowances. There was, moreover, talk of building a telephone line. An occasional car was met on the roads, and the first clumsy internal-combustion tractors began to clatter over the fields.

The change in the social side of existence was no less marked. To begin with, there was prohibition, which by legislation had tried to remove the age-old thirst from parched throats, but had succeeded only in banishing the sociability of a friendly drink in favour of furtive trips to a blind pig. The organizing of women's clubs to carry on Red Cross sewing and other war work had brought the community together into meetings. The dances and concerts which these groups had put on in an effort to raise money had all swelled the volume of social affairs. Since we lacked a hall, many of these functions were held at our place or in Dodson's house, as these contained the largest rooms in the area. The necessity of a hall was clearly indicated.

At first these dances were simple affairs, where the women brought lunches and a fiddler was paid by a silver collection. Candles were shredded and sprinkled over the floor to polish it. One fiddler sat and played away all night, except when he got a chance to slip out and have a quick drink of some locally distilled product. There were waltzes, one-steps, two-steps, and three-steps, minuets, the heel-and-toe polka, and cabbage dances; and every third or fourth number was a square dance. Two or three times during the evening Frank Redlin, with his red neckerchief, did a step-dance—a relic of the old Red River Jig. Shorty Rogers, too, and George Allen or George Brock, took turns step-dancing.

Young men who had spent their first earnings on a good horse and a buggy or cutter, brought their girls as far as fifteen miles to a dance. The younger married people brought their one or two children, and these were put to sleep in various rooms of the house. Dancing lasted until about three o'clock. In summer, of course, the sun was showing in the east by that time, but most of these entertainments were held during the winter. As well as plain dances, there were masquerades and box and shadow socials. There were always two or three belles of the ball—girls perhaps better looking, smarter, or of a better disposition than the others, and girls who, because of these qualities, were either "going with" or engaged to one of the young men with a buggy and a quick-stepping horse. It was understood that such couples would soon marry.

At a box social every woman made up a good lunch and placed it in an ornate box decorated with coloured paper and ribbons. At intermission these boxes were put up for auction, it being understood that the girl who made up the lunch would eat with whoever bought it. A variation of this was the shadow social, in which the men on one side of an improvised curtain bought the shadows cast on it by their girl friends on the other. Competition was keen for a few select silhouettes, but I always thought these affairs to be cruel to the less attractive girls, who in this manner were forced to run the gauntlet of adverse comment and humorous remarks.

Humour is relative. So is pride. And rural pride, like all other pride, hinges on the belief—perhaps not too wide of the mark—that the other fellow "thinks himself much better than you."

Rural people are sensitive about the social ease of city folk, their dressier clothes, the uncalloused hands and unbroken finger-nails of the men, and the women's hands not reddened by toil or by delving into the earth but only, at their smooth fingertips, by lacquer. Silly, you say? Sure it is, but so is most pride. We could all live in glass houses if we left it to those without silly pride to cast the first stone.

I remember an instance of it one night when a talented visitor from Edmonton, a guest of one of the more cultured ladies of our community, was the main attraction in a concert at the school-house. The pianist played many selections, and the applause showed how much we enjoyed them. I noticed that the man I sat next to, a bachelor with brains, did not clap, and I asked why. "She's good," he said, "but if we all clap our hands off, these city folk will think we've never heard anything like it in our lives."

The school-house was also the scene of Tom Bowen's services and Sunday-school classes, every other Sunday. He was stationed in Westlock and had several other charges, including the community of Eastburg. He was tall, thin, bald, and austere; and he feared his God and flayed his people over a large territory. He was the last of the old-time preachers, who for the love of his God and for the sake of the souls of his people, lived on a pittance and ranged far and wide over the bush trails. At first he rode horseback. Later he came with team and buggy, and, before his ministry at Eastburg closed, Tom Bowen acquired a Model T Ford. With it he sped along the dry roads, rattled and bumped over the corduroy, wrestled with the mud-holes, and of a Sunday morning roared into the school grounds. Sitting high in his wobbling chariot he tilted at all the powers of darkness. Roaring through the forests he railed at the opponents of prohibition. His services in Cotswold School were well attended, considering the backsliding nature of the community, but poorly attended considering the zeal of the man. How often he must have been discouraged at what surely appeared to him his failure to interest the indifferent of our area; and yet attendance at divine service in a country school-house is no measure of how much good a man like Tom Bowen did.

After two years of regimentation in the army, Dad was overjoyed to be back in Eastburg. It was like starting out on a long holiday. He appreciated the improvements Mother had made on the homestead, and he decided to set to work to make a real farm of it. He reviewed our assets—thirty acres broken, some land cleared ready for breaking, some good-looking cattle, three large horses, one boy of thirteen, and another of ten—and the picture was bright. The thirty-five cents he had saved from his two years' service in the army had now been spent, but the shortage of cash could be overcome if we got a good crop on the twenty-eight acres which he planned to sow to wheat.

The wheat flourished. It started well, stooled well, and grew thick, strong, and vigorous. Just at the right time the rains came, and by the beginning of August it was heavy of head and would be ripe in a week. This crop, Dad hoped, would buy two more horses and some machinery, and then he would be on easy street. Everything looked rosy. Everything except Mother. She was definitely ill, and all summer had looked like the wrath of God. All that had kept her going was her courage and a will-power which would not let her give in. The doctors could not put their finger on anything specific. This was in the days when there were two great panaceas, if other remedies had failed. First, they took out your appendix; and then, if that did not work, they murmured "Pyorrhoea," and took out your teeth.

Mother had no symptoms of appendicitis, so it was decided that her teeth must come out. They were strong and white and even. She had always been proud of them and had taken good care of them. But if the doctors said so, why all right then, she would have them taken out as soon as the crop was threshed.

In the meantime, on a hot Sunday morning during the first week of August, she and Dad walked around the rolling fields of wheat. Beyond the wheat to the north and west rose the remains of the old forest, and beyond that, great cumulus clouds exploded in puffs far up into the blue sky. It was good to see the wind walking over the yielding surface of this field of strong stems, the proud heads bowing before it, alternately rising and falling in waves that rippled right across the field. Surely those proud golden heads would produce fifty bushels to the acre of hard, rich kernels. Dad and Mother returned to the house well satisfied. "One more week," they said, "and it will be ready to cut."

After lunch, as the afternoon wore on, the great fleecy masses of clouds swept closer. Higher they mounted and higher, piled on each other till they looked like a grey wall bearing down over us. The uppermost clouds twisted and turned and writhed, and ever they rolled on like an angry sea till they obscured the sun.

With a feeling of awe, we four gathered on the north verandah to watch them. They looked so much like the painting by a famous artist in the encyclopaedia, depicting the fall of Babylon. At first the cloud bank was six miles away. In five minutes it was only three miles away, and an unreal calm pervaded the hushed air. Relentlessly the clouds pressed on and suddenly the wind struck. Dad and Mother, Bill and I, watched in silence. Out of the black heavens, like a pistol shot, a hailstone hit the ground and bounced ten feet into the air. Then, with a bang, another one hit the roof and then ten hit, and finally millions of them struck the yard in front of us, and all rebounded crazily. Just as suddenly as it had swept upon us, the storm sped away, except for the odd vengeful stone which, although left behind by its fellows, still pursued its diabolical purpose.

None of us had ever seen a hailstorm like that. Bill and I watched awed and fascinated. When it had swept away, we turned to look at Mother. She was sitting on the bench staring straight ahead, while the tears dropped down her cheeks. Only then did Bill and I realize what this great spectacle of nature meant to us.

The storm cut right through Eastburg, its centre passing through our place and its flanks sweeping over the country for three miles on each side. Not one of the farmers whose crops were ruined by it had any insurance. There had been a minor storm ten years previously, but we all believed that we were in an area not subject to hail. The following year everybody insured. It was well that they did, because in 1919 and the following years, hail struck Eastburg five years in succession. Of course, even if you are insured, the insurance at best gives you only half of the revenue you might have had if the crop had been harvested.

Although in the country as a whole times were good, that fall of 1918, they were not good in Eastburg. The price of grain was high but the price of commodities was high too, and Eastburg had no grain to barter for goods. Times were stringent, and particularly so on the North-West of 16. Mother was ill and had been waiting until after the harvest to have her teeth pulled out. There was no use waiting any longer. It would cost possibly twenty-five dollars to have the job done in town; but that amount of money, in addition to our own farm produce, would probably feed us for two or three months. She and Dad talked it over; Dad urged her to go to town, and said that in some way we would find the money to pay the bill, but Mother was adamant. The money must not be wasted on teeth. In the end she persuaded Dad to dig out the forceps he had used for the relief of so many a pioneer.

When a tooth is solid, hard and firm, extracting it is no mean feat. Even with the skill of a modern dentist and with his kindly anaesthetic, it is an ordeal not to be faced lightly. But to sit on the front steps while an amateur, fitted out with inefficient forceps, pulls them one after another without any anaesthetic—that takes grit. And that is the kind of grit Mother had. One evening after supper she sat on the front steps while Dad pulled the first one. "That's all for tonight," he said. "In two or three days we'll take out another."

Two or three days, nothing! Next night Mother led Dad and his forceps out again, and this time he took out two more. So it went every night, until all thirty-two of Mother's sound white teeth were gone. The last seven were pulled out on two successive nights, three one evening and four the next. Mother was resolute of soul and firm of purpose. When a job had to be done, she wanted to get it over. So did poor Dad. If it takes grit to sit and have your teeth pulled out, it takes no less grit to pull thirty-two sound teeth from someone you love. The pity of it was that after this ordeal shared by Dad and Mother, there was no appreciable improvement in her health.

Even though it appeared that Dad could accomplish the work of a dentist without money, it soon became evident that he could not accomplish the work of a farmer without it. The Soldier Settlement Board had been created by this time, and since Dad was eligible for a loan, he applied for one, and got it. I'm not sure of the exact amount, but it was either $800 or $1,000—a tremendous amount of money at that time. With this, in the spring of 1919, he bought a sulky plough, a cultivator, a mower and a rake and two more good horses, and our potential horsepower was increased by a new colt which Molly brought us that spring. At last it appeared that the North-West of 16 was to become a farm. What an improvement the sulky plough was! It turned two furrows at once, and had a seat so that one could plough sitting down. In the fall of 1919, when the crop was ripe, a binder was added to our equipment.

But the old homestead, the old home of bear and beaver, the ancient haunt of snipe and swan, the one-time haven of honeysuckle and tiger lily, did not take kindly all at once to this rattling machinery. It accepted the sulky and the cultivator without comment, but the old-time stumps and trees in the meadows in the bush put up a hard and disabling fight with the rattling, roaring mower. In time the mower chewed pieces off the stumps until they were subdued, but not before we had made many trips to Westlock for new parts for the machine.

It was the binder, though, that put the thrill into farming. Dad hauled the parts home in the wagon and assembled them by the barn. He oiled and greased the machine and turned it with the hand crank, just itching to get into the field with this new binder. It was a wondrous thing, a McCormick, I believe, with a seven-foot platform. It was all slats and canvases, all gears and chains, with a bundle-kicker and that greatest of all inventions, a knotter. The very track of the bull-wheel in the soft ground was the mark of the Great God of the Harvest.

Finally word spread over the farm, from house to barn, and from henhouse to hog pen, that on Monday morning, as soon as the dew had lifted, the new binder was to try conclusions with the long strip of wheat on the new breaking south of the house. You know what the first crop on a strip of new breaking is like. It's rank and heavy, lodged and uneven. The breaking itself is all hills and hollows and holes, with roots sticking up into the grain. You know also what the borders of such a field are like, with their hazelnuts, raspberries, willows and young poplars. Hidden amongst these are stones rolled off the field and roots too big or too wet to burn. All of these, concealed in the rank growth six inches away from the grain, lie in wait for the unwary binder. The first round of the binder in the fall is always an anxious one. It is then that a sprocket breaks, a chain slips, the knotter jams or the bundle-carrier hits a root and folds up like an accordion. That first round, with horses long broken to the rattle of machinery, is always a difficult one. How much more trying it is, then, on a piece of new breaking with a team unused to a binder and a man operating one for the first time in his life! In such circumstances anything can happen, and it usually does. And it generally happens all at once with a roar and a bang.

Monday morning was clear and bright. A light breeze dried the dew. A golden sun smiled effulgently over the golden grain. Blackbirds in great flocks swirled in the air, and wrens warbled in the bushes. By nine o'clock all was in readiness for the great event. The binder, red and shiny, glinted in the sun, while waving far above it was the thong of the bamboo binder whip. "Now Vickie," said Dad as he drove the horses up to show them the binder, "now

Vickie, we're going to do a little binding today. See, Nellie, it won't hurt you. As for you, Molly," he said, "you've seen binders before." He seemed anxious to be certain that the horses understood. If they did, none of them showed it. One ear after another was cocked back and then forward. One head after another turned to look at this monstrous red thing.

"Get up," ventured Dad, and sedately the four horses moved forward. All appeared to be going well. The click, click, click of the driving chain running unloaded over the idle gears did not disturb the horses. Even the swaying whip did not distract them. Mother viewed the procession from afar, feeling some safety in remoteness. Bill and I trotted along behind the empty binder, after warning Scotty, the dog, that this machine was ten times more terrible than the simple mower, with which he had had an unfortunate experience. We ran around to open the gate that would admit this equipage to the field, and team and clicking binder passed through and then swung at right angles to commence the first cut along the field. You know how an aeroplane takes on its load of passengers, taxies away across the airfield and then comes up to the edge of the runway and stops dead for a final check. Well, in the same way Dad stopped the binder, the quietly clicking binder with the tall bamboo staff towering over it. He pushed this lever and pulled that one. I forget where it is now, but amidst the armful of levers is a thingamee called a clutch which you twiddle with your foot to put the monstrous machine into gear. Dad twiddled that, took a firm grip on the seat, slapped at the bamboo whip with the palm of his hand and shouted "Get up!"—like Ivanhoe in the lists at Ashby-de-la-Zouche shouting "Laissez-aller!" Molly, always a nervous horse, jumped into her collar, and so did the other three.

The erstwhile quietly clicking binder, following docilely at the horses' heels, became a raging, flailing monster, striking out in all directions. With a roar of rolling chains and a growl of grinding gears, with a banging of the pitman and a clicking of the blade as it seared into the wheat, the monster started down the field at the heels of the horses. Just behind the team the reel flailed the air, and far above their backs the whip flapped frantically, scaring them out of four days' oats. They leaped ahead and tore down the field, sure that the devil himself was after them. Dad tugged at the reins, grabbed at the levers and clutched at the seat. "Bang!" went the bull-wheel against a stone, then clattered and squealed as it climbed over it. The impact and the jolt threw Dad against the three levers, which battered and bruised him and then, with a thud, flung him back into the seat. By this time the first sheaf of the new breaking was through the machine and tied. Then the ejecting forks threw it far over the bundle-carrier. For the horses, this bundle flying off towards the fence was the last straw. With one accord, they resolved to run away from the frantic, flailing demon behind them. As they broke into a gallop, Dad yelled and cursed and tugged at the reins. "Wham, wham, wham" went the sheaves as they were hurled far into the brush. The bull-wheel and the bundle-carrier banged and bumped against stones and logs. Scotty barked, while Bill and I ran to keep up with the rampant runaway. *Chug* went something, and silence settled over the binder, silence tempered only by the swish of a sickle no longer cutting but only dragging through the wheat. Even the flailing reel had stopped. "Whoa!" shouted Dad. "Whoa! Whoa!" And Molly stopped, dragging the other horses to a halt. White-faced heads turned and equine necks twisted backwards to see how successfully they had overcome this monster, while Dad climbed down to estimate the damage.

The damage was easy to see. This gear was gone, that sprocket was sprained, this chain was snapped, and that one was snagged helplessly around the support of the seat. Even the reel sagged drunkenly, while parts of the bundle carrier lay strewn along the wayside. "Unhitch the horses," said Dad. "After you put Nellie and Dolly into the barn, hitch Vickie and Molly to the wagon. We're going to Westlock."

Three hours later, we arrived there. That is the only time I can remember Dad telling a real lie. Perhaps, technically, it wasn't lying, but certainly he was not thrusting the truth forward. "Must have been a set of defective castings," he said. "Why, I hadn't gone twenty-five yards on the first round before all these broke." When an I.H.C. man had brought out all the new parts piled in a big box, we set off for home again.

Maybe the field was hoodooed, or perhaps it was old Molly's fault again, but in this same field on almost the identical spot where Dad's first epic ride on the binder ended, my first runaway with the harrows started. It was one of those sultry summer days when, as you trudge behind the harrows, you curse your luck for not having a cart to ride instead of having to plod sleepily, enveloped in a cloud of dust. The horses were lazy too, and had reduced their pace until only a discerning eye could tell that they were still moving, and even then only after watching closely. The sun beat

down, and the swish of the harrows in the yielding soil seemed
to intensify the silence. Old Molly, as usual, was hanging back,
trying to let her whiffle-tree rest against the evener. Poor old
Molly. How old she was we had never known, but she had seen
many, many summers. In spite of plenteous feeding she was thin,
and she suffered some of the same ills that plague humans. As they
get older, horses become increasingly subject to flatulency; and
Molly was very old.

The horses and I plodded slowly and silently along, the reins
slack in my hands while my feet moved past each other mechanic-
ally. As I looked straight ahead, peering through the dust, Molly's
tail suddenly went high in the air. With a crack like a rifle shot
(I have never heard a noise like it before or since), Molly burst
the sonic barrier. Undoubtedly it hurt her, but I think the sound
scared her as much as it scared me and the other three horses.
They all leapt as if lightning had struck them. From my favoured
position just behind Molly, I knew what had happened, but the
horses did not know and they leaped forward and jerked the lines
out of my hands. They gathered speed as they progressed and soon
the sections of the harrows were leaping and bouncing like larks
on the hills. Round and round the field went the horses, breaking
off bits of harness and chunks of evener, and scattering harrow
teeth far and wide, while I ran behind futilely shouting "Whoa!
whoa!"

About this time in the long history of the development of farm
machinery, it occurred to someone to attach a light cart behind
the harrows. The purchase of such a cart was urged on Dad without
avail. A similar concession to comfort would have been the purchase of a spring seat for our wagon, but that too was considered
unnecessary, so we continued to ride the wagon into Westlock
sitting in Spartan austerity on a flat board placed across the top
of the box.

If Dad was reluctant to buy these conveniences, he was no less
reluctant to waste time going to Westlock for groceries before
we were practically out of everything. It was on occasions like this
that Mother regretted the sale of the store. Then, one day, she
conceived the idea of hiding his plugs of tobacco. That was a
stroke of genius. The plugs of smoking tobacco were piled on
a shelf in a cupboard. When Mother anticipated a shortage of
necessary groceries, she began abstracting plug after plug from this
pile until there was only one left. As soon as Dad found that he

was down to his last plug of tobacco, he always suggested another trip to Westlock.

The winter of 1919–20 was long and severe, with heavy snows which lay on the ground into May. That year we had plenty of wild hay, a fair amount of alfalfa, and much straw from what had been a good crop before the hail struck; so that was the year, of all years, when Dad decided to augment our small herd of cattle. With a further loan from the Soldier Settlement Board, he bought six yearling heifers of a good Shorthorn strain from a man who had brought up two hundred head from the south of the province to winter them where feed was said to be more plentiful. As we drove these six starved creatures the five or six miles to the bountiful feed of our haystacks, they were so weak that one of them could not make the trip. We lifted her into the sleigh, but she died during the night on a pile of alfalfa which she was too far gone to eat. Within three days, three more died; and later the green grass of early spring killed another, leaving Dad with one badly stunted heifer out of his original six. That was a poor investment.

Had we secured these cattle a couple of weeks earlier, it is possible that all of them would have pulled through the winter. The five that died only shared the fate of hundreds of thousands of cattle that winter and spring of 1919–20. It was a tragic winter. The snow lay deep and crusted, preventing the cattle from feeding on the stubble or on any natural meadows. Every morsel they ate had to be hay or straw, and by February most of these feeds in the country had been eaten. All our neighbours had a few cattle and some of them had many. In desperation they began buying hay and even straw, which sold for sixteen dollars a load. Finally they were reduced to buying stacks two and three years old, and even to unearthing the bottoms of long-forgotten straw stacks.

In spite of the straw that was bought at such a cost and hauled at such great effort, the cattle began to die. Each morning as you walked out to your dwindling straw-pile, you found one or more of the cattle "down." From the straw-pile, those cattle that were left followed you to the well, but they did so with leaden footsteps. There was no frisking, no jumping about, no cavorting and bellowing amongst these cattle that exposure and starvation had marked for death, these cattle that were nearly all minus one or both ears and generally deprived of their tails from frost-bite. As you watched them wobbling over to the well you wondered which of them was making its last tottering trip to the trough. In spite of their weakness, they drank a lot of water, or at any rate it seemed so to a farm boy pumping away endlessly while the cattle soaked up the water and the wind whitened his freezing nose and cheeks. Then, when they finally got filled up, they crawled back slowly, uncertainly and hopelessly to the straw-pile to live out, if they could, another day.

Meanwhile the farmer hitched up a team, and with a logging chain, dragged away those cattle that had died during the night. These might still perform a useful function, for, if they were placed strategically over the field within rifle shot of the barn, it might be possible on a moonlight night to shoot a coyote or two when these animals gathered around to feed on the carcasses. For these creatures, too, would have starved during the winter of 1919-20 if it had not been for the abundance of dead cattle.

In those post-war years, Bill and I worked hard to clear the land. With a four-horse team we broke up about twenty acres each summer. There were a few stones on our quarter and, needless to say, clearing stony land is hard on axes. Bill and I cleared all day, and it seems to me that we sharpened axes all evening. Sharpening axes is a necessary and a purposeful evil if you are using them yourself, but to me in earlier years when I used to turn the grindstone for Dad, the purpose was not so manifest. In fact, I was quite sunk in the drudgery of my task.

In the beginning, the grindstone had been about eighteen inches in diameter. During the first years, of course, Mother had turned it. It gradually wore away as, year after year, for what seemed hours at a time, my weary arms turned it, until it became a trifling, eccentric, wobbly stone of about eight inches in diameter. Some of our neighbours had a treadle arrangement affixed to the stone, so that one could sit down and pedal the thing in much the same manner as a bicycle. To me this seemed like an ideal arrangement. Many times I suggested it to Dad, but he, ever a Spartan in outlook, could not see the need of such a contrivance when we had a boy perfectly able to turn the stone by hand. As he often said, "What's the good of having a dog and barking yourself?"

You can turn a grindstone in a mood of rebellious disapproval. Or, if that becomes too boring, you can dream of the day you will leave the farm; or you can resort to doing problems in mental arithmetic. On some of these occasions it seemed to me that if it took one thousand revolutions of the stone to sharpen one axe, and if three axes were dulled in a day, then by the end of a year the stone would have revolved about a million times. Now, multiply that by the number of years it takes to clear up a farm in the bush, and you get quite a respectable figure for the total revolutions of a grindstone.

About this time one of the neighbour lads, whose active mind was still too young to bother about girls or sex, had come up with a new definition of eternity. Suppose, he said, that once in a million years a little sparrow lighted on the peak of Mount Everest. And suppose that, when he did so, he rubbed his bill ever so lightly on the highest point of the mountain, once on this side and once on that, and then flew away for another million years. The time it would take, said this neighbour boy, to wear Mount Everest away would be eternity. While I spun the grindstone I kept turning this idea over in my mind, and concluded that, if Mount Everest had been made into grindstones and if all these grindstones had been shipped to Alberta farms to use to sharpen axes, then Mount Everest would have been worn away by the generation that cleared the bush off Alberta.

My wife says that I have big hands. Well, they got that way from gripping the handle of a grindstone, or that of the sharpened axe. And every fieldstone that dented or dulled its precious edge was my personal enemy.

One day as we were clearing down by the creek, our axes glanced off many more stones than usual. When we had cleared away all the poplars, balms and the willows, we soon discovered the reason for this. Here, in an erratic row for some hundreds of feet along the upper bank of the creek, lay the remains of half a dozen old Indian fireplaces. These were stones arranged in a circle so as to contain a fire, and each stone was cracked and burned red with the heat of fires extinguished long ago. When the nearby field was ploughed we found arrowheads and scrapers of all ages, and also turned up a thing which we called a hoe. Some of the projectile points were of the Yuma type, and as such, may have been eight thousand years old.

Here was a new thought, a sobering one. Fifteen years previously Dad had seized this quarter from the primeval forest. He had been the first white man to lay claim to this portion of the land and blithely assumed that he had been the first man ever to regard these hills and grasses as his own. Yet here before him lay evidence that once this creek bank had been the home of other men. If the hoe proved anything, then parts, at least, of these large fields had been cultivated by a people who claimed this as their land. Beside this little creek had burned other hearth fires. Beside this little brook had burned all the passions of other hearts, the fond loves and the fierce hates of other hearts. Here, other men and women, loving this land no less than Dad, had worked and worried, lived and died, and in the end, except for this old fireplace long since covered and hidden by the forest, had left no trace. Perhaps this very quarter, this North-West of 16 which Dad had claimed for himself and his children's children for all time, would some day bear the imprint of their feet no longer. Perhaps alien races would some day live here when all traces of the MacGregors, or even of Canadians, or probably even of the white race, had vanished. Perhaps the forest, older and more patient and persistent than man, would regain and cover this land.

As Dad turned over in his hand these relics of another civilization, he wondered what objects future peoples might unearth from this field as traces of its occupation by white men. If such people were to look for relics, what would they discover? They would not find these wooden buildings nor these modern farm machines. For even during the short span of fifteen years, what had happened to the earlier machines we had owned? As each outlived its usefulness, it still contained valuable iron. This metal which had made up its most enduring parts was periodically sold for scrap. In a few years, of the disks, the seed drill and the binder which we now owned, nothing would remain but rusted nuts which had worked loose as they traversed the field. All that would remain would be these stray nuts, rusted pliers dropped from pockets, and small miscellaneous items. Possibly the most common objects that future peoples might find in what had been the bush country would be old axe-heads and the heads of grub hoes, badly rusted by the passing of hundreds or thousands of years, but still recognizable as the tools of the race that once had lived here.

16

Preacher Bowen's Ford was soon followed by Henry ter Horst's. Because of Henry's knowledge of and aptitude for things mechanical, his Model T ran with much less fuss than Tom Bowen's. Many a trip Henry and I took in this shaking steed, bumping over the corduroy at a snail's pace, and then, when we reached a straight, smooth piece of road, roaring along, watching the fence-posts fly by at fifteen and sometimes twenty miles an hour. I'll tell you, that car could go! In fact it cut the round trip of twenty-five miles to Westlock to only two and a half hours.

Henry ter Horst was a hard and ambitious worker. By the end of the war the amount of land under cultivation in the community was increasing by leaps and bounds, and the difficulty and delay in getting the crop threshed by Hughes' steamer was irksome. There was room for a thresher in Eastburg, and Henry mortgaged his future and bought one of the new makes of small separators. In place of the towering steam tractor and the forty-two-inch separator of former years, the new threshing-machines were run by internal-combustion tractors of about thirty horsepower and the small separators had a cylinder about twenty-two inches long. In a day they could thresh only a fraction of what the huge old-time machines could handle, but they did so with a small crew, and in every way were more practical for use on small farms such as those in Eastburg. The bang of Henry ter Horst's one-cylinder Mogul tractor and the purr of his little separator were welcome sounds in Eastburg.

For one thing, this thresher, being an Eastburg institution, was expected to thresh only a limited area. As a result, many of the

Eastburg farmers would be threshed soon enough after harvest that their grain could be handled without the necessity of stacking it. In other words, those farmers near enough to ter Horst's place could rely on being stook-threshed. This saved all the labour of hauling in the sheaves and stacking them.

In the fall of 1919, Henry ter Horst gave me the job of spike-pitcher on his machine. He must have had some doubt about the ability of a spindly boy of fourteen to stand the grind of pitching bundles twelve to fourteen hours a day, or as long as the light lasted, for six days a week over a period of seven weeks, but he took a chance. Except for the labour of breaking land with a four-horse team, it was the hardest toil I have ever performed. At the same time, I have never been more fit than I was then; I may have been tall and skinny, but I was strong and as hard as nails. Never before or since have I been happier than on this, my first real paying job.

When on a Saturday night it became too dark to work any more, the thresher, of course, was left where it was. This might be six or more miles from home. On Monday mornings we had to leave home early in order to have the thresher ready as soon as there was sufficient light to be able to distinguish stook from stubble. Henry ter Horst and his brother Bill would come along about three o'clock, and we would drive in the democrat the six or seven miles to the thresher, arriving there maybe an hour and a half later. Then Bill busied himself with the separator while Henry and I started the engine.

For threshing we liked good cold nights with hard frosts, because these were almost certain to be followed by clear days. On the very cold mornings we would sweep the snow and frost off the engine, pour in some ether so that it would fire readily, and crank the flywheel. While at times it may have been stiff, usually it was not too hard to start. Then the engine and the separator had to be oiled up. We usually carried a forkful of straw over beside the engine and set it afire to warm our hands and to heat the can of lubricating oil. Morning after morning we stood around this fire of straw, glad of its light in the early dawn, and more grateful for its heat. I remember particularly the peculiar blue flame that clings to burning straw after the main burst of flame has subsided. Whatever gases burn with a clear blue flame, like that of a well-adjusted natural-gas burner, these gases were present in burning wheat straw.

Soon the engine would be idling away and the separator oiled and ready. Then we would unwind the great black belt and stretch it from the engine pulley to the separator. The threshing-machine was then ready to run. It remained only for its three votaries, Henry, Bill, and I, to go in and have another breakfast with the farmer, and for the other servants of the machine—the bundle teams and the grain teams—to rally round, and then the day's threshing would begin.

There were always one or two racks that had been drawn up to the separator the evening before, and while the taste of the last cup of coffee still lingered in my mouth, I would climb onto one of these racks and, with poised fork, await the full-throated roar of the separator that announced that it was ready for the sacrificial sheaves. From that moment until noon, the insatiable feeder gobbled sheaves. Each one of these had to be thrown into it by the spike-pitcher, and that animal was I. Except for an hour at noon and for rare interruptions when some part of the machinery broke, the endless cycle was repeated till dark: throw off one load, jump out of the empty rack and climb into the succeeding rack as it was being drawn up to the feeder, and then begin pitching sheaves off it. Finally, when it became too dark to see, we stopped for supper and were through for the day. But on moonlight nights, especially if another hour or two of work would finish off the farmer's crop and enable the machine to move on to the next farm during the late evening—on such occasions supper was of short duration.

I believe my longest day of spike-pitching was some fifteen hours. At six o'clock that morning we started the machine, and at seven the first sheaf had been dropped into the separator. Fifteen hours later, after an hour's break each at noon and supper, the last sheaf shone in the moonlight as I passed it up to the feeder. The hard work of the day was over then. In the morning, the field extending far to its forested borders had lain covered with rows of stooks so thick that a team could not drive through a row. At night, in the moonlight, the field was bare and garnered; a great pile of fresh, clean straw glistened in the pale light, and hard by in the field granaries a thousand bushels of flinty, golden kernels lay where they had spilled from the spout. The rest was easy: roll up the big belt, couple the separator to the tractor and hitch on the utility cart with its barrels of oil and grease, then climb on it and ride in solemn procession along the moonlit trail a mile to the next farmer's place, so as to have the machine there for the morning.

Yes, those were great days and good ones for the threshing crews. Working long hours in the crisp fall air, amidst the happy camaraderie of harvest time, eating wonderful meals prepared by the farm wives, and enjoying the sleep of the weary in cozy bed, aromatic barn or scented haymow—for the young men, at any rate, they were the happiest days imaginable. After the noise and the roar of the day, the silence of the night was soothing; a silence punctuated by the rattle of hay racks straggling home in the darkness, the rumble of bundle wagons that rocked over Alberta's trails from Athabasca in the north to Lethbridge and Manyberries in the south, from Edson in the west to Lloydminster and Medicine Hat in the east. That was the era when the Mogul or Hart-Parr tractor and the Peoria separator ruled the harvest.

Those were the days when I earned my first wages. For forty days at four dollars a day, I laboured joyfully. The days of the week slipped by in an atmosphere of cheerful work and good fellowship, and on Saturday nights Mother was always waiting with a light in the window and the kettle boiling. On Sundays I would finally emerge from the blankets to find her ready with a lunch fit only for a king or a farm boy; and the rest of the day was before me, with not one stroke of work to do.

Each fall and winter, in those post-war years, Bill and I cleared more land, and each summer we broke it up. By the time I left the farm, little of it remained unbroken. With the rapid increase in our cultivated areas and the natural increase in our cattle, we began to make some progress as farmers, in spite of hail losses of varying degrees for five years in a row. About this time Dad's sister Nellie, in Glasgow, died, and part of her estate came to him. This legacy completed the process of putting us on our feet. With the money Dad bought an International 15-30 Tractor, just in time to break the last bit of land on the quarter. This was the extreme north-west corner where in the early days the bulk of our lumber had been cut. It was still a tangle of spruce stumps and roots. We had dreaded breaking it with the horses, but with the new tractor, the heavy breaking-plough sailed squarely through the stumps, slicing them off like cheese or uprooting them like jackstraws. The old days of clearing and breaking by hand and with horses were over. The machine age had reached the North-West of 16.

Social changes of similar magnitude were sweeping over the land. Up to that time, the farmers had always failed to make their voice heard. While they tended to blame all their misfortunes on some remote monsters called the Big Shots or the Capitalists, and regarded themselves as poor but honest—mere lambs led to slaughter—there was indeed much merit in their belief that various governments were crooked and that the grain companies were defrauding them. This is no place to go into the history of agrarian movements which started in the United States a hundred years ago and at least sixty years ago were rampant on Canada's prairies. Actually they made little headway until after the First War. When they did start to roll, they swept on to success. Both the Wheat Pool idea and the United Farmers of Alberta movement gathered momentum in the years after the war.

Those great corporations, the Wheat Pools, had their start at this time in little meetings in the country schools all over the province. These gatherings led to other meetings and conventions, and eventually Dad, and other men in Eastburg, took around Wheat Pool contracts to be signed. Nearly everyone in Eastburg signed, and so did a majority of the other farmers in Alberta. Soon the Wheat Pool was in the midst of growing pains which have resulted in the gigantic corporation of today.

Hand in hand with this went the plunge of the United Farmers of Alberta into politics. Meetings were held in the school-house. Regional conferences were held in Westlock or Barrhead, and larger conventions in Edmonton and Calgary. All were attended by the most thoughtful farmers, but at each meeting much of the time of the delegates was wasted by the niggling little local politicians who, in a desperate effort to catch a place on the bandwagon, argued and quibbled, trying to establish a reputation for mental acuity. Farmers may be too much inclined to believe that panaceas for their ills can be brought about by legislation, but they rarely make a mistake in picking out their most level-headed members to serve them in politics or in any of their organizations. The U.F.A. movement, headed by the clear wisdom and the social philosophy of Henry Wise Wood and aided by such far-seeing and level-headed men as George MacLachlan, Herbert Greenfield, George Church, R. G. Reid, Norman Priestley, George Johnston, and many more, was a solid organization.

In 1921 the leaders of the U.F.A. assessed the unrest in rural communities correctly. They entered politics and felt confident that in the next legislature the U.F.A. would be represented by many members, but they were not prepared for the resounding response which the movement was to get. When the election returns came in, we were still in the days before radio, but by means of telephones and cars, the word soon spread to rejoicing rural communities. The U.F.A. had elected thirty-nine members out of a total of sixty-one. It was necessary for the leaders of the organization to find themselves a premier, and to do so quickly. They chose our remote neighbour of the ample girth and the clarion voice, Herbert Greenfield, from over south of Westlock. Rejoicing was the order of the day. The millennium had arrived. We, the farmers, had elected a farmers' government, and now all our problems would be legislated away. In such an atmosphere was the U.F.A. Government elected—the first good government Alberta had possessed, and one that lasted and did faithful work for fourteen years.

The farmers of Eastburg, who had worked together so well for the Wheat Pool and for the U.F.A., now put their shoulders to the wheel and set out to build a community hall. There was, alas, little money to spare, but there was plenty of willing labour. The hall could be built of logs, but fir was needed for the floor, and lumber and shingles had to be bought for the roof. Dad, who at this time still retained some of his recent legacy, offered to lend the money for this material, and the hall became assured.

I like to remember the erection of the first hall. The best place to cut building-logs was on Doc Phillips's old quarter which Dad had recently purchased as a farm for Bill. A bee was organized and a dozen or so neighbours with axes, saws and teams, met in the best stand of poplar; and, for a day or so, the forest rang with merriment and the crash of falling trees. As fast as each tree was felled, half a dozen of us descended on it with axes and saws, and reduced it to a building-log. Other men loaded these on sleighs, and by the end of the second day the logs for the hall were piled on the site half a mile from the school. In the spring, when the weather was not too cold for working with bare hands, but before seeding time, the hall was erected. Four good axe-men each took one corner and mortised the ends of the logs. These were Paul Cantin, Charlie Caron, Axel Clausen and someone else whose name I have forgotten. To be a good axe-man was something of which to be proud, and these men vied with each other. The logs went up quickly, and the corners of the building were neat and true. After the logs were up, all of us turned to boarding the roof, and soon the building was ready for the floor and the inside finishing. A local carpenter was paid to lay the fir floor.

The work of building the hall went quickly in the hands of so many willing neighbours. From that time on, we had a place for meetings, concerts and dances; and a barn was built to shelter the horses of those who attended. The barn was useful for only a few years, because even as its logs were being laid one on the other, automobiles were starting to domicile themselves in the community. With more and more of the young people going to dances by car, the hall itself, such a glorious achievement when it was built, soon became too small. In a few years it was replaced by a much larger frame building which still serves as Eastburg's community hall and is likely to do so for some years to come, even though there is no longer an Eastburg post office and the word Eastburg does not appear on modern maps.

The woodwork of the kitchen and of the stage of this new hall kept Dad busy. Day after day he walked down there, and, working all by himself, he put most of the finishing touches to the hall. This labour, freely given, was a hobby that occupied him for many months. Amongst other things, to frame the stage he made an elaborate and detailed Doric portico modelled exactly after the Parthenon. When last I peeked into the hall, his handiwork still formed an impressive part of the building.

I did not stay on the farm long after the log hall was built, but while I was there, I never missed a dance. As people travelled further and further to attend them, and there was more money to spend for music, the local fiddler found himself pushed over to make way for a pianist. In a year or so a set of drums was added, and we now had three performers to pay; but the added expense was justified because these three did pep up our dances. Not long after I left the farm I heard that Eastburg had a dance at which a hired orchestra from Edmonton played. Progress was really reaching the community.

For the first years that I attended the University of Alberta, I returned each spring to help Bill finish clearing up the North-West of 16, so that for a few more summers I was able to enjoy the dances in the hall. At first, of course, I had to go over and get Dolly with a neighbour's buggy, but about this time we acquired an old buggy of our own, so that I never had to resort to the lumber wagon. Then, one spring when exams were over, Dad arrived at the University with a brand new Star car, and I could go to dances in style. Those were great days—driving home from a dance in summer just as the sun was getting up.

. . . . . .

The rest of the story will not take long to tell. By 1926 Bill was assuming the full responsibility of running the farm. Dad worked harder attending to roads and municipal problems as a councillor of the Municipal District of Lockerbie than he did on the farm. A branch railway line had been built from Busby to Barrhead about that time, and now that grain could be hauled to the new railway stations of Arvilla, Highridge, and Manola, the framework of roads had to be re-oriented.

When the wind was favourable, it was possible at times to hear the whistle of locomotives on their way to Manola, for at one point the railway track was only about three miles from the farm. The first time we heard that whistle was on a fall evening. Over the hedge bordering the garden we could look out to the lengthening shadows cast by the thick rows of stooks marching across the west field. Their black shadows contrasted sharply with the rosy glow of the setting sun. The grass of the lawn was still green, and although many of the flowers had gone to seed, the pastel shades of the asters, the flaming red of dwarf dahlias, and the haunting blue of delphiniums still remained. The leaves of the native birches were yellow, and through the thinning foliage of the rowan trees the flaring red of their clusters of berries glowed pleasantly.

It was harvest time, a time of fruition for all. Mother and I were sitting on the porch steps while Dad was bending over his flowers. Suddenly through the still, clear air, mellowed and softened by the distance, came the unmistakable notes of a train whistle. We all straightened up and looked at each other. For the first time in history the sound of a train had been heard on the North-West of 16. Dad came over and sat beside Mother. "Did you ever believe that you would hear that? When you unpacked your china over there," he said, pointing to a spot in the field of stooks, "if I had said that in less than twenty years we would sit here and listen to a train whistle, would you have believed it?"

That whistle, like the stooks, the yellow leaves and the rowan berries, was a sign of fulfilment—of harvest. That whistle marked a turning point in the lives of Mother and Dad. The days of struggle and anxiety, of denial and hardship, were over. Henceforth, for many years, we hoped, they would reap the harvest that Dad's love of this country and Mother's courage had sown. More and more, from then on, Dad and Mother began to enjoy life—life on this farm that Dad had always loved, this farm that had changed Mother's fear and hatred to a deep content.

Late in 1929 Bill married a local girl and brought his bride to live on the old place. Dad and Mother turned over the big house to them, and built a smaller one in the clump of poplar and choke-cherry trees a hundred yards west of where the first log shack had stood. Both of them devoted much time to planting lawns, flower beds, and hedges in the place they had cleared out of the trees, in the only spot on the farm that had never been cleared. Here, where twenty-five years earlier they had felled the logs for the old shack, they now planted mountain ash trees. Where on crude skidways they had rolled building-logs over the stumps, they now pushed the lawnmower over a velvety turf. When these occupations palled, Dad would drive down to the river to fish, while Mother, carrying her lard pail, went down to the bush on Bill's place to pick wild strawberries. But if Dad took only a passing interest in breaking, seeding, and threshing, he yielded to no one his privilege of burning brush piles on Bill's clearing. Many an evening Mother wandered down there to call him to a supper long since cold, and joined him sitting on a log to watch the sparks rise from his burning pyres. Then, together in the gathering dusk, they walked home through the incense of soft willow smoke.